Lecture Notes in Computer Science   8915

Commenced Publication in 1973
Founding and Former Series Editors:
Gerhard Goos, Juris Hartmanis, and Jan van Leeuwen

Editorial Board

More information about this series at http://www.springer.com/series/7412

Utpal Garain · Faisal Shafait (Eds.)

Computational Forensics

5th International Workshop, IWCF 2012
Tsukuba, Japan, November 11, 2012 and
6th International Workshop, IWCF 2014
Stockholm, Sweden, August 24, 2014
Revised Selected Papers

Springer

Editors
Utpal Garain
Indian Statistical Institute
Kolkata
India

Faisal Shafait
School of Electrical Engineering
 and Computer Science
National University of Sciences
 and Technology
Islamabad
Pakistan

ISSN 0302-9743   ISSN 1611-3349   (electronic)
Lecture Notes in Computer Science
ISBN 978-3-319-20124-5   ISBN 978-3-319-20125-2   (eBook)
DOI 10.1007/978-3-319-20125-2

Library of Congress Control Number: 2015942810

LNCS Sublibrary: SL6 – Image Processing, Computer Vision, Pattern Recognition, and Graphics

Springer Cham Heidelberg New York Dordrecht London

Springer International Publishing AG Switzerland is part of Springer Science+Business Media
(www.springer.com)

Preface

Computational forensics is an emerging research domain concerned with the investigation of forensic problems using computational methods. The primary goal is to use different computational frameworks for the discovery and advancement of forensic knowledge and the establishment of forensic findings with scientific rigor. Computational forensics refers to the specific discipline that involves computational modeling, simulation, analysis, and recognition in studying and solving forensic problems.

During the last decade, many researchers and practitioners have been attracted to this discipline and have formed several research groups. The International Association for Pattern Recognition (IAPR) has also formed a similar group under its Technical Committee-6. This group aims to further promote research, development, and education in computation forensics, and to provide a platform for cooperation and exchange for researchers, practitioners, and teachers from the various disciplines of computational and forensic sciences. The International Workshop on Computational Forensics (IWCF) is one such platform for nurturing recent areas of research in computational forensics. The workshop has been organized regularly since 2007 and addresses different areas of forensic sciences. The sixth version of this event aimed at dealing with the forensic analysis of documents.

The workshop was organized with the 22nd International Conference on Pattern Recognition (ICPR) in Stockholm, Sweden. The event was held as a single-track, full-day workshop on August 24, 2014. The workshop focused on the use of pattern recognition principles for forged document analysis both in hard copy and digital medium. Analysis of handwriting or signature, detection of change in original documents, writer/speaker identification and verification, and copyright violation were some of the areas of emphasis. Efforts were made to bring researchers together who work on these issues in different areas including document and speech processing, music analysis, digital security, forensic sciences, etc.

The 6th IWCF received an overwhelming response from related academic groups and industry practitioners. The preparation of the workshop started as soon as the proposal was accepted by the ICPR Workshop Committee. Abstracts for 23 papers were registered and 18 full papers were submitted. After a rigorous review process, 13 papers from research groups in ten different countries were accepted for presentation at the workshop. Paul Lahmi, CEO of Send Only Oked Documents (SOOD), France, delivered the workshop keynote address and the workshop invited talk was delivered by IAPR TC-10 Chair Jean-Marc Ogier.

For the first time, there was a call for holding a shared task in IWCF. One research group from Malaysia responded to this call and organized a competition on Recognition of Android Malware Patterns (RAMP). Several groups registered to participate in this shared task and one group finally submitted their results. A special session, the discussion forum, was organized in the workshop. The session was chaired by the IAPR TC-6 Vice Chair Marcus Liwicky. Participants who attended the workshop without any papers or talks were initially given the chance to present their research or products by making brief presentations. Later discussions identified niche areas of computational forensics on which collaboration among different groups was discussed. The preparation of sharable data and systems was emphasized.

After the workshop, authors of selected contributions were invited to submit expanded versions of their papers for this edited volume. The authors were encouraged to include the ideas and suggestions that arose during the discussions at the workshop. Thus, this volume contains reviewed and improved versions of papers presented at IWCF 2014. We intend to give a snapshot of state-of-the-art research in the field of computational forensics.

It should be noted that because of some unavoidable reasons, the proceedings of IWCF 2012 were not published on time. Therefore, the authors of the papers presented at IWCF 2012 were also invited to submit their extended and updated work to be included in this edited volume. Hence, this volume can be considered as the joint proceedings of the 5th and 6th IWCF. Altogether, this volume contains 17 papers; 12 from IWCF 2014 and the rest from IWCF 2012. The papers are divided into three broad areas, namely, biometrics, document inspection, and applications.

Finally, we would like to sincerely thank those who helped to ensure IWCF 2014 was a success: Kim Boyer (Past President, IAPR), Simone Marinai (2nd Vice President, IAPR), Apostolos Antonacopoulos (IAPR Treasurer), Cris Luengo and Ola Friman (ICPR 2014 Workshop Co-chairs), and other ICPR organizers for their generous support; the members of the IWCF Program Committee for reviewing and commenting on all of the submitted papers; IAPR for its sponsorship of the workshop. Our sincere thanks to Katrin Franke, Gjovik University College, Norway; Mario Koeppen, Kyushu Institute of Technology, Japan; and Andre Arnes, Gjovik University College, Norway – the workshop chairs of the 5th IWCF 2012.

March 2015   Utpal Garain
Faisal Shafait

Organization

Workshop Chairs

Utpal Garain   Indian Statistical Institute, Kolkata, India
Faisal Shafait   National University of Sciences and Technology, Pakistan

Program Committee

Ali Dehghantanha   University of Salford, Manchester, UK
Arun Ross   Michigan State University, USA
C.J. Veenman   Netherlands Forensic Institute, The Hague, The Netherlands
David Doermann   University of Maryland, College Park, USA
Hiroshi Sako   Hosei University, Japan
Jean-Marc Ogier   University of La Rochelle, France
Josep Lladós   Computer Vision Center, Barcelona, Spain
Karthik Nandakumar   IBM Research Collaboratory, Singapore
Katrin Franke   Gjøvik University College, Norway
Marcus Liwicki   University of Kaiserslautern, Germany
Massimo Tistarelli   University of Sassari, Italy
Muhammad Imran Malik   German Research Center for Artificial Intelligence (DFKI), Germany
Rajesh Kumar   Institute of Forensic Science, India
Sargur N. Srihari   The State University of New York (SUNY), USA
Sergio Damas   European Centre for Soft Computing, Spain
Thomas Walmann   ØKOKRIM, Norway
Venu Govindaraju   The State University of New York (SUNY), USA
Yoshinori Akao   National Research Institute of Police Science, Japan
Zeno Geradts   University of Amsterdam, The Netherlands

Contest Organizer

Ali Dehghantanha   University of Salford, Manchester, UK

Local Arrangements Chairs

Ola Friman   SICK IVP, Sweden
Cris Luengo   Uppsala University, Sweden

Sponsoring Institute

Contents

Applications

Biometrics

Voice Passphrase Variability Evaluation
for Speaker Recognition

Vladislav Sukhmel[1], Sergei Aleinik[2,3(✉)], and Vadim Shchemelinin[3]

[1] St. Petersburg State University, St. Petersburg 198504, Russia
sukhmel@apmath.spbu.ru
[2] Speech Technology Center, Krasutskogo-4,
St. Petersburg 196084, Russia
[3] ITMO University, St. Petersburg 196084, Russia
{aleinik, shchemelinin}@speechpro.com

Abstract. We propose a method of voice passphrase variability calculation. To calculate the variability, we transform an acoustic passphrase into a sequence of formants, then into a multi-dimensional histogram. We then compute a value which characterizes the entropy of the sequence. We provide a computer simulation and conclude that using this variability for passphrase creation (e.g. during the enrollment process) helps to significantly increase the performance of speaker verification and speaker identification systems.

Keywords: Passphrase · Speaker recognition · Speech processing · Preprocessing

1 Introduction

Voice passphrase comparison is a popular technique in speaker verification / identification (SVI) systems. In particular, during the enrollment process, an SVI user is prompted to utter a short phrase into a microphone. Various acoustic parameters (frequencies, pitch and other physical characteristics of the vocal tract, etc., often called "acoustic features" [1, 2]) are then measured and determined, using this phrase. These acoustic parameters, referred to as a "voiceprint," are then stored in a database together with the user ID. During the verification process, the user is asked to repeat the same (or different) phrase. A voice verification algorithm calculates the user's current voiceprint and compares it to the voiceprint stored in the database in order to allow or deny security access.

One of the main problems in the aforementioned verification technique is the phonetic variability of the voice passphrase. The variability of a passphrase is said to be low if the passphrase contains a limited number of unique phonemes. If a voice passphrase is phonetically poor (i.e. has low variability), it is impossible to obtain an adequate estimation of the physical characteristics of the speaker's vocal tract. As a result, an ineffective voiceprint is created, and the efficacy of the SVI system degrades sharply.

It should be noted that this problem is different from the problem of text password cryptographic security. If a text password contains a limited number of unique text

U. Garain and F. Shafait (Eds.): IWCF 2012 and 2014, LNCS 8915, pp. 3–9, 2015.
DOI: 10.1007/978-3-319-20125-2_1

characters, its cryptographic security is low. This means that the password is easily guessable by an attacker. In contrast, in the case of SVI systems, the lack of acoustic sounds in a passphrase makes it impossible to create an effective voiceprint. The result is low speaker recognition quality during the verification /identification process.

This paper is organized as follows. Section 2 describes the basic idea of the proposed method. Section 3 presents the acoustic passphrase PV calculation algorithm. Section 4 describes the corresponding algorithm for text passphrase PV calculation. Section 5 describes the experimental results. Diagrams and Conclusions are provided in Sects. 6 and 7, respectively.

2 Basic Idea

Recent comparative studies have demonstrated that the use of new features and some additional processing of short, phonetically-constrained utterances increases SVI system performance [3–5]. Our approach is quite different. In this paper, we propose a method for calculating the phonetic variability (PV) of the voice passphrase, which can then be used to either generate phonetically rich passwords in text-dependent SVI systems or to estimate the variability of input passphrases in text-independent systems during the enrollment process.

We have selected and investigated the following values as characteristics of phonetic variability:

- Absolute pseudoentropy PE_{abs}
- Relative pseudoentropy PE_{rel}

We selected PE_{abs} and PE_{rel} as characteristics of phonetic variability because we discovered in our previous experiments that dependence between PE_{abs}, PE_{rel} and Equal Error Rate [2] (EER) provided improved accuracy than dependence between the well-known "classical" entropy E and EER.

3 Simplified Diagrams

Logic simplified diagrams illustrating possible embodiments of the proposed method are shown in Fig. 1–2.

Figure 1 is a block diagram of a method for creating speech passphrases during the enrolling process in text independent systems. The passphrase establishment process can begin in step 1, where a user can be prompted to audibly provide an acoustic speech password. In step 2, audio input signal is received in response to the password prompt. In step 3, the calculation apparatus calculates the variability of the input acoustic signal. Next, the threshold unit 4 compares the calculated variability value with the predefined threshold level.

When the calculated variability value exceeds the threshold, the process can progress to step 5, where the password entry for the speaker is created and stored in a database. When the threshold is not exceeded, a warning message and a prompt to choose and input a new (more variable) password is generated in step 6, then the

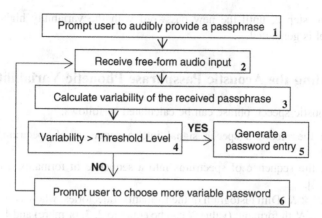

Fig. 1. Creating a password in a text-independent system.

process can loop from step 6 to step 2, until the new password with high PV is received.

Figure 2 is a block diagram of a method for creating speech passphrases during the enrolling process in text dependent systems. The passphrase establishment process begins in step 1, where the system is requested by a user to provide a voice passphrase. In step 2, the text passphrase is generated by a system.

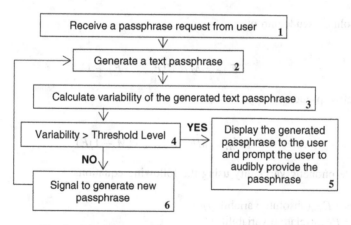

Fig. 2. Creating a password in a text-dependent system.

Next, in step 3 the calculation apparatus calculates the phonetic variability of the text passphrase. Next, the threshold unit 4 compares the calculated variability value with the predefined threshold level. When the calculated variability value exceeds the threshold, the process can progress to step 6, where the generated text passphrase is displayed to the user with the prompt to speak. When the threshold is not exceeded, a signal to generate a new more variable password is created in step 5, then the process can loop from step 5 to step 2, until the new password with the variability higher than the threshold level is generated.

4   Calculating the Acoustic Passphrase Phonetic Variability

PV of the acoustic speech phrase can be calculated as follows:

- Transform the recorded speech signal into a sequence of spectrums (e.g. [6], Lecture 3).
- Transform the sequence of spectrums into a sequence of formants (formants trajectories) [2].
- Calculate $N \times K$- Dim histogram of the formants trajectories, where coordinates are: 1-st, 2-nd ... N-th formant, (value N can be equal to 2, 3, or more) and 1, 2 ... K bin (we chose $K = 10 ... 20$ in our experiments).
- Calculate entropy E as:

$$E = \sum_{i=1}^{L} H(i) \log_2 \frac{1}{H(i)} \tag{1}$$

where L is the number of non-zero histogram bins and i is the index of the non-zero bin.
- Calculate:

  - Absolute pseudoentropy:

$$PE_{abs} = M/(M(E_{max} - E) + 1) \tag{2}$$

  - Relative pseudoentropy:

$$PE_{rel} = ME/(ME_{max} - (M - 1)E) \tag{3}$$

- Calculate phonetic variability using the following equations:

  - $V_a = PE_{abs}$(absolute variability)
  - $V_r = PE_{rel}$(relative variability)

In (2) and (3): $E_{max} = \log_2 L$; M is the maximum value for values of PE_{abs} and PE_{rel}, introduced to prevent the appearance of infinity in extreme cases (equal to 1000, for example). Absolute variability depends on the absolute value of the difference between estimated maximum entropy E_{max} and current value E. Relative variability depends on the ratio between entropy E and E_{max}.

Given the formants sequence, the $N \times K$-Dim histogram can be obtained using the well-known multi-dimensional histogram calculation algorithm:

- Choose the number of formants to be analyzed $(2, 3, \ldots N)$.
- Choose the number of bins in every coordinate $(K$, we used: $10 \ldots 20)$.
- For every formant in the sequence (for every $n = 1, N$ coordinate), calculate minimal and maximal frequency values $ValMin_n$ and $ValMax_n$, respectively.
- Divide each $ValMax_n - ValMin_n$ interval into K equal bins (so there is $N \times K$-dimensional hypercube H').
- For every formant vector in the time domain, place a single unit into the corresponding bin of the hypercube.
- For $N \times K$ bins of hypercube H', find a set of non-zero bin indices $\Lambda, H(i) \neq 0 \Leftrightarrow i \in \Lambda$, and normalize H' as:

$$H(i) = H'(i) \ / \ S_H, \ i \in \Lambda, \tag{4}$$

where $S_H = \sum_{i \in \Lambda} H'(i)$.

5 Calculation of Text Passphrase Phonetic Variability

We are able to calculate the PV of a given *text* (not speech) passphrase using a single additional pre-step. Using the text and some speech synthesis algorithms (for example, [6], chapters 12-13, also [4, 5]) an artificial phonogram is created. This artificial phonogram is then simply used as an input speech signal in the algorithm described above for acoustic passphrase processing. We should note here that text passphrase PV can be calculated without this "text-to-speech" conversion step. In this case, the generated text passphrase is transformed into a sequence of phonetic symbols using pronunciation rules for the selected language [6, 7]. Subsequently, every phoneme in the sequence of phonetic symbols is transformed directly to formants, using known algorithms [8] and the sequence of formants is then used to calculate formants trajectories, etc. This algorithm provided slightly worse results, as this method does not take into consideration natural variability in pronunciation of the same phonemes.

6 Experiments and Results

In our experiments, we used a speaker verification system based on i-vectors, as described in [9]. Standard MFCC-39 were used as feature vectors, and the UBM and Total variability matrix dimensions were taken as 512 and 400, respectively. The experimental corpus consisted of 190 speakers (127 males and 63 females), uttering numbers from zero to nine. Original phonograms were recombined into separate databases containing different passphrases and consisting of different sets of unique words. There were databases starting from an extremely low amount of sounds (e.g. "two" repeated ten times), and stopping with the most varied phrase (numbers from zero to nine). EER for each database, and mean values of PE_{rel}, PE_{abs} were calculated.

Figures 3 and 4 demonstrate an example of the improvement in speaker identification system efficacy when voice passphrase variability evaluation is used to generate passwords with higher variability. Figure 3 shows the EER of the identification system as a function of Absolute pseudoentropy and Fig. 4 shows the EER of the identification system as a function of Relative pseudoentropy.

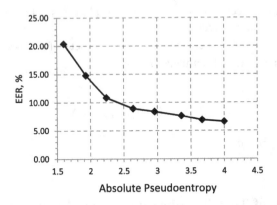

Fig. 3. EER as a function of absolute pseudoentropy.

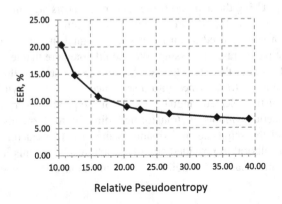

Fig. 4. EER as a function of relative pseudoentropy.

It is clearly demonstrated that when passphrase variabilities increase, the EER decreases significantly, i.e. system efficacy increases.

7   Conclusions

The paper has presented a relatively simple method for calculating password phonetic variability. The major advantage of the proposed approach is that it enables SVI systems to control the enrollment process more effectively. The calculated PV (if it is low) can be used directly in the first stage of the user registration process as a signal to the user, prompting him or her that the acoustic passphrase being input needs to be changed, or as a signal to the text password generator to regenerate the text password. Either directive improves the efficacy of the SIV system. We also point out here that the proposed method is the subject of a pending US patent application and is protected by US and international copyright laws.

This work was partially financially supported by the Government of the Russian Federation, Grant 074-U01.

References

1. Cohen, A., Zigel, Y.: On feature selection for speaker verification. In: Proceedings of COST 275 Workshop on The Advent of Biometrics on the Internet, pp. 89–92 (2002)
2. Jain, A.K., Flynn, P., Ross, A.: Handbook of Biometrics Springer. Springer, Heidelberg (2007)
3. Larcher, A., Bousquet, P., Lee, K., Matrouf, D., Li, H., Bonastre, J.F.: I-vectors in the context of phonetically-constrained short utterances for speaker verification. In: Proceedings of IEEE International Conference on Acoustics, Speech and Signal Processing, ICASSP-2012, pp. 4773–4776 (2012)
4. Larcher, A., Bonastre, J.F., Mason, J.S.D.: Reinforced temporal structure information for embedded utterance-based speaker recognition. In Proceedings of INTERSPEECH-2008, pp. 371–374 (2008)
5. Gupta, H., Hautamäki, V., Kinnunen, T., Fränti, P.: Field Evaluation of Text-Dependent Speaker Recognition in an Access Control Application. Speech and Image Processing Unit. Department of Computer Science, University of Joensuu, Finland (2005)
6. Brookes, M.: Speech Processing. 20 lectures in the Spring Term. http://www.ee.ic.ac.uk/hp/staff/dmb/courses/speech/speech.htm
7. Keller, E.: Fundamentals of Speech Synthesis and Speech Recognition: Basic Concepts, State of the Art, and Future Challenges. Wiley, Hoboken (1994)
8. Holmes, J.N., Holmes, W.J.: Speech Synthesis and Recognition, 2nd edn. Taylor and Francis, London (2001)
9. Kozlov, A., Kudashev, O., Matveev, Y., Pekhovsky, T., Simonchik, K., Shulipa, A.: SVID speaker recognition system for NIST SRE 2012. In: Železný, M., Habernal, I., Ronzhin, A. (eds.) SPECOM 2013. LNCS, vol. 8113, pp. 278–285. Springer, Heidelberg (2013)

Minutiae Based Palmprint Indexing

Alfredo Muñoz-Briseño$^{(\boxtimes)}$, José Hernández-Palancar, and Andrés Gago-Alonso

Advanced Technologies Application Center (CENATAV), Havana, Cuba
{amunoz,jpalancar,agago}@cenatav.co.cu

Abstract. Nowadays, palmprint identification has emerged as a very competitive and used technique in biometric systems. In these applications, efficiency is a very important but challenging problem for some reasons. The area of a palmprint is bigger than the one in a fingerprint. In this way, the amount of minutiae is also bigger and distortions are much more critical. On the other hand, reduction of the search space is essential in the process of identification. In this paper, a new palmprint indexing algorithm based on minutiae is proposed. Minutiae are very used by experts in order to perform manual matching, so this proposal can use features corrected by humans. The presented algorithm also uses a representation of palmprints based on an expanded triangle set, that proves to be very tolerant to minutia displacements on impressions. With this representation, a small set of features is extracted from minutia triplets. This aspect is very critical in the context of palmprints where the amount of minutiae can be over 900. The accuracy reached by this method in the performed experiments, is higher than $99,5\,\%$ for any value of penetration rate.

1 Introduction

Biometrics can be defined as the automated use of physiological or behavioural characteristics to identify or verify the identity of a person. Nowadays, palmprints matching is one of the most useful techniques [1,2]. The ridge patterns found on the palms of hands are unique, and they provide enough information to distinguish a specific person from the rest. Since the palm area is much larger, more distinctive features can be captured in comparison with fingerprints. This fact turns palmprints into a suitable technique for identification systems.

Despite having some similarities with fingerprint, the use of palmprints in recognition tasks brings additional problems. These issues are given mainly because the useful area of a palmprint is very large: palmprints usually have more than 900 minutiae. Thence, the computational cost of a matching operation has a significantly increment, since palmprints recognition process can not be implemented by searching over every possible entry stored in a gallery.

For these reasons, the reduction of the search space in which an exhaustive search will be performed is essential. Unlike fingerprints [3], palmprints can not be classified by any standard efficient criteria. Also, even when some proposals are found in the literature [4,5], the number of clusters in which the search

© Springer International Publishing Switzerland 2015
U. Garain and F. Shafait (Eds.): IWCF 2012 and 2014, LNCS 8915, pp. 10–19, 2015.
DOI: 10.1007/978-3-319-20125-2_2

space is divided is small. Therefore, the reduction of the potential candidates is minimal using this approach.

The classical solution for this kind of problem is the use of some indexing and retrieving process. There are many proposals focused on indexing approaches in fingerprint recognition [6–8]; however, in palmprints it is a relatively new topic. Moreover, Delaunay triangulations and other similar structures have never been used in palmprint indexing as in fingerprints identification [9–11].

There are a few proposals in the literature using different techniques for palmprints indexing. Some of these techniques are line features for building hierarchical classifiers [12], texture features [13,14], Haar wavelets and Zernike moments [15], palmprint pre-alignment and coarse matching [16], SIFT points [17] and KD-trees [18]. However, all of these works use images of a palm and they do not use minutiae information.

The main advantage of our proposal, is that, unlike other methods found in the state-of-the-art, it reaches a high accuracy using only minutiae information. These characteristic points are very used by experts in the field, so our method can be used even with manually edited features, in a more intuitive way.

The general structure of all indexing methods is very similar. When a new object (palmprint in our case) is inserted in the gallery, some information in form of indices is extracted from it and stored in an index table. Then, when a query is performed, their indices are obtained in the same way, in order to find correspondences with the index table. Using this information, the algorithm must be able to return a list of candidates ordered by a similarity value (see Fig. 3).

The present work is organized as follows. In Sect. 2, the representation used for processing palmprints is described. Section 3 is dedicated to the selection of the features used and the construction of the index table. In Sect. 4, the process of retrieving is presented and in Sect. 5 some experimental results validating our proposal are shown. Finally, in Sect. 6, our conclusions are given.

2   Representation

In this proposal, a previously introduced representation [8] in the literature is used, in order to assign a unique topological structure to each palmprint. This representation, based on the Delaunay triangulation, has been successfully used in fingerprints. Formally, a generalization of the Delaunay triangulation [19] can be defined as follows:

Definition 1. *Let $P = \{p_1, \cdots, p_n\}$ be a set of points in $\mathbb{R}^2$, for $p_i, p_j, p_k \in P$:*

- *$(\overline{p_i p_j})$ is a Delaunay edge of order k if there is a circumcircle to $(\overline{p_i p_j})$ that contains at most k point of P.*
- *$\triangle p_i p_j p_k$ is a Delaunay triangle of order k is its circumcircle contains at most k points of P.*
- *A triangulation of P is a Delaunay triangulation of order k if every triangle in the triangulation is from Delaunay of order k and will be denoted as $TD_k(P)$.*

The Delaunay triangulation of order k is unique for a specific set of points if there is no circumcircle with three or more points of P on the border. This characteristic is very useful in many areas of image and shape recognition.

As was mentioned earlier, some proposals build representations based on the previous definition, by constructing the set P with minutiae coordinates [6,8]. However, Delaunay triangulations may suffer great local changes in some cases. This situation may occur even with small variations on the points coordinates. In the process of palmprint recognition, these changes may represent a serious issue. The human skin is elastic, so the position of some minutiae may be different in two impressions of the same palm. This problem is more evident in palmprints since the area of interest is much bigger than in fingerprints. In Fig. 1(a) and (b) we can see the structural change in a triangulation when a point p is slightly displaced.

In order to deal with this problem, an expanded triangle set $ET_k(P)$ [8], defined as follows is used:

$$ET_k(P) = TD_0(P) \bigcup TD_k(P) \tag{1}$$

As it is shown in Fig. 1(c), this representation generates the triangles that would be found if minutiae were displaced. In this way, some matches will be found even if there are variations in coordinates produced by noise.

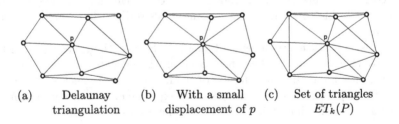

(a)   Delaunay   (b)   With a small   (c)   Set of triangles
      triangulation   displacement of p $ET_k(P)$

Fig. 1. Triangles generated with the expanded representation.

The expanded triangle set has many advantages regarding other existing representations. Besides dealing with displacements of minutiae, the number of triangles generated in $ET_k(P)$ remains linear over the size of P, as is enunciated in the following property:

Theorem 1. *The number of triangles in $ET_k(P)$ is smaller than $8|P| - 5|CH(P)| - 8$ for any value of k, where $|P|$ and $|CH(P)|$ are the number of points of the set P and the number of edges in $CH(P)$, respectively (see proof in Muñoz-Briseño et al. [8]).*

This property is very desirable in palmprints recognition, since the number of minutiae found in a palm is considerably bigger than in a finger. Delaunay triangles of order k are obtained using a variation of the algorithm described by Gudmundsson et al. [19].

As in a previous proposal [8], a strategy was used in order to eliminate the triangles of $ET_k(P)$ that may be affected by noise in the impression. To perform this operation, bad quality zones of the palmprints are computed by using a state-of-the-art method [20].

Finally, those triangles belonging to $ET_k(P)$ with sides crossing more than r pixels of a bad quality zone in the palmprint, are eliminated. In Fig. 2 the final representation used in the present proposal can be seen.

Fig. 2. Palmprint representation.

3   Indexing Stage

In this stage, the index table H that will be used in the retrieving stage is designed. The values of the keys introduced in H are indices that describe distinctive characteristics of the palmprints stored in the database.

In order to index a palmprint using its respective representation $ET_k(P)$, a feature vector $f(s_t, a_1, a_2, a_2, c_{ij}, c_{jk}, c_{ki})$ of each triangle $\triangle p_i p_j p_k \in ET_k(P)$ made up by the following features is extracted:

- s_t: triangle sign. $s_t = 0$ if the expression $x_i(y_j - y_k) + x_j(y_k - y_j) + x_k(y_i - y_j)$ is less than 0, and $s_t = 1$ otherwise.
- a_1, a_2 and a_3: relative directions of the minutiae represented by the points p_i, p_j y p_k, with respect to their opposite side in $\triangle p_i p_j p_k$, with $0 \leq a_i \leq 7$ since the value of this feature is discretized.
- c_{ij}, c_{jk} and c_{ki}: ridge counters between the segments $(\overline{p_i p_j})$, $(\overline{p_j p_k})$ and $(\overline{p_k p_i})$, respectively.

Using the minimum amount of bits for representing each component of f, the feature vector can be represented with 22 bits. Taking this into account the index function is defined as follow.

Definition 2. *The index function of a feature vector f is defined as $h : \Phi \to K_{22}$, such that $h(f(s_t, a_1, a_2, a_2, c_{ij}, c_{jk}, c_{ki}))$ is the integer number obtained by concatenating the binary representation of each component of f.*

With the previous definition the index table H is built. In Algorithm 1 this process is illustrated, given a set of tuples $E = \{\langle ET_{k1}(P_1), ID_1 \rangle, \langle ET_{k2}(P_2), ID_2 \rangle, \ldots, \langle ET_{kn}(P_n), ID_n \rangle\}$, where $ET_{ki}(P_i)$ is an extended triangle set, and ID_i is the identifier assigned to the palmprint represented by $ET_{ki}(P)$.

Algorithm 1: Indexing process.

Input: E
Output: H
$H \leftarrow \emptyset$
foreach $\langle ET_{ki}(P_i), ID_i \rangle \in E$ **do**
    foreach $\triangle p_l p_m p_n \in ET_{ki}(P_i)$ **do**
        $f \leftarrow extractFeatureVector(\triangle p_l p_m p_n)$
        $H \leftarrow H \cup \{h(f), \langle \triangle p_l p_m p_n, ID_i \rangle\}$
    end
end
return H;

Firstly, an empty table H is initialized (line 1). Then, for each $\triangle p_l p_m p_n$ in each $\langle ET_{ki}(P_i), ID_i \rangle$ the respective feature vector f_i is obtained. Using this information, an entry of the form $\langle \triangle p_l p_m p_n, ID_i \rangle$ is inserted in H under the key $h(f_i)$ (lines 2–7). It is important to note that more than one entry can be stored in H under the same key.

4   Retrieving Stage

In the retrieving stage, the candidate list to match with a given palmprint (query) is constructed using a correspondence count structure called R. Each element of R is composed by a key and a numerical counter. The whole process is detailed in Algorithm 2.

The first step is to obtain the representation $ET_{kq}(P_q)$ of the query, using the same process explained in previous sections. Then, for each $\triangle p_l p_m p_n \in ET_{kq}$ the following process is performed. Let f be the feature vector computed from $\triangle p_l p_m p_n$, and let $L = \{\langle \triangle p_{l1} p_{m1} p_{n1}, ID_1 \rangle, \langle \triangle p_{l2} p_{m2} p_{n2}, ID_2 \rangle, \ldots, \langle \triangle p_{lr} p_{mr} p_{nr}, ID_r \rangle\}$ be the set of tuples of H stored under the index $h(f)$.

Using this matches, new tuples $\gamma_i = \langle ID_i, T_i \rangle$ are built where T_i is a geometric transformation performed on $\triangle p_l p_m p_n$ composed by the values of translation and rotation that minimize the average euclidean distance between the transformed points of $\triangle p_l p_m p_n$ and their corresponding points in $\triangle p_{li} p_{mi} p_{ni}$ (lines 5–6). Then, γ_i is used as key to insert a new entry in R. If an element with the same key already exists in R, the associated counter is incremented by 1. Otherwise, a new element is created in R with the counter set to 0, using γ_i as key (lines 7–11). Notice that if there are no entries stored with the key $h(f)$ in H, no operation is performed. In Fig. 3 the general scheme of this proposal is illustrated.

Finally, the candidate list is obtained from R by sorting their elements in decreasing order, by the values of the counters. This method is based on the idea that if indices are extracted from two different impressions of a same palm, they will match with very similar geometric transformations.

The retrieving process of our approach is very efficient since every operation in this stage can be performed by using some kind of index. Both structures, H and R, can be implemented using hashtables or similar data structures, so every operation over them has a constant order. In addition, the size of L is considerably smaller than the amount of elements contained in H in a real environment. In this way, the final number of operations depends on the amount of indices generated by the queries.

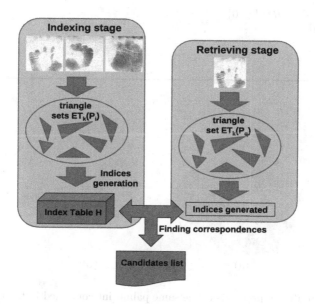

Fig. 3. Final scheme of the indexing and retrieving stages.

5   Experimental Results

In our research we could not find any free palmprint dataset in order to perform our experiments. The only dataset available was provided by the authors of a previous work [16]. That is why comparisons where performed with this proposal as reference. In order to test the accuracy of our proposal, experiments were performed using the first 100 palmprints of a dataset introduced by Yang et al. [16]. As in the mentioned work, the results reported were obtained by selecting one impression for each palmprint to create the gallery, while the other seven were used as queries (700 palmprints in total). As can be seen in Fig. 4, some images of this dataset are very rotated. Also, 12 616 single impressions were added as background, totalling 13 316 images in the gallery.

Algorithm 2: Retrieving process.

Input: $ET_{kq}(P_q)$
Output: R - count structure
foreach $\triangle p_l p_m p_n \in ET_{kq}$ **do**
    $f \leftarrow extractFeatureVector(\triangle p_l p_m p_n)$
    $L \leftarrow FindTuplesUnderIndex(h(f), H)$
    foreach $\langle \triangle p_{li} p_{mi} p_{ni}, ID_i \rangle \in L$ **do**
        $T_i \leftarrow ComputeTrans(\triangle p_l p_m p_n, \triangle p_{li} p_{mi} p_{ni})$
        $\gamma_i \leftarrow \langle ID_i, T_i \rangle$
        if $\gamma_i \in R$ **then**
           | $IncrementCounter(R[\gamma_i])$
        end
        else
           | $R \leftarrow R \cup \{\gamma_i, 0\}$
        end
    end
end
return R;

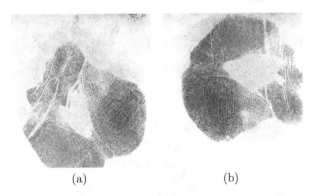

(a)   (b)

Fig. 4. Two rotated impressions of the same palmprint contained in the test dataset.

To extract minutiae from the elements of the dataset a similar method to the one reported in literature was used [21]. This approach is based on the computation of black-white transition count around each point in the skeletonized image of palmprints. A very simple segmentation of the images was performed in order to eliminate blank areas. For the calculation of ridge counters a simple method that uses the binarized image was developed.

Table 1 illustrates the average amount of minutiae and triangles computed in the extraction stage with different values of k in our palmprints representation. As we can see, the proportion remains linear.

The classical measure used for the evaluation of indexing algorithms, is the trade-off between Penetration Rate (PR) and Correct Index Power (CIP). For this reason, the accuracy of our results is expressed in function of this. More formally we can define $CIP(N) = 100 \times c(N)/E$ and $PR(N) = 100 \times N/E$,

Table 1. Efficiency.

	Average number of minutiae	Average number of triangles
k = 0	912	1726
k = 1		2496
k = 5		4243
k = 10		4796

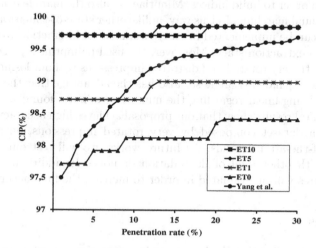

Fig. 5. Comparison of indexing palmprints algorithms.

where E is the number of experiments and $c(N)$ is the number of times that the correct result is within the list of the first N hypothesis.

In Fig. 5 the results obtained by our approach using representations with different values of k is shown. From these results, we can conclude that for $k \geq 5$ the accuracy is almost the same. Also, we can see that our proposal outperforms a method proposed by Yang et al. [16]. In fact, we return the correct impression in first place in the candidate lists of 698 queries. The two remaining queries are very degraded palmprints in which our method fails to collect proper features.

The introduced approach not only reaches a high accuracy but also presents a good efficiency compared with the proposal of Yang et al. [16], as evidenced by Table 2. Execution times in both processes, features extraction and retrieving are

Table 2. Average execution time (in seconds) of features extraction and retrieving processes for each palmprint.

	Proposed approach	Yang et al.
Features extraction	2.3 s	22 s
Retrieving	0.15 s	0.22 s

lower than the previously mentioned work. The same programming environment was used to compute the average execution time of both algorithms.

6   Conclusions

In the present work, a new palmprint indexing algorithm is proposed. One of the advantages of the introduced method is that it only works with minutia information in order to build indices. Minutiae are also the main features used by experts in manual matching. In this way, unlike other state-of-the-art algorithms, our proposal can be implemented in an environment of interaction with humans in the features extraction stage. Moreover, the used palmprint representation is able to deal with very rotated and distorted impressions without losing accuracy. The use of the expanded triangle set also has the advantage that the amount of indices keeps being linear regarding the number of minutia found.

Experimental results show that our proposal achieves high accuracy and good efficiency in a dataset composed by very rotated impressions, outperforming other state-of-the-art proposals. As future works, we will test our method in palmprints with other kind of degradation or noise. In addition, some other triangle features will be evaluated in order to increase the final accuracy.

References

1. Zhang, D., Zuo, W., Yue, F.: A comparative study of palmprint recognition algorithms. ACM Comput. Surv. **44**(1), 2 (2012)
2. Somvanshi, P., Rane, M.: Survey of palmprint recognition. Int. J. Sci. Eng. Res. **3**, 1–7 (2012)
3. Liu, M.: Fingerprint classification based on adaboost learning from singularity features. Pattern Recogn. **43**(3), 1062–1070 (2010)
4. Fang, L., Leung, M.K.H., Shikhare, T., Chan, V., Choon, K.F.: Palmprint classification. In: SMC, pp. 2965–2969 (2006)
5. Wu, X., Zhang, D., Wang, K., Huang, B.: Palmprint classification using principal lines. Pattern Recogn. **37**(10), 1987–1998 (2004)
6. Liang, X., Bishnu, A., Asano, T.: A robust fingerprint indexing scheme using minutia neighborhood structure and low-order delaunay triangles. IEEE Trans. Inf. Forensics Secur. **2**(4), 721–733 (2007)
7. Cappelli, R., Ferrara, M., Maltoni, D.: Fingerprint indexing based on minutia cylinder-code. IEEE Trans. Pattern Anal. Mach. Intell. **33**(5), 1051–1057 (2011)
8. Muñoz-Briseño, A., Gago-Alonso, A., Hernández-Palancar, J.: Fingerprint indexing with bad quality areas. Expert Syst. Appl. **40**(5), 1839–1846 (2013)
9. Bebis, G., Deaconu, T., Georgiopoulos, M.: Fingerprint identification using delaunay triangulation. In: IEEE International Conference on Intelligence, Information, and Systems, ICIIS, pp. 452–459 (1999)
10. Ross, A., Mukherjee, R.: Augmenting ridge curves with minutiae triplets for fingerprint indexing. In: Proceedings of SPIE Conference on Biometric Technology for Human Identification IV, vol. 6539 (2007)
11. Iloanusi, O.N.: Fusion of finger types for fingerprint indexing using minutiae quadruplets. Pattern Recogn. Lett. **38**, 8–14 (2014)

12. Li, F., Leung, M.K.H.: Hierarchical identification of palmprint using line-based Hough transform. In: ICPR, vol. 4, pp. 149–152 (2006)
13. Paliwal, A., Jayaraman, U., Gupta, P.: A score based indexing scheme for palmprint databases. In: ICIP, pp. 2377–2380 (2010)
14. Li, W., You, J., Zhang, D.: Texture-based palmprint retrieval using a layered search scheme for personal identification. IEEE Trans. Multimedia 7(5), 891–898 (2005)
15. Nagasundara, K.B., Guru, D.S.: Article: Multi-algorithm based palmprint indexing. In: IJCA Proceedings on International Conference and Workshop on Emerging Trends in Technology (ICWET 2012) vol. 2, pp. 7–12 Published by Foundation of Computer Science, New York, USA, March 2012
16. Yang, X., Feng, J., Zhou, J.: Palmprint indexing based on ridge features. In: IJCB, pp. 1–8 (2011)
17. Badrinath, G.S., Gupta, P., Mehrotra, H.: Score level fusion of voting strategy of geometric hashing and SURF for an efficient palmprint-based identification. J. Real Time Image Process. 8(3), 265–284 (2013)
18. Anitha, M.L., Rao, K.A.R.: An efficient palmprint identification system based on an indexing approach. In: IEEE ICACCI, pp. 688–693 (2013)
19. Gudmundsson, J., Hammar, M., van Kreveld, M.J.: Higher order delaunay triangulations. Comput. Geom. 23(1), 85–98 (2002)
20. Maltoni, D., Maio, D., Jain, A.K., Prabhakar, S.: Handbook of Fingerprint Recognition, 2nd edn. Springer Publishing Company Incorporated, London (2009)
21. Kasaei, S., Boashash, B.: Fingerprint feature extraction using block-direction on reconstructed images. In: IEEE Region TEN Conference on Digital Signal Processing Applications, TENCON, pp. 303–306 (1997)

Studies in Individuality: Can Students, Teachers and Schools Be Determined from Children's Handwriting?

Sargur N. Srihari[✉], Gang Chen, Zhen Xu, and Lisa Hanson

CEDAR, Department of Computer Science and Engineering University at Buffalo,
The State University of New York, New York, USA
srihari@buffalo.edu
http://www.cedar.buffalo.edu

Abstract. The individuality of handwriting is the principal underpinning of forensic handwriting examination. Studies of individuality have considered different statistical extremes to obtain handwriting samples. The first is a representative population drawn from a country. The second is a population of twins– so as to reflect genetic similarity. A third approach is to study whether teachers and schools have an influence on individuality. This paper presents preliminary results of individuality studies with data from children's handwriting, in grades 2–4, to identify the school, teacher and student. Considering the single handwritten word *and* we evaluate the performances of two methods, one based on feature values assigned by human questioned document examiners and the other based on automatically computing image features. Results are given for determining the school, the teacher and the student from images using restricted Boltzmann machines. Results of identifying the school with human assigned features and support vector machines are also given.

Keywords: Computational forensics · Handwriting individuality · Questioned document examination · Restricted Boltzmann machine

1 Introduction

Forensic identification based on handwriting rests on the premise: *no two people write the same way and no one person writes the same way twice* [1,4,10]. Various types of quantitative support for the hypotheses of identifiability have been proposed using computational methods. One of these is to determine error rates for the writer verification problem using writing samples from a representative human population [13]. While the accuracies achieved were high, it was felt that a diverse population would make the task unrealistically easy. A second approach was to factor-in genetic attributes and study the discriminability of the handwriting of twins [14]. A third approach takes the other side of the nature vs. nurture argument – one where the handwriting samples are from individuals taught by the same method. Taking this third approach we study here the handwriting traits of children.

© Springer International Publishing Switzerland 2015
U. Garain and F. Shafait (Eds.): IWCF 2012 and 2014, LNCS 8915, pp. 20–30, 2015.
DOI: 10.1007/978-3-319-20125-2_3

Data for the present study consists of samples of handwriting of elementary school children. In the present paper we describe the analysis of the handwriting of children in Grades 2–4 using : (i) images of handwritten *and* and (ii) characteristic values assigned by forensic document examiners (FDEs) to the handwriting of each student. The tasks reported reported upon here are on whether it is possible to determine the student, the teacher and the school.

2 Data Sets

The handwriting samples are from a large number of students (approx. 1800) as they are learning (2nd grade) or have just learned (3rd and 4th grade) how to produce cursive and printed writing (2012). Five independent school districts were chosen to participate in this study. The students wrote a paragraph twice in cursive writing and twice by hand printing using the Zaner-Bloser style of handwriting taught to them. The Zaner-Bloser Copy Book Handwriting Style [5], Fig. 1, is the hand printing / hand writing copy book style being taught in elementary schools in Minnesota to introduce children to writing. The paragraph consists of the following text: The brown fox went into the barn where he saw the black dog. After a second, the black dog saw the fox too. The brown fox was fast and quick. The black dog was not fast and he lost the fox. The fox hid in a hole and waited for the black dog to go home. After the black dog went home, the fox was able to go to the hole he called home and saw all the other foxes. The other foxes were glad to see him and they all asked him to tell them about his day.

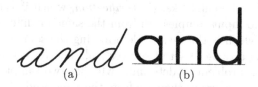
(a)   (b)

Fig. 1. Zaner-Bloser copy book style for word *and*: (a) cursive, and (b) printed.

A sample of printed handwriting of a student is shown in Fig. 2. All the writing samples were collected using the same forms to control variation due to document size and/or format. All students received the same instructions, as each of the teachers read the same instruction paragraph prior to collecting the writing samples.

The word *and* appears five times in the paragraph and was chosen as the focus of this study. The word *and* was chosen because it is one of few words that children write over and over during their early writings and have therefore began to develop individual handwriting characteristics rather than words that are not written often. There are an average of 5 to 10 samples of the word *and*

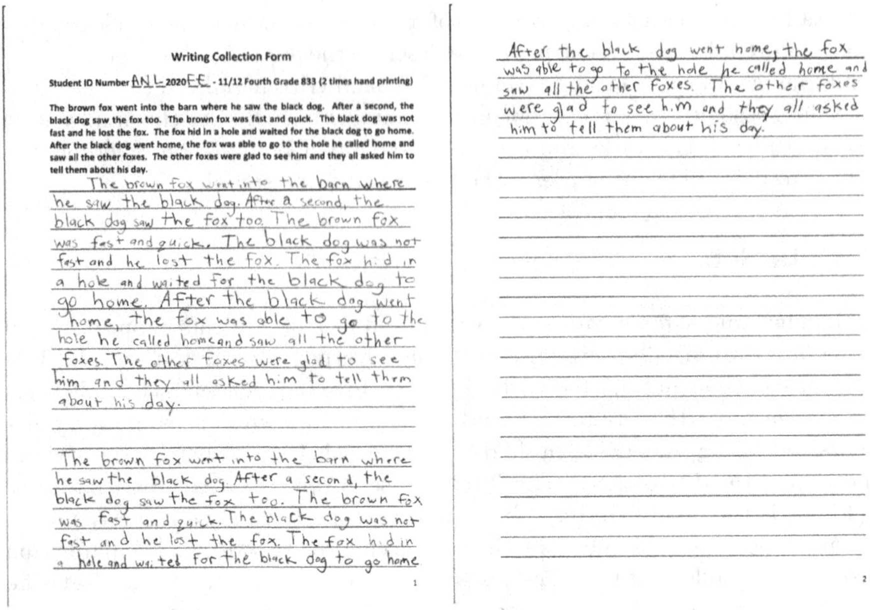

(a)

Fig. 2. School children's writing sample: hand-printed.

per student in hand printing and in cursive (except for second graders). Five of the datasets were used in the analysis described here: *printed writing* from the 2nd, 3rd and 4th grade and *cursive writing* from the 3rd and 4th grade.

We studied two different tasks: (i) *verification*, which is the task of determining whether two input samples are from the same or different sources, and (ii) *identification*, which is the task of determining the source of a single input sample from among a (closed) set of sources [13]. The verification problem is a binary classification problem to determine whether two samples of writing are from the same source– whether they are from the same student, same teacher or same school. The identification problem is a multi-class problem, to determine the source of an input sample among one of several (individuals, teachers or schools).

Two types of inputs for each of verification and identification were conducted. The first type of input were whole images of *and* as described in Sect. 3 and in the second we used a vector of handwriting characteristics of *and* as provided by human FDEs (Sect. 4).

3   Image-Based Approach

For the verification task, we took the approach of providing as input to the system raw images of each pair of *and* and leaving it to an automatic system to learn the features. The classification algorithm was trained to produce as output whether or not the inputs are from the same source or from different sources.

3.1   Classifier

For the verification task we used the restricted Boltzmann machine (RBM), a cornerstone for many variant neural networks [2,6,8]. The RBM and its variants yield state-of-the-art results in various recognition tasks [6,7,11].

Given a training set $\mathcal{D} = \{(\mathbf{x}_i, y_i)\}$, with the i-th pair: an input vector $\mathbf{x}_i$ and a target class y_i, where $\mathbf{x}_i \in \mathbb{R}^d$ and $y_i \in \{1, C\}$, a RBM with n hidden units is a parametric model of the joint distribution between a layer of hidden variables $\mathbf{h} = (h_1, ..., h_n)$ and the observations $\mathbf{x} = (x_1, ..., x_d)$ and y. The RBM joint likelihood takes the form:

$$p(y, \mathbf{x}, \mathbf{h}) \propto e^{-E(y, \mathbf{x}, \mathbf{h})} \tag{1}$$

where the energy function is

$$E(y, \mathbf{x}, \mathbf{h}) = -\mathbf{h}^T \mathbf{W} \mathbf{x} - \mathbf{b}^T \mathbf{x} - \mathbf{c}^T \mathbf{h} - \mathbf{d}^T \mathbf{y} - \mathbf{h}^T \mathbf{U} \mathbf{y} \tag{2}$$

with parameters $\Theta = \{\mathbf{W}, \mathbf{b}, \mathbf{c}, \mathbf{d}, \mathbf{U}\}$ and $\mathbf{y} = (1_{y=i})_{i=1}^C$ for C classes. And we can compute the following conditional likelihood:

$$p(\mathbf{h}|y, \mathbf{x}) = \prod_j p(h_j|y, \mathbf{x}) \tag{3a}$$

$$p(\mathbf{x}|\mathbf{h}) = \prod_i p(x_i|\mathbf{h}) \tag{3b}$$

$$p(y|\mathbf{h}) = \frac{e^{d_y + \sum_j U_{jy} h_j}}{\sum_{y^*} e^{d_{y^*} + \sum_j U_{jy^*} h_j}} \tag{3c}$$

$$p(x_i = 1|\mathbf{h}) = \text{logistic}(b_i + \sum_j W_{ji} h_j) \tag{3d}$$

where $\text{logistic}(x) = 1/(1 + e^{-x})$. To learn RBM parameters, we need to optimize the joint likelihood $p(y, \mathbf{x})$ on training data $\mathcal{D}$. Note that it is intractable to compute $p(y, \mathbf{x})$, because it needs to model $p(x)$. Fortunately, Hinton proposed an efficient stochastic descent method, namely contrastive divergence (CD) [3] to maximize the joint likelihood.

For classification problem, we need to compute the conditional probability for $p(y|\mathbf{x})$. As shown in [12], this conditional distribution has explicit formula and can be calculated exactly, by writing it as follows:

$$p(y|\mathbf{x}) = \frac{e_y^d \prod_{j=1}^n \left(1 + e^{c_j + U_{jy} + \sum_i W_{ji} x_i}\right)}{\sum_{y^*} e_{y^*}^d \prod_{j=1}^n \left(1 + e^{c_j + U_{jy^*} + \sum_i W_{ji} x_i}\right)} \tag{4}$$

Grade 2

Grade 3

Grade 4

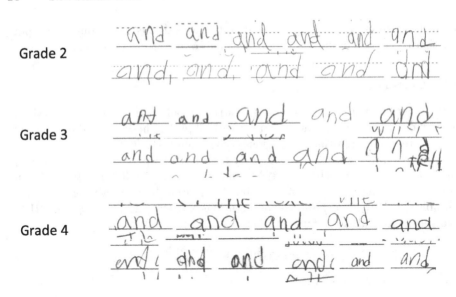

Fig. 3. "and" samples cropped from grades 2, 3 and 4 text images on Print dataset. The first 2 rows are from grade 2, the middle 2 rows are from grade 3, and the last 2 rows are from grade 4.

Table 1. Distribution of students for handprint samples.

Number	Group distribution		
	Grade 2	Grade 3	Grade 4
Students	193	324	336
Teachers	12	16	13
Schools	3	4	4

3.2   Input Images

We cropped the word "and" as our training samples from print dataset (see Fig. 3). We sampled a total of $7,782$ images, which are distributed among grade 2 to grade 4 with 2241, 2752 and 2789 samples, respectively. In this subset, we have a total of 6 schools, 41 teachers and $1,184$ students. Then, we divide students into groups according for each grade. Then, for each grade we categorize the verification problem into three levels: school level, teacher level and student level (Table 1).

Considering the different sizes of "and" images, we first resize them into the same average width and height. Then, we do some preprocessing to all resized "and" images. For example, we binarize each image, and then vectorize it as its feature representation. Then, we construct pairs from all the given vectorized images. Basically, we concatenate the two corresponding feature vectors (see Fig. 4 and give it a positive label if these two images from the same group, otherwise a negative label.

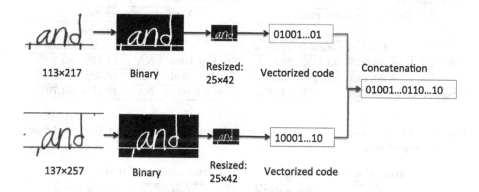

113×217   Binary   Resized: 25×42   Vectorized code   01001...01

Concatenation
01001...0110...10

137×257   Binary   Resized: 25×42   Vectorized code   10001...10

Fig. 4. Vectorization for image-based verification.

For student level, we have around 6–10 "and" images for each student, so we can construct positive pairs for all students. However, the negative pairs are very large, thus we random sample negative pairs so that the number of samples are roughly equal to that of positive pairs. Given sampled pairs, we can train RBM with 10-folder cross validation. For teacher level, each teachers have around 20 to 30 students, so the pairs grow rapidly. We random sample 10,000 pairs from both positive and negative pairs for each group, and then train RBM with 10-folder cross validation. For school level, it has the same situation as the teacher level. Thus we take the same strategy as what we did in the teacher level.

Parameter setting In all our experiments, we set the number of hidden units $n = 50$ and learning rate $\alpha = 0.1$ for RBM, and use 10-fold cross validation to evaluate performance.

Results We used RBM as the verification classifier and determined the error rates for each level in each group for handprint as shown in Table 2(a). The verification algorithm is unable to determine either teacher or school, since the error rate in this two-class problem is close to 50 %. On the other hand the student can be determined with better than random chance. Although the error rate is 45 %, it is promising in that we only used a single word as input.

Classification error rate into schools, using a multi-class RBM, is shown in Table 3 on both print and cursive datasets respectively. Here we see that the error rate gets progressively worse with each grade. This indicates higher degree of individualization with increasing grade.

Table 2. Results for handprinted (left) and cursive (right) images respectively.

(a) Verification error rates for groups on Print dataset.

Verification error rate			
Levels	Grades		
	Grade 2	Grade 3	Grade 4
Student level	44.92%	43.24%	46.52%
Teacher level	51.29%	47.92%	50.20%
School level	46.12%	50.58%	53.66%

(b) Verification error rates for groups on Cursive dataset

Verification error rate			
Levels	Grades		
	Grade 2	Grade 3	Grade 4
Student level	NA	44.22%	45.39%
Teacher level	NA	48.62%	49.93%
School level	NA	49.21%	54.79%

Table 3. Identification error rates for schools on Print (left) and Cursive (right) datasets respectively.

(a) Error rates on Print dataset.

Grade	Error Rate
2nd Grade (3 schools)	47.47%
3rd Grade (4 schools)	53.06%
4th Grade (4 schools)	68.76%

(b) Error rates on Cursive dataset.

Grade	Error Rate
3rd Grade (4 schools)	59.34%
4th Grade (4 schools)	68.35%

4   Characteristics-Based Approach

4.1   Handwriting Characteristics

QDEs assign different characteristics to handwriting manually, depending on whether the writing is *cursive* or *hand-print*. A handwritten letter, or a combination of letters such as the word *and*, can be represented by a set of D characteristics, $\mathbf{X} = \{X_i\}, i = 1, .., D$ where characteristic X_i takes one of d_i discrete values. Based on the characteristics defined in Fig. 6, the Zaner-Bloser Copy Book style of writing letter construct features can be assigned values as illustrated in Fig. 5.

The characteristics assigned to children's handwriting is represented in Fig. 6. The characteristic values were assigned by QDEs using a *truthing tool* [9].

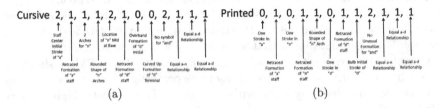

Fig. 5. Characteristics of handwritten *and* in Zaner-Bloser copy book style as specified by FDE.

Table 4. The number of handwriting samples for different schools.

School	Printed		Cursive	
	3rd	4th	3rd	4th
Liberty Ridge	67	65	82	77
Middleton	125	119	73	72
Royal Oaks	80	79	74	70
Red Rock	121	103	71	68
Woodbury	80	78	71	65

Table 5. Characteristics-based identification error for schools

Classification error	Cursive	Handprint
3rd Grade	45.45 %	51.19 %
4th Grade	48.57 %	58.33 %

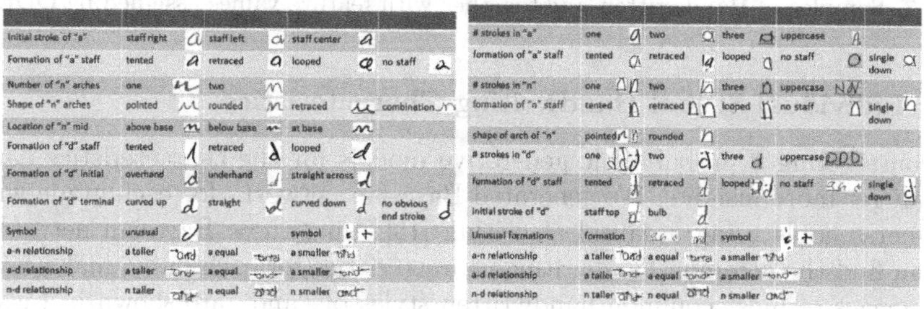

(a)   (b)

Fig. 6. Twelve characteristics of *and* together with their possible values: (a) cursive and (b) hand-print

Samples of handwritten *and* by children of grade 2, 3 and 4 and their respective feature values are shown in Fig. 7. Out of these, the samples for Handprint and Cursive writing in Grade 4 were extracted from the paragraphs in Fig. 2.

4.2 Classification

A support vector machine (SVM) was used to classify an input vector of characteristics into one of five schools: Liberty Ridge, Middleton, Royal Oaks, Red Rock, and Woodbury. An SVM is a two-class classifier which can be generalized to more than two classes using a one-versus-rest methodology.

The total number of samples are shown in Table 4. We randomly chose 90 % of the data as training set and the remaining 10 % as the testing data. The classification error is shown in Table 5. From the table we see that cursive handwriting has lower error or higher individuality.

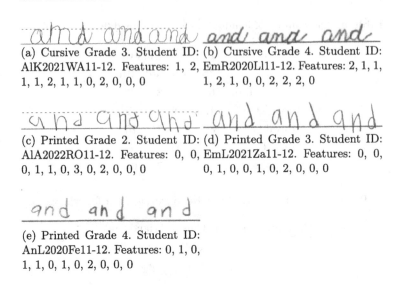

(a) Cursive Grade 3. Student ID: AlK2021WA11-12. Features: 1, 2, 1, 1, 2, 1, 1, 0, 2, 0, 0, 0

(b) Cursive Grade 4. Student ID: EmR2020Ll11-12. Features: 2, 1, 1, 1, 2, 1, 0, 0, 2, 2, 2, 0

(c) Printed Grade 2. Student ID: AlA2022RO11-12. Features: 0, 0, 0, 1, 1, 0, 3, 0, 2, 0, 0, 0

(d) Printed Grade 3. Student ID: EmL2021Za11-12. Features: 0, 0, 0, 1, 0, 0, 1, 0, 2, 0, 0, 0

(e) Printed Grade 4. Student ID: AnL2020Fe11-12. Features: 0, 1, 0, 1, 1, 0, 1, 0, 2, 0, 0, 0

Fig. 7. Samples of Handwritten *and* together with feature values assigned by QDEs.

4.3   Individual School Handwriting Characteristics

By constructing a probabilistic generative models for the characteristics data, we can get more insights. We generated Bayesian networks for each grade with different schools using a causal algorithm [15].Using these Bayesian networks, we can find the common handwriting characteristics for each individual school. The images of most common handwritten styles of "and" are shown in Figs. 8 and 9. We can find school handwriting characteristics by inference from Bayesian networks. Next we give some examples of what we have learned from the 3rd handwriting data.

Printed Handwriting Characteristics

– Students from Middleton are more likely to write tented 'n' (8 students), while for other 4 schools there are total 3 students writing in this way.
– Students from Middleton are more likely to write inconsistent 'a'-'n' and 'n'-'d' relationships (total 24 students), while for other schools the total number is 7.
– Only students from Royal Oaks write inconsistent number of strokes for 'a', 'n', and 'd'.

Cursive Handwriting Characteristics

– Students from Liberty Ridge are more likely to write pointed 'n' (9 students), while for other schools the biggest number is 2.
– Only students from Liberty Ridge write tented 'd'.
– Students from Middleton are more likely to write inconsistent number of 'n' arches (23 students), while for other schools the biggest number is 3.

- Only students from Red Rock write straight across 'd'.
- Students from Middleton are more likely to write no staff 'a' (23 students), while for other schools the biggest number is 4.
- Students from Woodbury are more likely to write no obvious end stroke of 'd' (9 students), while for other schools the biggest number is 2.
- Students from Middleton are more likely to write inconsistent formation of 'd' initial and terminal (total 32 students), while for other schools the total number is 7.

With printed handwriting, students in Liberty Ridge, 'a' is more likely to be smaller than 'd', while in other schools 'a' is usually taller than 'd'. For students in Middleton, 'n' is more likely tented. For students in Royal Oaks, the number of strokes for 'd' is usually larger. For students in Red Rock, the number of strokes for 'a' is usually larger. In addition, 'a' is more likely looped. For students in Woodbury, 'n' is more likely taller than 'd'.

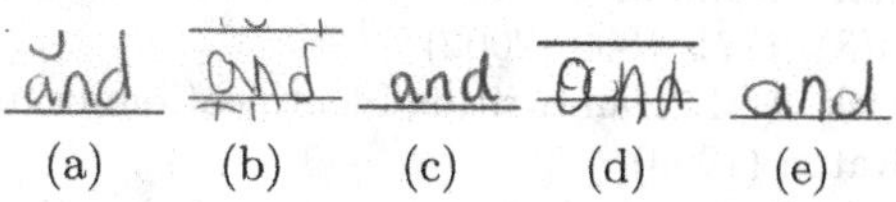

(a)   (b)   (c)   (d)   (e)

Fig. 8. The most common style of hand-printed *and* from five schools: (a) Liberty Ridge; (b) Middleton; (c) Royal Oaks; (d) Red Rock; (e) Woodbury.

(a)   (b)   (c)   (d)   (e)

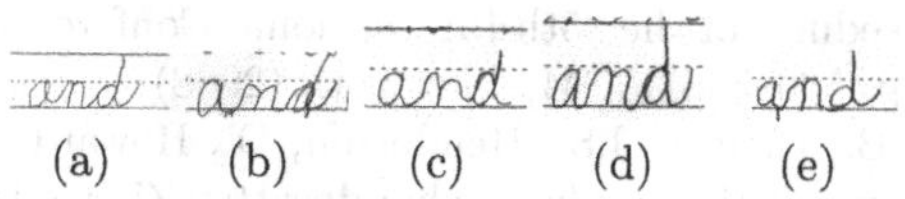

Fig. 9. The most common style of cursive *and* from five schools: (a) Liberty Ridge; (b) Middleton; (c) Royal Oaks; (d) Red Rock; (e) Woodbury.

5   Discussion

We have analyzed the handwriting of children using a single word of text, i.e., the word *and*. Both the verification task and the identification task were considered using (i) whole images and (ii) characteristics provided by FDEs.

Using image-based verification, we see that it is not possible to determine whether two samples are from the same school and teacher. On the other-hand, whether two samples are from the same student can be determined with better than random chance. This supports the individuality argument individuals are more distinctive than a collection of individuals. In image-based identification we see that the error rate increases with grade thereby supporting individuality with age as well.

Using characteristics-based identification the error rate is about 45 %, while a random assignment to schools would have only resulted in 80 %. This supports the hypothesis that schools have some distinctiveness which is captured by the characteristics specified by FDEs.

Acknowledgement. The work was supported by Award No. 2010-DN-BX-K212 of the NIJ, Office of Justice Programs, U.S. DoJ. The opinions expressed are those of the author(s) and do not necessarily reflect those of the DoJ.

References

1. Hilton, O.: Scientific Examination of Questioned Documents, Revised Edition. CRC Press, New York (1993)
2. Hinton, G.E., Salakhutdinov, R.R.: Reducing the dimensionality of data with neural networks. Science **313**(5786), 504–507 (2006)
3. Hinton, G.E.: Training products of experts by minimizing contrastive divergence. Neural Comput. **14**(8), 1771–1800 (2002)
4. Huber, R.A., Headrick, A.M.: Handwriting Identification: Facts and Fundamentals. CRC Press, Boca Raton (1999)
5. Kelly, J.S., Lindblom, B.: Scientific Examination of Questioned Documents, 2nd edn. CRC Press, Boca Raton (2006)
6. Krizhevsky, A., Sutskever, I., Hinton, G.E.: Imagenet classification with deep convolutional neural networks. In: Advances in Neural Information Processing Systems (2012)
7. Larochelle, H., Bengio, Y.: Classification using discriminative restricted Boltzmann machines. In: Proceedings of the 25th International Conference on Machine Learning, ICML 2008, pp. 536–543. ACM, New York (2008)
8. LeCun, Y., Boser, B., Denker, J.S., Henderson, D., Howard, R.E., Hubbard, W., Jackel, L.D.: Backpropagation applied to handwritten Zip Code recognition. Neural Comput. **1**(4), 541–551 (1989)
9. Puri, M., Srihari, S.N., Hanson, L.: Probabilistic modeling of children's handwriting. In: Document Recognition and Retrieval XX. SPIE (2014)
10. Osborn, A.: Questioned Documents. Nelson Hall Pub, Chicago (1929)
11. Rashid, S.F., Schambach, M.P., Rottland, J., von der Nüll, S.: Low resolution arabic recognition with multidimensional recurrent neural networks. In: Proceedings of the 4th International Workshop on Multilingual OCR, MOCR 2013, pp. 6:1–6:5. ACM, New York (2013)
12. Salakhutdinov, R., Mnih, A., Hinton, G.: Restricted Boltzmann machines for collaborative filtering. In: Proceedings of the 24th International Conference on Machine Learning, ICML 2007, pp. 791–798. ACM, New York (2007)
13. Srihari, S.N., Cha, S., Arora, H., Lee, S.: Individuality of handwriting. J. Forensic Sci. **44**(4), 856–872 (2002)
14. Srihari, S.N., Huang, C., Srinivasan, H.: On the discriminability of the handwriting of twins. J. Forensic Sci. **53**(2), 430–446 (2008)
15. Xu, Z., Srihari, S.: Bayesian network structure learning using causality. In: Submitted (2014)

Robust 2D Face Recognition Under Different Illuminations Using Binarized Partial Face Features: Towards Protecting ID Documents

Moazzam Butt[✉] and Wael Alkhatib

Competence Center Identification and Biometrics, Fraunhofer Institute for
Computer Graphics Research IGD, Darmstadt, Germany
{moazzam.butt,wael.alkhatib}@igd.fraunhofer.de

Abstract. Biometric recognition techniques have been widely employed in numerous applications, such as access control, identity check etc. In this paper we propose a method for protecting personal identity documents against forgery by using 2D face image on the ID document. The main components of this method includes detection of the face image from the document, extracting features from partial face images and converting the extracted features to binary feature vectors using Local Gradient Increasing Pattern (LGIP) approach. The binary feature vectors are concatenated to form a binary template which can be encoded and stored on the ID document in the form of a 2D bar code. This 2D bar code will be used to authenticate the ownership of the ID document. The face recognition method is evaluated using FRGC and FERET databases. The results show that this method can efficiently authenticate an ID document on the basis of the face image and the method can also be used to retrieve a subject from a database of images. The method is proved to be robust even if an ID document is scanned under different illuminations conditions. A report on document authentication where the face image is damaged is also presented.

Keywords: Biometrics · Face recognition · Document forgery · Verification and identification

1 Introduction

Biometric recognition techniques have been widely employed in numerous applications, such as access control, identity check etc. One of these applications is protecting the personal ID documents against forgery. In order to achieve a secure ID document, a Machine Readable Zone (MRZ) is commonly used, which basically protects against the manipulation of the alphanumeric data in an ID document. However, MRZ has not been used so far to protect the photo identity in an ID document. Another method is the use of electronic identity documents where the owner information is stored in an RFID chip. Although this method provides an enhanced security level, but it bears some disadvantages like unauthorized access on the wireless interface and higher costs. The limitations of previous methods motivate the use of biometric based techniques like face recognition to protect documents against falsification. However, with use of face recognition, challenges like sensor noise, illumination and quality of face image, size of

U. Garain and F. Shafait (Eds.): IWCF 2012 and 2014, LNCS 8915, pp. 31–43, 2015.
DOI: 10.1007/978-3-319-20125-2_4

the generated template needs to be properly addressed at ID document issuance and verification scenarios.

In this paper we propose a method for protecting personal identity documents against forgery by storing biometric face information in a 2D bar code on the document. This method shows robustness against illumination, white noise and generates a small binary feature vector that can be encoded in a 2D bar code. In addition to the biometric template, one may also store alphanumeric data in the 2D bar code 1, in order to protect the ID document against photo and alphanumeric data manipulation.

2 Proposed Approach

The proposed approach can be described in 5 steps: (i) face detection from ID document, (ii) partitioning of detected face image into vertical and horizontal sub-images (also referred as partial face images) and feature extraction from these partial face images, (iii) conversion of these extracted features to binary feature vectors using LGIP, (iv) concatenation of these binary feature vectors to a consolidated template and (v) storing this template as a 2D bar code on the document.

These steps are explained in the following sections:

2.1 Face Detection from Document

An image is detected from a document as shown in Fig. 1, where the region of interest is the face with forehead, hair and chin as shown in Fig. 1. The detection procedure comprises of the following four steps,

1. Conversion of the image to grayscale
2. Applying histogram equalization on the converted image
3. Detection of the face using the Cascade Classifier method [2]
4. Resizing of the image into 56 × 46 pixels (this step is performed in order to have equal size partial images in Sect. 2.2)

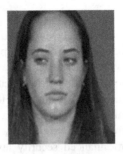

Fig. 1. (a) Original image (b) Detected face in 56 × 46 pixels gray scale image

2.2   Partial Face Features Extraction

This step extracts the face features from different portions of the face using projected random matrices as described in [3]. Initially, the face $X \epsilon R^{qXp}$ (where q is height and p is width in pixels of face shown in Fig. 1), is divided into different portions or sub-images in horizontal and vertical directions. The extraction of the features is carried on all horizontal and vertical sub-images. The feature extractions of each two dimensional sub-image matrix is done by using two projection matrices R_1, R_2, where R_1 is used in the feature extraction of the vertical face sub-images and R_2 is used in the feature extraction of horizontal face sub-images, respectively.

$R_1 \epsilon R^{k \times p}$ is a two dimensional matrix consisting of a sequence of the binary values "0" and "1", where k is an arbitrary number representing the height of the projection matrices and p is width of the face image. Based on a previous work [3], the height of the projection matrices (k) in this work is set equal to 5. The number of ones in each row is arbitrary. We assumed a series of 15 ones for each row [3]. This matrix R_1 is used to extract vertical features from the sub-image X with the same definition for R_2 $\epsilon R^{q \times k}$, which will be post-multiplied with the sub-image X, to get horizontal features. Figure 2 illustrates the projection matrices R_1 and R_2. Binary projection matrices will induce the effect of the data compression as it accumulates some selective pixels values (pixels at those positions where projection matrix bit is set to 1) and not all pixels. The cumulated value of all pixels will be the partial face (or sub-image) feature matrix, from which a binary feature vector is generated using LGIP approach as defined in Sect. 2.3.

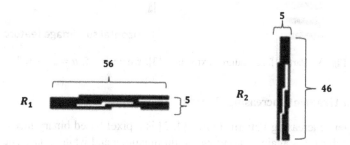

Fig. 2. Projection matrices R_1, R_2 (R_2 is transpose of R_1) [3]

To extract the partial face features, the original image is divided into n vertical and m horizontal partial face images, as shown in Fig. 3. In this work, n and m is set equal to 2 and 8, respectively. To extract features from vertical and horizontal sub-images, projection matrix R_1 is multiplied with vertical sub-images X_i, $i = 1, \ldots, n$ and projection matrix R_2 is multiplied with horizontal sub-images X_i, $i = 1, \ldots, m$. The resulting vertical and horizontal sub-images products $R_1.X_i \in R^{k \times q/n}$ and $X_i.R_2 \in R^{p/m \times k}$ are shown in Fig. 3.

The proposed method can be more robust against identity forgery by using different projection matrix to generate the binary vectors for individual users or documents. In case of document-specific projection matrix, a new ID document can be issued by selecting another projection matrix. It is to be noted that, the projection matrices can be interpreted as a random seed that is used to encode features. The projection matrix itself does not reveal any sort of personal information.

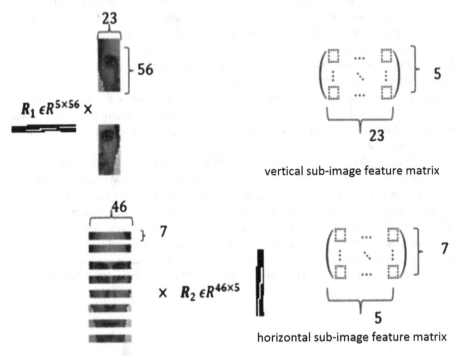

vertical sub-image feature matrix

horizontal sub-image feature matrix

Fig. 3. Partial face features extraction [3], where $k = 5$, $n = 2$, $m = 8$

2.3   Local Gradient Increasing Pattern

Local Gradient Increasing Pattern (LGIP) [4, 5] is a pixel-based binary face descriptor that shows robustness against variations in illuminations and white noise. Therefore, it is used to generate the binary vectors for the vertical and horizontal sub-image feature matrices resulted from the partial face division, shown in Fig. 3. LGIP employs Sobel masks [4, 5] $S_0, \ldots, S_7$ to calculate gradient responses in eight different orientations at each pixel. The gradient value resulted from each mask is converted into a single bit (1 or 0), depending on the sign of the gradient value. As a result, an 8-bit code descriptor of each pixel in the partial face image is obtained.

The Sobel gradient masks used in this work are shown in Fig. 4. These eight masks are applied on each pixel. If the pixel response to the mask is positive, a resultant bit is set to be 1, otherwise 0. As a result, an 8 bit value is generated for each pixel, where a single bit is the corresponding result of one mask. Since, the feature matrix is compressed (i.e., 56×23 pixels are reduced to 5×23 pixels in vertical sub-image and 7×46 pixels are reduced to 7×5 pixels in horizontal sub-image), it is necessary to take all the pixels in the binary vector generation. Therefore, a padding of 2 pixels is done at the boundaries of each generated feature matrix, so that 5 × 5 Sobel masks can also be applied on the boundaries of the vertical and horizontal sub-image feature matrix.

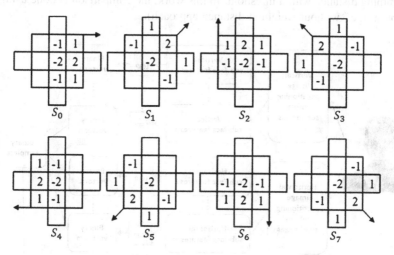

Fig. 4. Sobel gradient masks [4, 5]

2.4 Template Generation and Comparison

Each face image is divided into 2 vertical sub-images and 8 horizontal sub-images, the projection matrices R_1, R_2 are multiplied at fixed positions to cover all image pixels, where $R_1 \in R^{5 \times 56}$ and $R_2 \in R^{46 \times 5}$. The number of ones in each row for R_1 and each column for R_2 is set to 15. For an image, the size of each vertical features and each horizontal feature template is 5 × 23 pixels and 7 × 5 pixels, respectively. The binarization of these templates using LGIP as defined in Sect. 2.3, results in a binary feature vector of a length equal to 5 × 23 (pixels) × 8 (bits/pixel) = 920 bits and 7 × 5 (pixels) × 8 (bits/pixel) = 280 bits, respectively. The final binary feature vector of the image is generated by concatenating all vertical and horizontal binary feature vectors. This results in a total template size of 920 × 2 + 280 × 8 = 4080 bits per image. Figure 5 illustrates the overall workflow of the proposed scheme.

The comparison of the extracted binary feature templates from two images can be performed using hamming distance, in two ways. First is to calculate the hamming distance considering the complete binary vector, and this is a good option in case of uniform brightness or white noise. The second choice is to calculate the hamming distance by taking the binary vectors of individual partial face features and then fuse these hamming distances to get a final distance. In this case, the hamming distance generated from the comparison of different parts or partial features are weighted. The weights can be assigned to different hamming distance values depending on the confidence of the distance value. For instance, higher weights should be assigned to the distance values resulting from the comparison of partial face images with higher quality, higher entropy or higher discriminability and vice versa. The different weighted hamming distances can be combined to get a final hamming distance value.

In both options, the value of the hamming distance would depict the measure of closeness of two images whose feature templates are compared. The decision, if both compared templates are generated from the same face or not, can be done by comparing the hamming distance with a threshold. In this work, the comparison is done using the first option (i.e., without weighted distance approach).

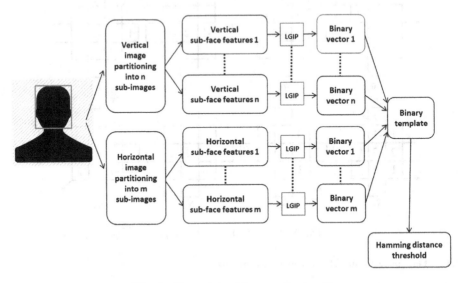

Fig. 5. Illustration of the overall scheme

2.5   2D Bar Code Generation

The generated binary vector consists of a series of ones and zeros, and by converting the binary vector to hexadecimal characters we reduce the vector size to 25 % of the original vector. For encoding the hexadecimal data, a QR code is used. The capacity of a QR code is up to 7000 digits or 4000 characters, and is highly robust. Zxing [6], a multi-format 1D/2D bar code image processing library, is used for generating the QR code and the Quricol library [7], is used for decoding the generated QR code. An illustration of the bar code generation application is shown in Fig. 6.

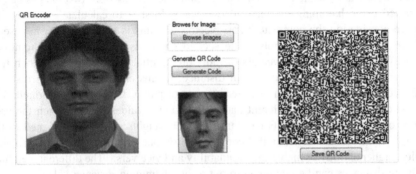

Fig. 6. QR code generation from binary template

It is possible that the 2D bar code also contains document owner personal information (like alphanumeric data [1], handwritten signature features [8, 9]) and other document information (like issuing and expiry dates) to detect a forgery in the ID document. Including personal data in the 2D bar code generation would be particularly useful to detect fake ID in case an attacker tries to replace both the face image and the bar code stored on the ID document simultaneously; thus additional information can be exploited to perform authentication of the ID document. However, it is not recommended to include the projection matrix information in the 2D bar code, as this may lead to function creep or attack on personal information.

3 Experimental Studies

In order to check the feasibility of given approach for ID document and its ownership authentication, three experimental studies were conducted. The first experimental study focuses on examining the effect of brightness during identity (ownership) verification of the subject on the ID document. The study has been carried out by comparing face image present on the ID document under different brightness with the compact 2D bar code feature representation also present on the ID document. The second experimental study focuses on the comparison of the binary feature vector extracted from 2D bar code stored on the ID document against the face image detected from the ID document or an image stored in a database. The result of the comparison is a hamming distance that can be compared with a threshold to make a decision, if the two images compared are matched or not matched. The third experimental study focuses on the identification of a person from a partially damaged face image. The original rank of the person is calculated given different kinds of damaged images. The test data set details and results of each of the experimental studies are explained as follows.

3.1 Robustness to Brightness

This experimental study was conducted on a data set of randomly selected 987 frontal posed images from 987 subjects (i.e., one image per subject). Out of these 987 subjects, 312 subjects were taken from the FRGC database [10] and the remaining 675 subjects were taken from the FERET database [11]. In each frontal image, the face region is detected and converted to a grayscale image of 46×56 pixels. Then from each frontal grayscale image, eight other images of different levels of uniform brightness were generated by adding a scalar value of ± 80, ± 60, ± 40 and ± 20 to the 2D grayscale frontal image, respectively. An example of a frontal image (labelled as 0 image) and the generated eight images is shown in Fig. 7. Partial face feature extraction was performed for all of these 987*9 images and the features were binarized using LGIP approach, as defined in Sects. 2.2 and 2.3, respectively.

In order to verify the robustness of features against the brightness, hamming distances were generated by comparing each subject (original image marked as intensity

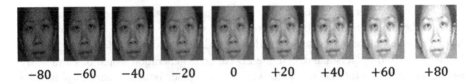

| −80 | −60 | −40 | −20 | 0 | +20 | +40 | +60 | +80 |

Fig. 7. Example of a frontal image (center image: labelled as 0) and the generated 8 images with different brightness levels (scalar value displayed as label under each individual image)

zero in Fig. 7) with its other 8 different brightness images (examples shown in Fig. 7) and with all other subjects (imposters) original image and their variants. Figure 8 shows the maximum and minimum distance values obtained for a genuine and imposter comparison, respectively. Analyzing this plot of scores obtained from genuine subject comparisons (intra-class comparisons) and imposter subject comparisons (inter-class comparisons), it can be estimated that the ID authentication system will classify very well between genuine and fake IDs with a threshold for hamming distance equal to around 400 bits. A very low decision threshold (approx. 400 bits) as compared to full feature length (4080 bits) shows effectiveness of the proposed approach.

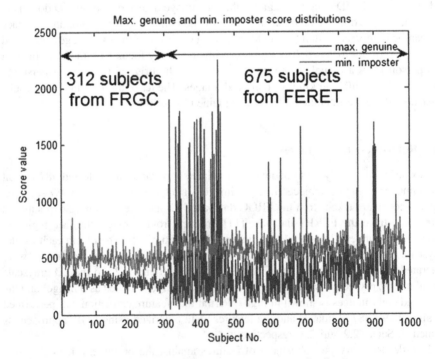

Fig. 8. Max. genuine and min. imposter score distributions

3.2   Identification and Verification

The aim of this experimental study is to check the quality of the discriminative feature represented by the binary feature vector, for the purpose of identification and verification of a person. The use case for identification can be a, (i) lost and found scenario, where an owner of a lost ID document needs to be identified, or (ii) duplicate enrolment check scenario, where a person asking for a reissue of another ID document can be detected by comparing his/her face image with face images of other persons already enrolled in the database. The experimental study was conducted on a dataset of 1203 images taken randomly from selected 295 subjects of the FRGC databases. Multiple images were taken from different subjects. The images taken were mainly frontal images with their intrinsic different illuminations and different expressions. Unlike Sect. 3.1; an explicit set of 8 different brightness were not generated in this case. Partial face feature extraction was performed for all of these 1203 images and the features were binarized using LGIP approach, as defined in Sects. 2.2 and 2.3, respectively.

For each image in the dataset we compare its binary feature vector with binary feature vectors extracted from other images in the database. The comparison scores were then ranked on the basis of least hamming distance, as lower distance would indicate high measure of closeness of both the images. The identification process carried was in closed-set identification scenario. i.e., the probe subject always had mate templates in the enrolment database.

To visualize the identification (1:N comparisons) and verification (1:1 comparisons) performances, the CMC (cumulative match curve) and the ROC (receiver operating characteristic) is plotted in Figs. 9 and 10, respectively.

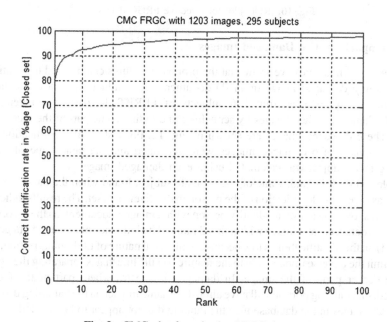

Fig. 9. CMC plot for selective FRGC data set

The CMC plot shows that the proposed method gives 80.3 % rank-1 performance for the given dataset. The ROC plot shows a true match rate of 58 % at false acceptance rate of 10 %. Figure 11 shows an illustration of identification application, where given an input test image, the top 8 closest images (based on hamming distance) were successfully retrieved.

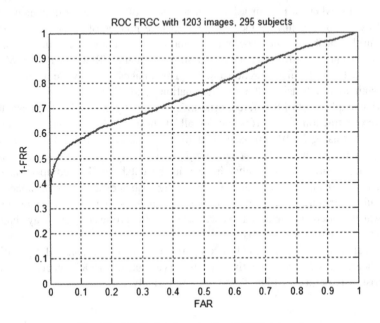

Fig. 10. ROC plot for selective FRGC data set

3.3   Comparison with Damaged Images

In this experimental study we show that the proposed features can be used to identify a person from a damaged image in an ID document. To conduct this study, a data set consisting of 449 images from 166 subjects of FERET database was taken. We manually damaged 6 face images by scratching and fading some part of the face in the image. These damaged images are shown in Fig. 12. For testing of identification, the binary templates of 6 damaged images were generated and the rank value of corresponding mate subject was calculated using each damaged image.

Table 1 shows the rank value of correct mate subject found when the damaged face image was given for identification of the person in the given data set. The results indicated in Table 1, shows the ability to identify person with damaged document, as the algorithm was able to detect correct image within first 3 ranks. The influence of damaged images (a, b, c and f) on the identification is low because of the local nature of LGIP binarization, as it would limit the adverse impact only to the features on the line that is separating the lighter and the darker parts of the image. In damaged image (e) where part of the face is scratched, this missing portion will have almost the same impact on the hamming distance against all images in the database thus the ranking did not appear to be affected.

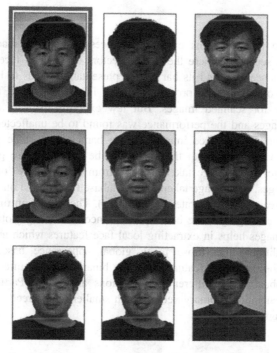

Fig. 11. Illustration of top ranked images (red highlighted: Input image)

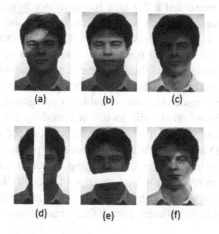

Fig. 12. Illustration of damaged images in an ID document

Table 1. Values of rank correctly detected under different damaged images

Damaged image	a	b	c	d	e	f
Rank of correct image	1	3	2	Face not detected	2	1

4 Discussion

It is important to note that this evaluation process should be made as close as possible to a real scenario, where the binary vectors of scanned face image from a document (using a scanner) and its bar code representation needs to be compared. It is evident that in our evaluation process, the used FRGC and FERET databases are not representative for scanned images. But few experiments were also performed using scanned images and the performance was found to be unaffected provided that both binary vectors for the face image and the bar code must be generated from images of same nature. i.e., both the vectors to be compared are generated either from digital images (i.e., image taken directly from the database) or are generated from scanned images. (i.e., image taken from database first printed on a paper using a printer and then scanned to generate the templates). The extraction of horizontal and vertical partial face image provide better performance than using global face images, because partial images helps in extracting local face features which are less sensitive to imaging conditions than those using global appearance based features [3]. Applying LGIP approach after feature extraction binarizes the features and makes the features more robust under different illuminations and noise. Partitioning of face image helps in generating a binary vector much smaller than directly apply LGIP on the complete image at once.

5 Conclusion and Future Work

In this paper, we have presented a 2D face recognition scheme based on extracting features from partial horizontal and vertical face images and feature level fusion (concatenation) of binary form of these features. These features are extracted using projection matrices and the extracted features are binarized using LGIP approach. The experimental results indicate 80.3 % rank-1 identification rate on a data set of FRGC database. The experimental results also showed that partial features are robust under different brightness conditions and are also suitable for recognition of faces even in case of damaged images. Future work will focus on encoding and compression of the generated binary template, so that it is as small as possible and can be easily printed using a much smaller 2D bar code. This will improve the practical usability of the face recognition approach for application of protecting ID documents. In addition, our future plan is to improve recognition performance in uncontrolled scenario (different illuminations with face expressions) by assigning optimum weights to different comparison scores extracted from different partial face binary features.

Acknowledgement. The work leading to these results has received funding from the European Community's Framework Programme (FP7/2007-2013) under grant agreement no. 284862

References

1. Zhou, X., Schmucker, M.: Securing of Personal Identity Documents against Forgery (Sichern von personen-identitätsdokumenten gegen Falschung). Patent WO 2009/074342 A1, June 2009
2. Cascade classifier. http://docs.opencv.org/doc/tutorials/objdetect/cascade_classifier/cascade_classifier.html. Acessed 4 June 2014
3. Oh, B.-S., Toh, K.-A., Choi, K., Teoh, A.B.J., Kim, J.: Extraction and fusion of partial face features for cancelable identity verification. Pattern Recogn. **45**, 3288–3303 (2012)
4. Lubing, Z., Han, W.: Local gradient increasing pattern for facial expression recognition. In: 19th IEEE International Conference on Image Processing (ICIP) (2012)
5. Zhou, L.B., Wang, H.: Local gradient increasing pattern (LGIP) for facial representation and gender recognition. In: Campilho, A., Kamel, M. (eds.) ICIAR 2012, Part II. LNCS, vol. 7325, pp. 46–53. Springer, Heidelberg (2012)
6. Odeh, S., Khalil, M.: Off-line signature verification and recognition: neural network approach. In: International Symposium on Innovations in Intelligent Systems and Applications (INISTA) (2011)
7. Karouni, A., Daya, B., Bahlak, S.: Offline signature recognition using neural networks approach. In: World Conference on Information Technology WCIT 2010, Procedia Computer Science (2011)
8. ZXing (zebra crossing), bar code image processing library. https://github.com/zxing/zxing. Accessed 4 June 2014
9. Quricol 2.0 QR Code Generator. http://delphi32.blogspot.de/2013/09/quricol-20-qr-code-generator.html. Accessed 4 June 2014
10. Phillips, P.J., Flynn, P.J., Scruggs, T., Bowyer, K.W., Worek, W.: Preliminary face recognition grand challenge results. In: 7th International Conference on Automatic Face and Gesture Recognition (2006)
11. Phillips, P.J., Moon, H., Rauss, P.J., Rizvi, S.: The FERET evaluation methodology for face recognition algorithms. IEEE Trans. Pattern **22**(10), 1090–1104 (2000)

Comparison of Multidirectional Representations for Multispectral Palmprint Recognition

Zohaib Khan[✉], Faisal Shafait, and Ajmal Mian

School of Computer Science and Software Engineering,
The University of Western Australia, Perth, Australia
{zohaib.khan,faisal.shafait,ajmal.mian}@uwa.edu.au

Abstract. Palmprint is emerging as a new multi-modal biometric for human recognition. Multispectral palmprint images captured in the visible and infrared spectrum not only contain the superficial structure of a palm, but also the underlying structure of veins; making them a highly discriminating person identifier. This study comparatively analyzes multidirectional representations for multispectral palmprint recognition which show promising results. Comprehensive experiments for both identification and verification scenarios are performed on three public datasets. The accuracies of state-of-the-art clearly indicate the viability of multidirectional coding methods for multispectral palmprint recognition.

1   Introduction

The information present in a human palm has an immense amount of potential for biometric recognition. Information visible to the naked eye includes the principal lines, the wrinkles and the fine ridges which form a unique pattern for every individual [13]. These superficial features can be captured using standard imaging devices. High resolution scanners capture the fine ridge pattern of a palm which is generally employed for latent palmprint identification in forensics [3]. The principal lines and wrinkles acquired with low resolution sensors are suitable for security applications like user identification or authentication [12].

Additional information present in the human palm is the subsurface vein pattern which is indifferent to the palm lines. Such features cannot be easily acquired by a standard imaging sensor. Infrared imaging can capture subsurface features due to its capability to penetrate the human skin. The superficial and subsurface features of a palm have been collectively investigated under the subject of '*multispectral palmprint recognition*'. Using *Multispectral Imaging (MSI)*, it is possible to capture images of an object at multiple wavelengths of light, in the visible spectrum and beyond. A monochromatic camera under spectrally varying illuminations can acquire multispectral palm images. Figure 1 shows palm images captured at three different wavelengths. The availability of such complementary features (palm lines and veins) makes palmprint suitable for recognition where user cooperation is affordable, e.g., at secure access gates, workplace attendance and identification records.

© Springer International Publishing Switzerland 2015
U. Garain and F. Shafait (Eds.): IWCF 2012 and 2014, LNCS 8915, pp. 44–54, 2015.
DOI: 10.1007/978-3-319-20125-2_5

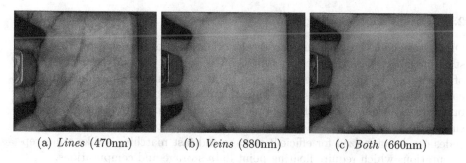

(a) Lines (470nm)   (b) Veins (880nm)   (c) Both (660nm)

Fig. 1. Examples of palmprint features in multiple bands. Three bands of a multispectral image captured using a contact based sensor. (a) Palm lines captured in the visible range. (b) Palm veins captured in the near infrared range. (c) A combination of the line and vein features at intermediate wavelengths.

The multi-modal nature of multispectral palmprints requires robust feature extraction methods. This work compares state-of-the-art orientation codes for *multispectral palmprint recognition*. Section 2 briefly describes the concept of orientation coding algorithms with details of the Contour Code (ContCode) [4], the Competitive Code (CompCode) [6], the Ordinal Code (OrdCode) [8] and the Derivative of Gaussian Code (DoGCode) [9]. Section 4 presents the multispectral palmprint verification and identification in various experimental settings and compares the performance of the state-of-the-art. These experiments are performed on three publicly available multispectral palmprint databases i.e. PolyU-Multispectral Palmprint Database, PolyU-Hyperspectral Palmprint Database and CASIA Multispectral Palmprint Database described in Sect. 3. Section 6 ends the paper with conclusions.

2 Multidirectional Palmprint Encoding

Palmprint recognition approaches can be categorized into line-like feature detectors, subspace learning methods and texture based coding techniques [5]. These three categories are not mutually exclusive and their combinations are also possible. Line detection based approaches commonly extract palm lines using edge detectors [2]. Recognition based solely on palm lines proves insufficient due to their sparse nature and the possibility of different individuals having highly similar palm lines [11]. Although, line detection can extract palm lines effectively, it may not be equally useful for the extraction of palm veins due to their low contrast and broad structure. A subspace projection captures the local and/or global characteristics of a palm by projecting to the most varying [7] or the most discriminative [10] dimensions. The palmprint subspace representations are not effective compared to the state-of-the-art techniques. The main reason is that subspaces learned from misaligned palms are unlikely to generate accurate representation of each identity.

2.1   Orientation Coding

Orientation codes extract and encode the orientation of lines which have shown state-of-the-art performance in palmprint recognition [13]. In the generic form of orientation coding, the response of a palm to a bank of directional filters is computed such that the resulting directional subbands correspond to specific orientations of line. Then, the dominant orientation index from the directional subbands is extracted at each point to form the orientation code. Orientation codes can be binarized for efficient storage and fast matching unlike other representations which require floating point data storage and computations.

Derivative of Gaussian Code (DoGCode) [9] is a compact representation which only uses vertical and horizontal gaussian derivative filters to extract feature orientation of a palmprint image, and then encodes the filter responses into binary code. The horizontal and vertical derivatives of 2D Gaussian filters used in DoGCode are given as

$$\mathcal{F}_x(x, y : \sigma) = -\frac{x}{2\pi\sigma^4} e^{\left(-\frac{x^2+y^2}{2\sigma^2}\right)} \tag{1}$$

$$\mathcal{F}_y(x, y : \sigma) = -\frac{y}{2\pi\sigma^4} e^{\left(-\frac{x^2+y^2}{2\sigma^2}\right)} \tag{2}$$

where σ is the scale of the filter.

Ordinal Code (OrdCode) [8] emphasizes the ordinal relationship of lines by comparing mutually orthogonal filter pairs to extract the feature orientation at a point. It uses six 2D elliptical Gaussian filters for filtering the palmprint image. The 2D elliptical Gaussian filter used in the OrdCode are defined as

$$\mathcal{F}(x, y : \theta, \delta_x, \delta_y) = e^{-\left(\frac{x\cos\theta + y\sin\theta}{\delta_x}\right)^2 - \left(\frac{-x\sin\theta + y\cos\theta}{\delta_y}\right)^2} \tag{3}$$

where (δ_x, δ_y) are the scales of the orthogonal Gaussian filters oriented at $(\theta, \theta + \pi/2)$. The ratio δ_x/δ_y is kept high to get an elliptical filter response.

Competitive Code (CompCode) [6] employs a directional bank of Gabor filters to extract the orientation of palm lines. The 2D Gabor filters for multidirectional filtering of palm images are given as

$$\mathcal{F}(x, y : \theta, \omega, \kappa) = -\frac{\omega}{\sqrt{2\pi}\kappa} e^{\frac{\omega^2}{8\kappa^2}(4(x\cos\theta + y\sin\theta)^2 + (-x\sin\theta + y\cos\theta)^2)} \left(e^{\iota\omega x} - e^{-\frac{\kappa^2}{2}}\right) \tag{4}$$

where $\omega = \kappa/\sigma$ is the radial frequency and θ is the orientation of the Gabor filter. The parameter $\kappa = \sqrt{2\log 2}\frac{2^\delta+1}{2^\delta-1}$, where δ is the bandwidth of the filter response.

Contour Code (ContCode) [4] uses pyramidal-directional filter banks to extract the orientation of palmprint features and uses a binary hash table encoding for efficient storage and matching. The pyramidal bandpass filter captures the details in the palm at a single scale. The pyramidal filtered component is subsequently convolved with a 2D directional filter bank of sinc filter.

$$\mathcal{F}(x, y : \theta) = P_f(x, y) * \frac{1}{\sqrt{2}} \frac{sin(x : \theta)}{x} \frac{sin(y : \theta)}{y} , \quad (5)$$

where $P_f(x, y)$ is the pyramidal filter. The combination of pyramidal and directional filter decomposition stages robustly capture line like features from palmprints.

2.2 Binary Encoding and Matching

Orientation codes can be integer coded according to the maximum (or minimum) filter response for directional subband at orientation θ

$$C(x, y) = \arg \min_i \quad I(x, y) * \mathcal{F}(x, y : \theta) , \quad (6)$$

where $\theta = i\frac{\pi}{K}$ where K is the total number of orientations. For storage and matching, orientation codes can be binarized and stored in efficient structures such as one proposed in [4]. All methods in this paper use the same binary encoding and matching scheme for a fair comparison.

3 Multispectral Palmprint Databases

Experiments are performed on the PolyU-MS[1], PolyU-HS[2] and CASIA-MS[3] palmprint databases. All databases contain low resolution (<150 *dpi*) palmprint images. Several samples of each subject were acquired in two different sessions. Detailed specifications of the databases are given in Table 1.

The PolyU-HS database was collected with the aim to find the minimum number of bands required for designing a multispectral palmprint recognition system rather than utilizing the complete set of hyperspectral bands. The number of bands of the PolyU-HS database were reduced from 69 to 4 according to the band selection method proposed in [1]. The four most informative bands were 580 nm, 620 nm, 760 nm and 940 nm.

---

[1] PolyU   Multispectral   Palmprint   Database   http://www.comp.polyu.edu.hk/~biometrics/MultispectralPalmprint/MSP.htm.

[2] PolyU   Hyperspectral   Palmprint   Database   http://www4.comp.polyu.edu.hk/~biometrics/HyperspectralPalmprint/HSP.htm.

[3] CASIA   Multispectral   Palmprint   Database   http://www.cbsr.ia.ac.cn/MS_Palmprint_Database.asp.

Table 1. Specifications of the PolyU-MS, PolyU-HS and CASIA-MS databases.

Database	PolyU-MS	PolyU-HS	CASIA-MS
Sensor type	contact	contact	non-contact
Identities	500	380	200
Samples per identity	12	11–14	6
Total samples	6000	5240	1200
Bands per sample	4	69	6
Wavelength(nm)	470, 525, 660, 880	420–1100 (10 nm steps)	460, 630, 700, 850, 940, White

Table 2. Individual performance of bands in PolyU-MS, PolyU-HS and CASIA-MS database.

	PolyU-MS			PolyU-HS			CASIA-MS	
Band	GAR(%)	EER(%)	Band	GAR(%)	EER(%)	Band	GAR(%)	EER(%)
470 nm	99.94	0.0784	580 nm	99.56	0.3003	460 nm	88.95	2.9246
525 nm	99.98	0.0420	620 nm	99.93	0.0779	630 nm	87.79	3.9065
660 nm	99.99	0.0242	760 nm	99.67	0.2475	700 nm	57.35	9.7318
880 nm	99.90	0.1030	940 nm	99.83	0.1495	850 nm	87.45	4.1398
						940 nm	90.73	3.4769

4   Multispectral Palmprint Recognition

The multispectral palm regions in each band are downsampled to 32×32 pixels using bi-cubic interpolation. Then, features are extracted using four state-of-the-art methods for subsequent use in recognition experiments.

4.1   Verification Experiments

Verification experiments are performed on PolyU-MS, PolyU-HS and CASIA-MS databases adapting the protocol of [13], where session based experiments are structured to observe the recognition performance. The evaluation comprises five verification experiments to test different techniques. The experiments proceed by matching

Exp.1: individual bands of palm irrespective of the session.
Exp.2: multispectral palmprints acquired in the 1st session.
Exp.3: multispectral palmprints acquired in the 2nd session.
Exp.4: multispectral palmprints of the 1st session to the 2nd session.
Exp.5: multispectral palmprints irrespective of the session (all vs. all).

In all experiments, the ROC curves, which depict the False Rejection Rate (FRR) versus the False Acceptance Rate (FAR) are reported. The Equal Error Rate (EER), and the Genuine Acceptance Rate (GAR) at 0.1 % FAR are also summarized to compare performance of the state-of-the-art techniques.

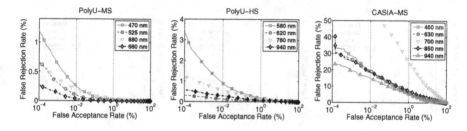

Fig. 2. Exp.1: ROC curves of ContCode on individual bands

Experiment 1: Band Discriminant Capability. This experiment compares the relative discriminant capability of individual bands in different databases. We compare the performance of individual bands of the PolyU-MS and CASIA-MS database using ContCode. Figure 2 shows the ROC curves of the individual bands and Table 2 lists their EERs. In the PolyU-MS database, the 660 nm band gives the best performance indicating the presence of more discriminatory features. A logical explanation could be that the 660 nm wavelength partially captures both the line and vein features making this band relatively more discriminative. In the PolyU-HS database, the 620 nm and 940 nm have the lowest errors followed by 760 nm and 580 nm. In CASIA-MS database, the most discriminant information is present in the 940 nm, 850 nm, 630 nm and 460 nm bands which are close competitors.

Experiment 2: Verification in the 1ˢᵗ Session This experiment analyzes the variability in the palmprint data acquired in the 1ˢᵗ session. Figure 3 compares the ROC curves of the ContCode with three other techniques on all databases. It is observable that the CompCode and the OrdCode show intermediate performance close to ContCode. The DoGCode exhibits a drastic degradation of accuracy implying its inability to sufficiently cope with the variations of CASIA-MS data. Overall, the CompCode and ContCode perform better on both databases while the latter performs the best.

Experiment 3: Verification in the 2ⁿᵈ Session This experiment analyzes the variability in the palmprint data acquired in the 2ⁿᵈ session. This allows for a comparison with the results of *Exp.2* to analyze the intra-session variability.

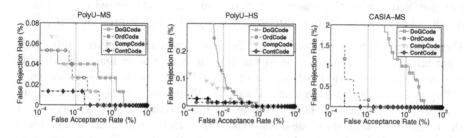

Fig. 3. Exp.2: Matching palmprints of 1ˢᵗ session.

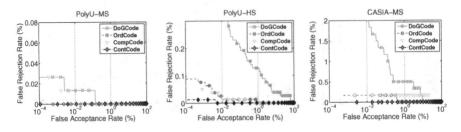

Fig. 4. Exp.3: Matching palmprints of 2nd session.

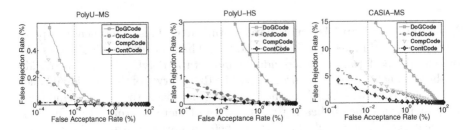

Fig. 5. Exp.4: Matching palmprints of the 1st session to the 2nd session. The verification performance is low relative to *Exp.2* and *Exp.3*. However, the performance degradation of the proposed ContCode is much less than the other techniques on both databases, indicating its robustness to image variability.

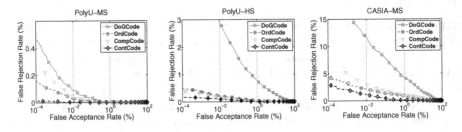

Fig. 6. Exp.5: Matching palmprints irrespective of the acquisition session.

Therefore, only the palmprints acquired in the 2nd session are matched. Figure 4 compares the ROC curves of all techniques. The small improvement in verification performance on the images of 2nd session can be attributed to the better quality of images and increased user familiarity with the acquisition system.

Experiment 4: Verification of 2nd Session from 1st Session This experiment mimics a verification scenario which incurs variation in image quality due to sensor aging or subject behavior over time. It analyzes the inter-session variability of multispectral palmprints. Therefore, all images from the 1st session are matched to all images of the 2nd session. Figure 5 compares the ROC curves of the techniques on all databases. Note that the performance of all techniques is relatively lower for this experiment compared to *Exp.2* and *Exp.3* because this

Table 3. Summary of verification results for *Exp.2* to *Exp.5*

		PolyU-MS			
		DoGCode	OrdCode	CompCode	ContCode
Exp.2	EER(%)	0.0400	0.0267	0.0165	0.0133
	GAR(%)	99.96	99.99	99.99	100.00
Exp.3	EER(%)	0.0133	0	0.0098	0
	GAR(%)	99.99	100.00	100.00	100.00
Exp.4	EER(%)	0.0528	0.0247	0.0333	0.0029
	GAR(%)	99.96	99.98	99.99	100.00
Exp.5	EER(%)	0.0455	0.0212	0.0263	0.0030
	GAR(%)	99.97	99.99	99.99	100.00
		PolyU-HS			
		DoGCode	OrdCode	CompCode	ContCode
Exp.2	EER(%)	0.0398	0.0130	0.0261	0.0130
	GAR(%)	99.97	99.99	99.99	99.99
Exp.3	EER(%)	0.1912	0.0128	0.0128	0.0045
	GAR(%)	99.79	99.99	99.99	100.00
Exp.4	EER(%)	1.1530	0.1598	0.0830	0.0866
	GAR(%)	97.56	99.80	99.93	99.92
Exp.5	EER(%)	0.8150	0.1043	0.0626	0.0596
	GAR(%)	98.42	99.88	99.96	99.96
		CASIA-MS			
		DoGCode	OrdCode	CompCode	ContCode
Exp.2	EER(%)	1.000	0.1667	0.0140	0
	GAR(%)	98.00	99.67	100.00	100.00
Exp.3	EER(%)	0.6667	0.1667	0.1667	0.0011
	GAR(%)	98.50	99.83	99.83	100.00
Exp.4	EER(%)	3.8669	1.2778	0.6667	0.2778
	GAR(%)	87.70	97.39	97.72	99.61
Exp.5	EER(%)	2.8873	0.8667	0.4993	0.2000
	GAR(%)	92.01	98.37	98.60	99.76

is a difficult scenario due to the intrinsic variability in the human behavior over time. However, the drop in performance of ContCode is the minimum. Therefore, it is fair to deduce that ContCode is relatively robust to the image variability over time.

Experiment 5: All-vs-All Verification. This experiment evaluates the overall verification performance by combining images from both sessions. All images

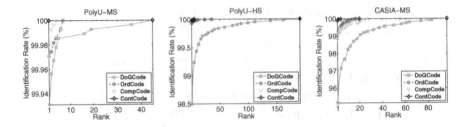

Fig. 7. CMC curves for the identification experiment. Note that ContCode has an average rank-1 recognition rate of 100 % on the PolyU-MS database.

Table 4. Comparison of rank-1 recognition rate and standard deviation on all databases.

Method	PolyU-MS (%)	PolyU-HS (%)	CASIA-MS (%)
DoGCode [9]	99.97±0.04	99.93±0.05	95.08±0.75
OrdCode [8]	99.93±0.05	98.50±0.28	99.02±0.11
CompCode [6]	99.97±0.03	99.99±0.01	99.52±0.11
ContCode [4]	100.0±0	99.98±0.03	99.88±0.08

in the database are matched to all other images, irrespective of the acquisition session which is commonly termed as an "all-versus-all" experiment. Figure 6 compares the ROC curves of all techniques. Similar to the previous experiments, the ContCode consistently outperforms all other techniques.

The results of *Exp.2* to *Exp.5* are summarized in Table 3 for the all databases. The ContCode consistently outperforms the other methods in all experiments. Moreover, CompCode is consistently the second best performer except for very low FAR values in *Exp.4* and *Exp.5* on the PolyU-MS database (see Fig. 5 and Fig. 6). It is also interesting to note that the OrdCode performs better than the DoGCode on all databases.

5   Identification Experiments

Palmprint identification is carried out in 5-fold cross validation experiment and the Cumulative Match Characteristics (CMC) curves are reported alongside the Rank-1 identification rates. The identification rates are averaged over the five folds. In each fold, one multispectral palmprint image per subject is randomly selected to form the gallery and the remaining images are considered as probes. This means that the identification is based on a single multispectral image for each subject in the gallery. This protocol is followed for all databases.

5.1   Experiment 1: Identification Experiment

The CMC curves on all databases are given in Fig. 7 and the identification results are summarized in Table 4. The ContCode achieved an average identification rate of 99.88 % on the CASIA-MS database, 99.91 % on the PolyU-HS database and 100 % on the PolyU-MS database. The ContCode clearly demonstrates better identification performance in comparison to state-of-the-art techniques.

6   Conclusion

In this study, state-of-the-art orientation based coding algorithms were compared for multispectral palmprint recognition. Various experiments were designed to cater for sessional affects in multispectral palmprint recognition. The results indicate that the ContCode is most accurate, followed by CompCode, OrdCode and DoGCode in both verification and identification experiments. Overall, the orientation coding techniques show promising results for extracting multimodal features of a palmprint. The MATLAB code of all techniques including the experiments conducted in this work is available at www.sites.google.com/site/zohaibnet/Home/codes.

Acknowledgements. This research was supported by ARC Grant DP0881813 and DP110102399. Authors acknowledge the Polytechnic University of Hong Kong for providing the PolyU-MS and PolyU-HS Palmprint database and the Chinese Academy of Sciences' Institute of Automation for providing the CASIA MS-PalmprintV1 database.

References

1. Guo, Z., Zhang, D., Zhang, L., Liu, W.: Feature band selection for online multispectral palmprint recognition. IEEE Trans. Inf. Forensics Secur. **7**(3), 1094–1099 (2012)
2. Huang, D.S., Jia, W., Zhang, D.: Palmprint verification based on principal lines. Pattern Recogn. **41**(4), 1316–1328 (2008)
3. Jain, A.K., Feng, J.: Latent palmprint matching. IEEE Trans. Pattern Anal. Mach. Intell. **31**(6), 1032–1047 (2009)
4. Khan, Z., Mian, A., Hu, Y.: Contour code: Robust and efficient multispectral palmprint encoding for human recognition. In: Proceedings of the International Conference on Computer Vision (ICCV), pp. 1935–1942. IEEE (2011)
5. Kong, A., Zhang, D., Kamel, M.: A survey of palmprint recognition. Pattern Recogn. **42**(7), 1408–1418 (2009)
6. Kong, A.K., Zhang, D.: Competitive coding scheme for palmprint verification. In: Proceedings of the International Conference on Pattern Recognition, pp. 520–523. IEEE (2004)
7. Lu, G., Zhang, D., Wang, K.: Palmprint recognition using eigenpalms features. Pattern Recogn. Lett. **24**(9), 1463–1467 (2003)
8. Sun, Z., Tan, T., Wang, Y., Li, S.Z.: Ordinal palmprint representation for personal identification. In: Proceedings of the Computer Vision and Pattern Recognition, pp. 279–284. IEEE (2005)
9. Wu, X., Wang, K., Zhang, D.: Palmprint texture analysis using derivative of gaussian filters. In: Proceedings of the International Conference on Computational Intelligence and Security, pp. 751–754. IEEE (2006)

10. Wu, X., Zhang, D., Wang, K.: Fisherpalms based palmprint recognition. Pattern Recogn. Lett. **24**(15), 2829–2838 (2003)
11. Zhang, D., Guo, Z., Lu, G., Zhang, L., Liu, Y., Zuo, W.: Online joint palmprint and palmvein verification. Expert Syst. Appl. **38**(3), 2621–2631 (2011)
12. Zhang, D., Kong, W.K., You, J., Wong, M.: Online palmprint identification. IEEE Trans. Pattern Anal. Mach. Intell. **25**(9), 1041–1050 (2003)
13. Zhang, D., Zuo, W., Yue, F.: A comparative study of palmprint recognition algorithms. ACM Comput. Surv. (CSUR) **44**(1), 2:1–2:37 (2012)

Efficient Iris Recognition System Using Relational Measures

Aditya Nigam, Lovish$^{(\boxtimes)}$, Amit Bendale, and Phalguni Gupta

Department of Computer Science and Engineering,
Indian Institute of Technology Kanpur, Kanpur 208016, India
{naditya,lovishc,bendale,pg}@cse.iitk.ac.in

Abstract. This paper proposes an efficient iris based authentication system. The segmented iris is unwrapped, normalized and enhanced using the proposed local enhancement technique. Occlusion mask determination is performed to detect eyelid, eyelashes and reflections using morphological and filtering operations. Features are extracted and matched from enhanced image using relative intensities of regions and encoding them into a binary template. The proposed recognition approach has obtained a CRR of 99.07 % on CASIA-4.0 Interval, 98.7 % on CASIA-4.0 Lamp and 98.66 % on IITK database. It has also achieved an EER of 1.82 % on CASIA-4.0 Interval, 4.2 % on CASIA-4.0 Lamp and 2.12 % on IITK database.

1 Introduction

Recently it is observed that personal authentication has emerged as a primary requirement of our society. Biometrics based characteristics are used to realize it either using physiological (such as face [18,19], fingerprint [7,25], iris [5,16, 20], palmprint [21], ear [23,24], knuckleprint [4,17,22] *etc.*) or behavioural such as gait, speech *etc.* characteristics, which are assumed to be unique for each individual. However, each trait has its own challenges and trait specific issues hence none of the biometric trait can be considered as the best one. The human eye is a well-protected internal organ and has rich texture information that can be used in identification. It has a very rich layered pigmentation structure composed of various colors and patterns. These patterns include ridges, furrows, spots, curves, etc.

The estimation of amount and location of iris occlusion is a very critical step. Hence it has to be carried out before recognition. In [10], parabola fitting has been used to detect upper and lower eyelids from original iris image. Eyelashes are detected using gray-level co-occurence matrix (GLCM) technique in [3]. GLCM is computed for windows of fixed size and fuzzy K-means algorithm is used to cluster them into skin, eyelash, sclera, pupil and iris using the computed GLCM values. In [13], the eyelids have been detected by line fitting on edge map of raw image within the inner and outer boundaries of iris.

In [8], iris recognition is done by creating a binary representation and has extracted a real-valued representation similar to [27]. Several filters have been

© Springer International Publishing Switzerland 2015
U. Garain and F. Shafait (Eds.): IWCF 2012 and 2014, LNCS 8915, pp. 55–66, 2015.
DOI: 10.1007/978-3-319-20125-2_6

proposed to extract useful features from the unwrapped iris image. In [15], discrete cosine transform(DCT) has been applied on overlapping rectangular patches rotated at 45° degrees from circumferential direction. Difference of DCT coefficients of adjacent patches is binarised and used to create the template. In [12], Dyadic wavelet transformation of a group constituting $1 - D$ row signals obtained from unwrapped iris image has been used to create a template. Ordinal measures proposed in [26] use relative intensities of image regions to generate a binary template. In [13], the quantised phase data from 1D Log-Gabor filters has been used to generate iris templates. Disadvantage of the Gabor-filter based approaches is that extensive parameter optimisation is required to get accurate recognition. The approaches which use real valued features use distance measures like Euclidean, Cosine, etc. In [2] four different features are extracted using Gabor filtering, histogram of phase coefficients, Daubechies wavelet and DCT to train a neural network. Statistical methods like PCA [9], and ICA [11], have been used as supplements to wavelets. Band-limited phase-only correlation($BLPOC$) based on $2D-$DFTs of two images has been used for matching in [14].

In this paper, initially occlusion mask is determined for each iris. Robust features using relative Gaussian filtering responses of neighbor regions are computed and matched using hamming distance. The paper is organized as follows: Sect. 2 describes the proposed algorithm. Section 3 presents the experimental results of the proposed system and last Section concludes the work.

2   Proposed Approach

The iris segmentation is done using the technique proposed in [6]. Iris region is normalized to a fixed size to deal with iris dilations. One of the major hurdles in iris recognition is occlusion (hiding of iris) due to eyelids, eyelashes, specular reflection and shadows. Occlusion hides the useful iris texture and introduces irrelevant parts like eyelids and eyelashes which are not an iris part.

2.1   Occlusion Detection

Occlusion is detected from the normalized image, instead of original iris image. It is done in three steps: eyelid, eyelash and specular reflection detection.

[A] **Eyelid Detection-** The major portion of the occluded iris area is constituted by lower and upper eyelids. Instead of traditional parabola/ellipse fitting, region-growing approach [1] has been used to determine the eyelids. For normalized image of size $r \times c$, two seed point $(r, \frac{c}{4})$ and $(r, \frac{3c}{4})$ are chosen to perform region-growing to detect lower and upper eyelid respectively. These points are chosen because after normalization upper and lower eyelids mostly at $\left(\frac{\pi}{2}\right)^c$ and $\left(\frac{3\pi}{2}\right)^c$ angles $w.r.t.$ horizontal axis. Region-growing begins with these seeds using a low threshold and expands the regions till they encounter similar region. This gives the expected lower and upper eyelid regions. Region-growing overcomes the problem of shape irregularity of eyelids and gives the exact area which is occluded by eyelids. It fails when eyelid boundary does not have good contrast because of which it grows outside the eyelid region. Therefore region-growing is repeated with a lower threshold so that it does not grow outside the eyelid regions. If region grows beyond a limit, it indicates that there is no eyelid. Finally, a binary mask is generated in which every eyelid pixel is set to 1, as shown in Fig. 1(b).

[B] Eyelash Detection - Eyelashes are of two types: separable and multiple. Separable eyelashes are like thin threads whereas multiple eyelashes constitute a shadow like region. Eyelashes have lower intensity as compared to iris texture; but absolute threshold that can separate them with the rest of iris cannot be determined properly, because it is very sensitive to illumination. Eyelashes have high contrast with their surrounding pixels but having low intensity. As a result, standard deviation in a small region around separable eyelashes will be high. The normalized image is convoluted with a 3×3 standard deviation filter. High filter response is used to localize he separable eyelashes. Multiple eyelashes do not have high value of filter response, but they have lower intensity value. Hence to give some weight to low intensity pixel value, filter response for each pixel is normalized with respect to the maximum response. A combined feature $CF(i,j)$ for every pixel $P(i,j)$ is computed as :

$$CF(i,j) = 0.5 \times SD(i,j) + 0.5 \times (1 - N(i,j)) \tag{1}$$

where SD is the normalized standard deviation filter response, N represents normalized intensity values $(0--1)$ of pixel (i,j) in normalized iris. This feature boosts up the gap between eyelash and non-eyelash part. The histogram CF_H of CF is computed, that has two distinct clusters - one corresponding to low CF values belonging to iris pixels while other with high CF values belonging to eyelash pixels. To identify these two clusters Otsu thresholding is used that considers all possible pairs of clusters and chooses the clustering that minimizes the intra-cluster variance. It thus separates the eyelash portion from the iris portion as shown in Fig. 1(c).

[C] Specular Reflection Detection Specular reflection can be detected by using simple thresholding method. Those pixels which exceed a threshold value of 200 (very bright) are declared as specular reflections. Absolute threshold can be used because specular reflections are very bright. A binary mask is generated in which all specular reflections pixels are set to 1 as shown in Fig. 1(d). The final occlusion mask is generated by addition (logical $OR - ing$) of the binary masks of eyelid, eyelash and specular reflection as shown in Fig. 1(e).

2.2 Enhancement

The normalized iris is enhanced to highlight its rich texture features. Non-uniform illumination is an important artifact introduced due to varying illumination condition. It adds different intensities to various iris regions and introduces

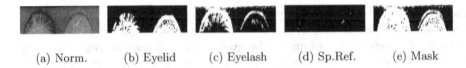

(a) Norm.   (b) Eyelid   (c) Eyelash   (d) Sp.Ref.   (e) Mask

Fig. 1. Determination of overall occlusion mask

noise. An example of such image is shown in Fig. 2(a). The mean intensity value of each 8×8 size block is used as an estimate of background illumination (e.g. Figure 2(b)) which is subtracted from the original image to obtain uniformly illuminated image (e.g. Figure 2(c)). The Contrast-Limited Adaptive Histogram Equalization ($CLAHE$) [28] is applied over uniformly illuminated image to obtain enhanced image (e.g. Figure 2(d)). The entire process of enhancement is shown in Fig. 2.

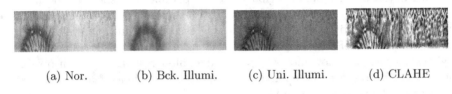

(a) Nor.   (b) Bck. Illumi.   (c) Uni. Illumi.   (d) CLAHE

Fig. 2. Overall Enhancement Process

2.3 Feature Extraction Approach

Raw iris image is very sensitive to translation, rotation, blurring, noises, occlusions and non-uniform illuminations. This sensitivity increases intra-class differences and may also mitigate inter-class differences that may lead to incorrect identification. Hence, a template is generated and used which represents the iris image in a robust, compact and unique manner.

In the proposed feature extraction approach, relational measures (RM) are calculated for various regions of enhanced image for iris encoding. The average intensities of an image region is compared with its four neighboring equi-spaced regions (as shown in Fig. 3(a)) at fixed distance and there sign is encoded into a bit. Hence for all selected regions, four bits corresponding to sign of such comparisons with four neighboring regions are obtained. Vertically and horizontally overlapping regions are chosen from the normalized image. The four bits per region are obtained and are concatenated to create a 2-D binary template.

Feature Extraction using Relational Measures (RM) Relational measures are features based on relational operators like $>,<,=$. These ordinal relationships are more robust than the "absolute difference". Single order relation (*i.e* greater than or less than) is encoded in a bit. The central region of size $b \times b$ is chosen and its four neighboring regions of size $b \times b$ are selected (as shown in Fig. 3(b)) at a particular distance d, where d is large as compared to b. The value of d is kept larger than b because distant regions provide comparison between uncorrelated regions which is more robust as compared to that with closer regions. A symmetric $2D$ Gaussian filter centrally clipped to size $b \times b$ is used for convolution with each of these five regions, as shown in Fig. 3(a). The symmetric $2D$ Gaussian filter is a bell-shaped probability function PDF defined as:

$$G(\boldsymbol{\mu}, \sigma) = \frac{1}{2\pi\sigma^2} e^{-\frac{(\boldsymbol{X}-\boldsymbol{\mu})(\boldsymbol{X}-\boldsymbol{\mu})^T}{2\sigma^2}} \tag{2}$$

where $\boldsymbol{\mu}$ is the spatial location of the peak (mean), σ is the standard deviation of the Gaussian and $\boldsymbol{X}$ is the spatial location. Assume that x-coordinate increases from top to bottom of image whereas y-coordinate increases from left to right. If the mid point of central region is $(0, 0)$, then the peaks of the four identical Gaussian filters used for its neighbors are at $(-d, 0)$, $(0, d)$, $(d, 0)$ and $(0, -d)$, as shown in Fig. 3(a).

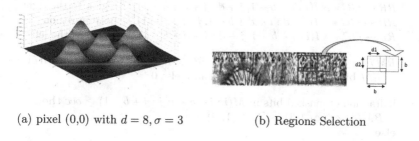

(a) pixel (0,0) with $d = 8, \sigma = 3$ (b) Regions Selection

Fig. 3. Region Filtering

The response of the central region is compared with those of its neighbors. If its response is greater than that of a neighbor, the information is encoded as 1 else 0. Thus, four bit code for this central region is obtained. Vertically and horizontally overlapping rectangular patches over the entire image are chosen as candidates for the central region, as shown in Fig. 3(b). These bits are concatenated according to the spatial location of their corresponding central regions in the image to generate a 2-D binary template (feature vector).

The occlusion mask is also generated for every iris image. A second level mask based on the feature vector calculation is generated as follows: if the central block has more than $80\,\%$ occluded pixels then the four bit code for that block is masked by values $[1, 1, 1, 1]$ in the second level mask. Otherwise, it is left unmasked or $[0,0,0,0]$ is put in the mask. The second level mask is essential because the feature vector is not pixel-based but block-based. Hence, the corresponding masking should also be brought down to block level. The algorithm to compute the feature vector and second level mask is given in Algorithm 1.

A $b \times b$ Gaussian filter GC is obtained by clipping the generalized Gaussian $G(\boldsymbol{0}, \sigma)$ centrally around the **zero** mean. Feature template RMT and block-level mask BM are initialized to zero values. Central block of size $b \times b$ is chosen from the normalized image NI and is convoluted with GC to obtain scalar response

---

Algorithm 1. *RM* Feature Extraction and Masking

Require: Normalized Iris image NI of dimension $m \times n$, Occlusion mask M of NI of same size, σ: scale of 2-D gaussian filter, d: inter-lobe distance, d_1 horizontal offset, d_2: vertical offset, b: clipped size of the filter, occ: occlusion threshold

Ensure: RMT (feature template) and BM(block-level mask)

1: $GC = clip2D(G(\mathbf{0}, \sigma), b)$ // Clip the filter obtained from Equation (2) centrally to $b \times b$
2: $RMT \leftarrow$ AllocateWithZero($\lfloor \frac{m}{d_2} \rfloor$, $4 \times \lfloor \frac{n}{d_1} \rfloor$) //Template initialisation
3: $BM \leftarrow$ AllocateWithZero($\lfloor \frac{m}{d_2} \rfloor$, $4 \times \lfloor \frac{n}{d_1} \rfloor$) // Mask initialisation
4: $c_1 \leftarrow 1$
5: **for** $i := d + 1$ to $h - d + 1$ in steps of d_2 **do**
6:     $c_2 \leftarrow 1$
7:     **for** $j := d + 1$ to $w - d + 1$ in steps of d_1 **do**
8:         $RC \leftarrow GC * NI(i : i + b - 1, j : j + b - 1)$ // convolution with central region
9:         $RT \leftarrow GC * NI(i - d : i - d + b - 1, j : j + b - 1)$ // top region
10:         $RR \leftarrow GC * NI(i : i + b - 1, j + d : j + d + b - 1)$ // region to the right
11:         $RB \leftarrow GC * NI(i + d : i + d + b - 1, j : j + b - 1)$ // bottom region
12:         $RL \leftarrow GC * NI(i : i + b - 1, j - d : j - d + b - 1)$ // region to the left

13:         $RMT(c_1, c_2 : c_2 + 3) \leftarrow [RC > RT, RC > RR, RC > RB, RC > RL]$
         // RM bits, a>b is 1 if a is more than b else 0

14:         **if** fraction of masked bits in $M(i : i + b - 1, j : j + b - 1) \geq occ$ **then**
15:             $BM(c_1, c_2 : c_2 + 3) \leftarrow [1, 1, 1, 1]$
16:         **else**
17:             $BM(c_1, c_2 : c_2 + 3) \leftarrow [0, 0, 0, 0]$
18:         **end if**
19:         $c_2 \leftarrow c_2 + 4$
20:     **end for**
21:     $c_1 \leftarrow c_1 + 1$
22: **end for**
23: **return** (RMT, BM)

RC. This convolution is also applied to neighboring regions to obtain responses RT, RR, RB, RL corresponding to top, right, bottom and left directions respectively. RC is compared to each of RT, RR, RB, RL and based on the sign of the comparison a '0—1' value is saved. Similarly, if the occluded bits in the central block exceeds a threshold, then $[1, 1, 1, 1]$ is placed in BM. This process is repeated for all overlapping central blocks chosen according to parameters d_1, d_2 and shown in Fig. 3(b). The feature and mask bits obtained are concatenated according to spatial position to generate RMT and BM.

2.4   Matching

Templates and second level masks of all the images in database are created in feature extraction stage. Matching between two iris considers their respective templates and corresponding masks and calculates their dissimilarity score. To calculate dissimilarity score between the binary templates, the hamming distance metric is used. Hamming distance between two $2D$ binary templates t_1 and t_2 of same size $M \times N$ is defined as in Eq. (3).

$$HD_{(t_1,t_2)} = \frac{\Sigma_{i=1}^{M}\Sigma_{j=1}^{N}(t_{1_{(i,j)}} \oplus t_{2_{(i,j)}})}{M \times N} \tag{3}$$

where $\oplus$ stands for bitwise exclusive-OR and $t_{1_{(i,j)}}$ is the $(i,j)^{th}$ bit value of t_1. Thus, HD is zero iff all the bits from both templates are of same value. Hence, HD is low for genuine matchings and high for imposter matchings. The pixels occluded are not considered while matching. To perform matching only in valid bits of the template, the second level occlusion masks are used. Equation (3) is be modified using occlusion masks m_1 and m_2 for the respective templates as:

$$HD_{(t_1,t_2)} = \frac{\Sigma_{i=1}^{M}\Sigma_{j=1}^{N}[t_{1_{(i,j)}} \oplus t_{2_{(i,j)}}] \mid [m_{1_{(i,j)}} + m_{2_{(i,j)}}]}{M \times N - \Sigma_{i=1}^{M}\Sigma_{j=1}^{N}[m_{1_{(i,j)}} + m_{2_{(i,j)}}]} \tag{4}$$

where operators $\oplus$, $\mid$, and $+$ stand for binary XOR, NAND and OR operations. $a \oplus b = 1$ if a and b are not same, else 0.

To perform recognition for a particular iris, template (and second level mask) of probe image P of same iris is computed. Its HD with all templates (and corresponding masks) stored in the database is calculated. If the minimum HD is obtained with the template (and second level mask) of image belonging to the same iris, it is considered as a hit otherwise a miss. Recognition accuracy is defined as percentage of hits obtained among all probe images used.

Rotational Invariance Rotation of the eye in Cartesian coordinate-space corresponds to horizontal translation in the normalized image. To account for head tilting while acquiring image, matching needs to be applied multiple times. Hence, while matching a template A with another template B, template B is circularly shifted in horizontal direction, to get the minimum hamming distance. This minimum distance is taken as final dissimilarity score. While rotating the gallery template, it is essential to rotate the corresponding mask too. This rotational matching is demonstrated in Fig. 4. Accounting for rotation in this manner makes the matching.

3   Experimental Results

Performance evaluation of the proposed iris recognition system on challenging and voluminous databases is essential to assess its applicability. The iris database is partitioned into gallery set and probe set and all probe images are matched with the gallery images.

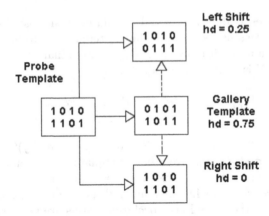

Fig. 4. Calculation of minimum HD

3.1 Databases

Two publicly available CASIA-4.0 Interval, CASIA-4.0 Lamp databases and the self-collected IITK database have been used for performance analysis. The CASIA-4.0 Interval database consists of 2,639 images, each of size 320 × 280, from both eyes of 249 people. Images from this database have clear iris texture taken by NIR camera. Images are taken in two sessions separated by a month. The CASIA-4.0 Lamp database consists of 16,212 images using both eyes of 411 subjects, with 20 images per eye. All images in this database are taken in single session. Each image is of size 640 × 480 pixels. This database has variable illumination introduced by switching of external lamp. The IITK database contains 20,420 images, each of size 640 × 480 using both eyes of 1021 subjects. This database has been collected using a circular LED based NIR camera. Images are acquired in two sessions. In each session, 5 images per eye per subject have been captured.

3.2 Recognition Results

The database is divided into probe set P and gallery set G. Each image from P is matched with all images of G. Those matchings where the image from G and P belong to same iris are called genuine matchings GM while those belonging to different irides are called impostor matchings IM. Those genuine and impostor matchings having combined mask of more than 85 % of the image size are discarded as they are highly occluded. This is done because when occlusion is very high, less evidence is available for the matching score to be authentic.

For CASIA-4.0 Interval first session images are taken as gallery set and second session images are taken as probe set. Those eyes which have less than 4 images are not used for identification because not enough gallery images are available for them. Thus, there are 1047 gallery and 1509 probe images. For CASIA-4.0 Lamp first ten images are taken as gallery while rest ten are considered as probe images. Thus there are 7830 images in gallery and probe set. For IITK database first session images are taken as gallery set and second session images are used as probe. Thus, there are $10,210$ images in both gallery and probe sets.

The performance of the proposed system on these databases is summarized in Table 1. The *ROC* graph for CASIA-4.0 Interval, CASIA-4.0 Lamp and IITK databases are shown in Figs. 5a, b, c respectively. The *EER* on Lamp database is higher because there is severe occlusion present in its images as compared to other databases. The best *EER* obtained is on IITK database due to better image acquisition conditions.

Table 1. Recognition Performance on Various Databases

Database	CRR	EER
CASIA-4.0 Interval	99.07 %	1.82 %
CASIA-4.0 Lamp	98.7 %	4.2 %
IITK	98.66 %	2.12 %

Since the iris template extraction in the proposed approach is based on comparison between regions and not on absolute measurements, it remains fairly stable with variable illuminations and small amounts of noises. Also, template extraction is efficient since only a single filter has to be applied to multiple regions using only basic convolution, which can be optimized by pre-calculation of the filter. Since binary values are stored instead of real values, feature vectors are compact. Flexibility can be provided by varying the distance parameters and the scale of Gaussian filter to achieve optimal performance.

However, the proposed approach cannot handle too much translation or torsional eye rotation because it does not track the features in two irides. It assumes one-to-one correspondence between image regions and is flexible to some extent. Also in case of failed segmentation, it cannot perform recognition because of this non-correspondence.

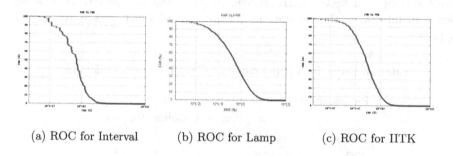

(a) ROC for Interval   (b) ROC for Lamp   (c) ROC for IITK

Fig. 5. ROC Curves for various Database

3.3 Comparison with Previous Approach

Comparison with Gabor filtering has been performed on the basis of feature extraction capability. Image preprocessing involving segmentation, normalization, occlusion masking and enhancement has been kept common for the sake of comparison. All possible cross-session matchings have been performed on CASIA-4.0 Interval, Lamp and IITK databases using the Gabor filtering approach. The performance metrics obtained for this experimentation are summarized in Table 2. It is evident from results on CASIA-4.0 Interval database that proposed approach gives slightly better results as compared to Gabor filtering, but results on Lamp and IITK database shows a significant amount of improvement in the result. It should be noted that the database size is small for CASIA-4.0 Interval (2,639 images) as compared to large size of Lamp (16,212 images) and IITK (20,420 images). Results on larger and more challenging databases usually are more reliable. Hence, it can be concluded that the proposed approach is at par and even better than the Gabor filtering approach.

Table 2. Comparative Results on Various Databases

Database	CRR		EER	
	Gabor	Proposed	Gabor	Proposed
Interval	99.47 %	99.07 %	1.88 %	1.82
Lamp	98.90 %	98.69 %	5.59 %	4.21
IITK	98.85 %	98.66 %	2.49 %	2.12

3.4 Effect of Enhancement

The effect of enhancement approach has also been studied. Results of the proposed approach and the gabor filtering approach are obtained both with and without enhancement on CASIA-4.0 Interval database, as shown in Table 3. It can be inferred that enhancement produces significant discrimination among irises leading to a better *EER*. Hence, enhancement has proved to be a key factor in improving the recognition performance of the proposed recognition approach.

Table 3. Recognition Performance on CASIA-4.0 Interval database

Enhancement	CRR		EER	
	Gabor	Proposed	Gabor	Proposed
Without	98.81 %	97.41 %	5.49 %	5.62 %
With	99.47 %	99.07 %	1.88 %	1.82 %

4 Conclusion

In this paper, a robust and efficient iris recognition approach based on Relational Measures (RM) has been proposed. Experimental results on large databases of CASIA-4.0 Interval, CASIA-4.0 Lamp and IITK have proved that the efficiency and reliability of the proposed approach is comparable to state-of-the-art recognition approaches. Novel occlusion detection approaches of region-growing for eyelid, combined feature for eyelash improve the quality of mask generated. The proposed recognition approach has obtained a CRR of 99.07 % on CASIA-4.0 Interval, 98.7 % on CASIA-4.0 Lamp and 98.66 % on IITK database respectively. The CRR becomes 100 % when top 10 matches are considered for identification instead of top 1. It has also achieved an EER of 1.82 % on CASIA-4.0 Interval, 4.2 % on CASIA-4.0 Lamp and 2.12 % on IITK database. Since this is a new algorithm there exist scope of result improvement by adding more constrains and fine parametric tuning for result optimization.

References

1. Adams, R., Bischof, L.: Seeded region growing. IEEE Trans. Pattern Anal. Mach. Intell. **16**(6), 641–647 (1994)
2. Alim, O., Sharkas, M.: Iris recognition using discrete wavelet transform and artificial neural networks. In: IEEE International Symposium on Micro-NanoMechatronics and Human Science. vol. 1, pp. 337–340. IEEE (2003)
3. Bachoo, A., Tapamo, J.: Texture detection for segmentation of iris images. In: Proceedings of the 2005 annual research conference of the South African institute of computer scientists and information technologists on IT research in developing countries. pp. 236–243. South African Institute for Computer Scientists and Information Technologists (2005)
4. Badrinath, G.S., Nigam, A., Gupta, P.: An efficient finger-knuckle-print based recognition system fusing SIFT and SURF matching scores. In: Qing, S., Susilo, W., Wang, G., Liu, D. (eds.) ICICS 2011. LNCS, vol. 7043, pp. 374–387. Springer, Heidelberg (2011)
5. Bendale, A., Nigam, A., Prakash, S., Gupta, P.: Iris segmentation using improved hough transform. In: Huang, D.-S., Gupta, P., Zhang, X., Premaratne, P. (eds.) ICIC 2012. CCIS, vol. 304, pp. 408–415. Springer, Heidelberg (2012)
6. Bendale, A., Nigam, A., Prakash, S., Gupta, P.: Iris segmentation using improved hough transform. In: Huang, D.-S., Gupta, P., Zhang, X., Premaratne, P. (eds.) Emerging Intelligent Computing Technology and Applications. Communications in Computer and Information Science, pp. 408–415. Springer, Heidelberg (2012)
7. Cappelli, R., Ferrara, M., Maltoni, D.: Minutia cylinder-code: a new representation and matching technique for fingerprint recognition. IEEE Trans. Pattern Anal. Mach. Intell. **32**(12), 2128–2141 (2010)
8. Daugman, J.: Biometric personal identification system based on iris analysis, US Patent (1 March 1994)
9. Dorairaj, V., Schmid, N., Fahmy, G.: Performance evaluation of iris based recognition system implementing pca and ica encoding techniques. In: Society of Photographic Instrumentation Engineers (SPIE). vol. 5779, pp. 51–58. Citeseer (2005)

10. He, Z., Tan, T., Sun, Z., Qiu, X.: Robust eyelid, eyelash and shadow localization for iris recognition. In: 15th IEEE International Conference on Image Processing (ICIP), pp. 265–268. IEEE (2008)
11. Huang, Y., Luo, S., Chen, E.: An efficient iris recognition system. In: Proceedings 2002 IEEE International Conference on Machine Learning and Cybernetics, vol. 1, pp. 450–454. IEEE (2002)
12. Ma, L., Tan, T., Wang, Y., Zhang, D.: Efficient iris recognition by characterizing key local variations. IEEE Trans. Image Process. 13(6), 739–750 (2004)
13. Masek, L., et al.: Recognition of human iris patterns for biometric identification. M. Thesis, The University of Western Australia (2003)
14. Miyazawa, K., Ito, K., Aoki, T., Kobayashi, K., Nakajima, H.: An efficient iris recognition algorithm using phase-based image matching. In: IEEE International Conference on Image Processing (ICIP), vol. 2, pp. II-49. IEEE (2005)
15. Monro, D., Rakshit, S., Zhang, D.: Dct-based iris recognition. IEEE Trans. Pattern Anal. Mach. Intell. 29(4), 586–595 (2007)
16. Nigam, A., Anvesh, T., Gupta, P.: Iris classification based on its quality. In: Huang, D.-S., Bevilacqua, V., Figueroa, J.C., Premaratne, P. (eds.) ICIC 2013. LNCS, vol. 7995, pp. 443–452. Springer, Heidelberg (2013)
17. Nigam, A., Gupta, P.: Finger knuckleprint based recognition system using feature tracking. In: Sun, Z., Lai, J., Chen, X., Tan, T. (eds.) CCBR 2011. LNCS, vol. 7098, pp. 125–132. Springer, Heidelberg (2011)
18. Nigam, A., Gupta, P.: A new distance measure for face recognition system. In: International Conference on Image and Graphics, ICIG (2009), pp. 696–701 (2009)
19. Nigam, A., Gupta, P.: Comparing human faces using edge weighted dissimilarity measure. In: International Conference on Control, Automation, Robotics and Vision, ICARCV, pp. 1831–1836 (2010)
20. Nigam, A., Gupta, P.: Iris recognition using consistent corner optical flow. In: Lee, K.M., Matsushita, Y., Rehg, J.M., Hu, Z. (eds.) ACCV 2012, Part I. LNCS, vol. 7724, pp. 358–369. Springer, Heidelberg (2013)
21. Nigam, A., Gupta, P.: Palmprint recognition using geometrical and statistical constraints. In: 2nd International Conference on Soft Computing for Problem Solving, (SocProS), pp. 1303–1315 (2012). http://dx.doi.org/10.1007/978-81-322-1602-5_136
22. Nigam, A., Gupta, P.: Quality assessment of knuckleprint biometric images. In: International Conference on Image Processing, ICIP. pp. 4205–4209 (2013). http://dx.doi.org/10.1109/ICIP.2013.6738866
23. Prakash, S., Gupta, P.: An efficient ear recognition technique invariant to illumination and pose. Telecommun. Syst. 52(3), 1435–1448 (2013)
24. Prakash, S., Jayaraman, U., Gupta, P.: Connected component based technique for automatic ear detection. In: 16th IEEE International Conference on Image Processing (ICIP), 2009, pp. 2741–2744. IEEE (2009)
25. Singh, N., Nigam, A., Gupta, P., Gupta, P.: Four slap fingerprint segmentation. In: Huang, D.-S., Ma, J., Jo, K.-H., Gromiha, M.M. (eds.) ICIC 2012. LNCS, vol. 7390, pp. 664–671. Springer, Heidelberg (2012)
26. Sun, Z., Tan, T.: Ordinal measures for iris recognition. IEEE Trans. Pattern Anal. Mach. Intell. 31(12), 2211–2226 (2009)
27. Wildes, R.: Iris recognition: an emerging biometric technology. In: Proceedings of the IEEE, 85(9), pp. 1348–1363 (1997)
28. Zuiderveld, K.: Contrast limited adaptive histogram equalization. In: Graphics gems IV. pp. 474–485. Academic Press Professional, Inc. (1994)

On Latent Fingerprint Image Quality

Soweon Yoon[1], Eryun Liu[1,2], and Anil K. Jain[1](✉)

[1] Department of Computer Science and Engineering,
Michigan State University, East Lansing, MI, USA
{yoonsowo,liueryun,jain}@cse.msu.edu
[2] Department of Information Science and Electronic Engineering, Zhejiang
University, Hangzhou, Zhejiang, China
eryunliu@zju.edu.cn

Abstract. Latent fingerprints which are lifted from surfaces of objects at crime scenes play a very important role in identifying suspects in the crime scene investigations. Due to poor quality of latent fingerprints, automatic processing of latents can be extremely challenging. For this reason, latent examiners need to be involved in latent identification. To expedite the latent identification and alleviate subjectivity and inconsistency in latent examiners' feature markups and decisions, there is a need to develop latent fingerprint identification systems that can operate in the "lights-out" mode. One of the most important steps in "lights-out" systems is to determine the quality of a given latent to predict the probability that the latent can be identified in a fully automatic manner. In this paper, we (i) propose a definition of latent value determination as a way of establishing the quality of latents based on a specific matcher's identification performance, (ii) define a set of features based on ridge clarity and minutiae and evaluate them based on their capability to determine if a latent is of value for individualization or not, and (iii) propose a latent fingerprint image quality (LFIQ) that can be useful to reject the latents which cannot be successfully identified in the "lights-out" mode. Experimental results show that the most salient latent features include the average ridge clarity and the number of minutiae. The proposed latent quality measure improves the rank-100 identification rate from 69 % to 86 % by rejecting 50 % of latents deemed as poor quality. In addition, the rank-100 identification is 80 % when rejecting 80 % of the latents in the databases assessed as 'NFIQ = 5'; however, the same identification rate can be achieved by rejecting only 21 % of the latents with low LFIQ.

Keywords: Latent fingerprints · "lights-out" latent identification · Latent value determination · Latent fingerprint image quality (LFIQ)

1 Introduction

Fingerprints have been widely used for reliable human identification in forensics and law enforcement applications for over a century. Law enforcement agencies routinely collect tenprint records of all apprehended criminals in two forms: *rolled*

© Springer International Publishing Switzerland 2015
U. Garain and F. Shafait (Eds.): IWCF 2012 and 2014, LNCS 8915, pp. 67–82, 2015.
DOI: 10.1007/978-3-319-20125-2_7

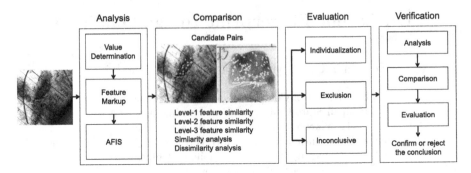

Fig. 1. ACE-V methodology in latent identification.

and *plain* (or *slap*). Rolled fingerprints are obtained by rolling a finger from nail to nail to capture the complete ridge details on a finger while plain fingerprints are captured by pressing down a finger on the flat surface of a fingerprint card or a live-scan sensor [1]. Both rolled and plain fingerprints, collectively called reference (exemplar) fingerprints, are believed to contain sufficient ridge details for individualization. To ensure good quality of fingerprint images, reference fingerprints are acquired under the supervision of a human operator; this way, fingerprints can be recaptured in case of poor quality impressions.

Automated Fingerprint Identification Systems (AFIS) are used by almost every major law enforcement agency worldwide to facilitate tenprint search; rolled or plain fingerprints are submitted as a query to an AFIS to search large-scale reference fingerprint databases. The FBI's Integrated AFIS (IAFIS) receives tens of thousands of requests everyday to search a reference database containing tenprint cards of over 72 million criminals and 34 million civilian job applicants [2]. The matching accuracy of tenprint search has already reached an impressive level; the 2003 Fingerprint Vendor Technology Evaluation (FpVTE) [3] reported that the best performing commercial matcher achieved 99.4 % true accept rate at 0.01 % false accept rate in searching plain fingerprints against a reference database with 10,000 plain fingerprints.

Another type of important fingerprint identification involves searching *latent* fingerprints against reference fingerprint databases. Latent fingerprints (or simply *latents*) refer to the fingerprints captured at crime scenes, and are regarded as an extremely important source of evidence in crime scene investigations to identify suspects. Unlike rolled or plain fingerprints, latents are often of poor quality; latent impressions typically contain partial ridge patterns of a finger, incomplete or missing ridge structures, mixture of ridge pattern and complex background noise or friction ridge structures from other fingers. Due to low quality of latent fingerprints, human intervention is inevitable in latent search, especially for feature markup (i.e., manually marking region of interest, minutiae, core, delta, and extended features). In matching latents to reference prints, latent fingerprint examiners are expected to follow a methodology, called Analysis, Comparison, Evaluation and Verification (ACE-V) [4]. Figure 1 illustrates the ACE-V methodology. In the analysis phase, an examiner evaluates the ridge information contained in latent images. If the latent is determined to contain sufficient information for identification or exclusion (called "of value" latent), the features in the latent are manually marked by the examiner to search for its mate using an AFIS. In the comparison phase, the examiner compares the "of value" latent with the candidate mates retrieved from the reference database side-by-side and ascertains the similarity between the latent and mated reference print pairs using feature markup in the latent. In the evaluation phase, one of the following decisions is made about the latent in question: individualization, exclusion or inconclusive[1]. Finally, in the verification phase, the decision made by the first examiner is confirmed by having a second examiner analyze the results independently.

Although the ACE-V methodology is widely accepted by forensic community for latent print examination, the influence of human factors in the ACE-V procedure has raised concerns about their reliability and consistency. A noteworthy case is the erroneous identification of Brandon Mayfield as a suspect in the Madrid train bombing incident based on an incorrect match between Mayfield's reference fingerprint and the latent print captured at the bombing site [6,7]. The National Research Council's report on limitations and recommendations of forensic science [8] pointed out two major shortcomings in the current forensic science discipline: (i) "lack of mandatory and enforceable standards" that can be globally referred to in crime labs and (ii) "unacceptable case backlogs in state and local crime labs which likely make it difficult for laboratories to provide strong evidence for prosecutions and avoid errors that could lead to imperfect justice". Along with the efforts to understand the human factors in latent fingerprint examination [9], standards and guidelines for latent examiners' practices have also been set up. As an example, the Science Working Group on Friction Ridge Analysis, Study and Technology (SWGFAST) published standards which define terminologies and establish the sufficiency level for decisions at each step of the ACE-V methodology to alleviate subjectivity involved in feature markups and decision makings among examiners [5].

Based on the guidelines in SWGFAST standard, latent examiners' practices have been evaluated from various aspects (e.g., reliability of decisions, degree of consensus and consistency of decisions) [10–12], mainly on two critical decisions that the examiners make in ACE-V methodology: (i) latent value determination in the analysis phase and (ii) latent individualization conclusion in the evaluation phase. Latent value determination assigns one of the following labels to each latent: value for individualization (VID), value for exclusion only

---

[1] Individualization is the decision that a latent examiner makes on a pair of latent and a reference print indicating that the pair originates from the same finger based on a sufficient agreement between the two ridge patterns. Exclusion, on the other hand, is the decision where an examiner concludes that the pair did not originate from the same finger based on a sufficient disagreement between the two ridge patterns. An inconclusive decision is made when an examiner cannot make a decision of either individualization or exclusion due to insufficient ridge details or small corresponding area between latent and reference print [5].

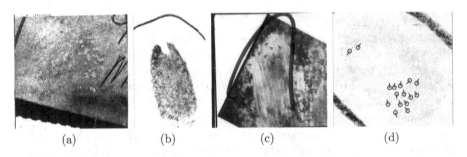

Fig. 2. Latents that are assessed as either VEO or NV, but the mated rolled prints are retrieved at rank-1 by AFIS. (a) NIST SD27 (U237): VEO (minutiae from AFIS) and (b) WVU (W514F02C_N): VEO (minutiae from AFIS), (c) NIST SD27 (U254): NV (minutiae marked by an examiner), and (d) WVU (W605F01C_I): VEO (minutiae marked by an examiner).

(VEO), and no value (NV). Only VID and VEO latents are further considered for comparison. However, recent studies on the consensus and consistency of latent examiners' value determination indicate that a significant amount of subjectivity and variation exists in latent value determination. In [11], the consensus of the latent examiners' value determinations was evaluated; among the 356 latents which were reviewed by the examiners (each latent was reviewed by 23 examiners, on average), unanimous decisions (either VID or not-VID) were made only for about 43 % of the latents. In terms of consistency, Ulery *et al.* [12] found that 85 % of NV decisions and 93 % of VID decisions were repeated by the same examiner after a time gap while only 55 % of VEO decisions were repeated. More importantly, an examiner's value determination is not always reliable; the ELFT-EFS (Evaluation of Latent Fingerprint Technologies: Extended Feature Sets) report [13] emphasizes that a significant portion of the latents assessed as being of VEO or NV can still be successfully identified by AFIS. Figure 2 shows examples of latents in the NIST SD27 database [14] and the WVU latent database [15] that were assessed as either VEO or NV by latent examiners, but whose mated reference prints were correctly retrieved at the top rank by an AFIS.

One of the most desirable properties of a latent fingerprint identification system is its ability to process latents in a "lights-out" identification mode with high accuracy. A "lights-out" fingerprint identification system refers to a system that requires only fingerprint images as input (query) and returns a short list of reference prints as potential mates [16]. The advantages of "lights-out" latent identification mode include: (i) avoiding subjectivity in latent print examination and (ii) increasing throughput of latent print matching, given the growing workload on latent examiners. While state-of-the-art latent fingerprint identification systems have already shown excellent performance in matching latents to reference databases[2] [13,17], more research efforts are needed to continue to improve this performance.

---

[2] The best performing matcher for latent search in the ELFT-EFS achieved 63.4 % rank-1 identification rate in the "lights-out" identification mode [13].

The first and the most significant step in achieving "lights-out" latent identification capability is the quality assessment of latents to (i) determine whether or not they have sufficient fingerprint ridge structure for either automatic feature extraction or manual feature markup and (ii) predict the reliability of latent to reference print matching with the given feature set. Although, in principle, the objectives of latent quality assessment are the same as those of tenprint or reference print quality assessment, defining a latent fingerprint image quality (LFIQ) measure is lot more difficult. Further, while the tenprint quality measures are mainly used to determine if they need to be recaptured, the main purpose of defining a latent quality measure is to expedite latent print examination by identifying 'good' quality latents which can be processed in "lights-out" mode. An appropriate latent quality measure will also help avoid potential erroneous subjective decisions regarding latent value.

Latent fingerprint quality can be assessed as latent value determination, and the latent value can be determined by two different ways: (i) latent examiners and (ii) AFIS. Latent value determination by examiners simply refers to the current practice of assigning one of the following values (i.e., VID, VEO and NV) to a latent by an examiner. However, as mentioned before, the latent values determined by examiners are not always correlated to the latent identification performance. Considering that one of the major goals of defining latent quality measure is to predict latent matching performance (assuming that the mated print in the reference database is of fairly good quality), we define a value determination by AFIS, following the comparison protocol in the ACE-V methodology: a latent fingerprint is declared to be VID in value determination by an AFIS if its mated print in the reference database is retrieved within the top rank-100; otherwise, the latent is declared as not-VID in value determination by the AFIS.

One of the challenges in defining a value determination by AFIS is to find salient features in latents which are directly related to the latent identification performance. Features that can be used in estimating latent fingerprint quality are generally comprised of (i) quality for value and (ii) quality for identification. Quality for value (often referred to as *qualitative* quality [10,18]) measures the sufficiency of Level-1 features such as fingerprint ridge clarity, pattern class, size of region of interest, fingerprint position (e.g., center, side, or tip of a finger), and determines the utility of the latent for either exclusion or identification. Quality for identification (often referred to as *quantitative* quality [10,18]) measures the sufficiency of Level-2 (i.e., minutiae) and Level-3 (e.g., pores) features which are directly used in fingerprint identification, and determines the reliability of matching results by an AFIS in the "lights-out" mode.

Another important consideration in defining a latent quality measure is whether it should depend on a specific AFIS. The issue of interoperability of AFIS in latent search is well known [19]. Given that the matching results of AFIS from different vendors on a given latent print can be significantly different as revealed in ELFT-EFS [13], we believe that a latent fingerprint quality measure should be designed for a specific AFIS. We call this a matcher-dependent latent quality measure.

In this paper, we report results of our preliminary study on defining LFIQ. First, we investigate a set of Level-1 features for qualitative quality and Level-2 features for quantitative quality that can be effectively used to define latent fingerprint image quality. The features are evaluated by constructing a 2-class classifier to determine whether a latent is VID or not-VID. The class labels (VID and not-VID) are determined either by latent examiners or an AFIS; this way, two different classifiers – one for value determination by examiners and the other for value determination by an AFIS – are obtained. Based on the observations from latent value estimation, we define a latent quality measure by combining a qualitative quality feature (i.e., the average ridge clarity) and a quantitative quality feature (i.e., the number of minutiae) to estimate the objective target quality: the probability that the mated reference print of a latent will be retrieved within the top rank-100.

2 Latent Fingerprint Image Quality (LFIQ)

To find the most significant features to represent latent fingerprint quality, a latent quality assessment is viewed as a 2-class classification problem: ω_{VID} versus $\omega_{\overline{VID}}$, where ω_{VID} represents the class of VID latents and $\omega_{\overline{VID}}$ represents the class of not-VID latents. Feature vectors with different composition of ridge clarity features and minutiae features are evaluated in terms of the resulting classification accuracy. Based on the empirical results, a latent quality measure is defined by combining the two most significant features: average ridge clarity in the convex hull enclosing all the minutiae and the number of minutiae.

2.1 Ridge Clarity Feature

Given a latent fingerprint image I, the quality of its local ridge structure is measured by the ridge strength in a local block and the ridge continuity in the block's neighborhood. The computation of local ridge clarity map, **RC**, involves the following steps:

1. Preprocessing: The contrast-enhanced latent image, I^*, is obtained by [20]:

$$I^* = \text{sign}(I - \bar{I}) \times \log(1 + |I - \bar{I}|), \tag{1}$$

   where $\bar{I}$ is the smoothed version of I by applying a 15×15 averaging filter, and sign$(x)= 1$ if $x > 0$, otherwise sign$(x)= -1$.
2. Fourier analysis: The contrast-enhanced image I^* is divided into 16×16 pixel blocks. The 64×64 subimage, $I^*_{mn}(x, y)$, is constructed by taking a 32×32 subimage of I^* around the center of the block at $[m, n]$ and padding with 0's to get high frequency resolution in the Fourier domain. The subimage is transformed into the Fourier domain, $F_{mn}(u, v)$. The top two local amplitude maxima within the frequency range of $\left[\frac{1}{16}, \frac{1}{5}\right]$ are selected [21]. Let (u_1, v_1) and (u_2, v_2) be the locations of the first and the second amplitude maxima

in $F_{mn}(u, v)$. Then, a 2-dimensional sine wave corresponding to the i-th local maximum of the block at $[m, n]$ can be written as:

$$w_{mn}^{(i)}(x, y) = a_{mn}^{(i)} \sin(2\pi f_{mn}^{(i)}(\cos(\theta_{mn}^{(i)})x + \sin(\theta_{mn}^{(i)})y) + \phi_{mn}^{(i)}), \ i = 1, 2, \quad (2)$$

where

$$a_{mn}^{(i)} = |F(u_i, v_i)|, \ f_{mn}^{(i)} = \frac{\sqrt{u_i^2 + v_i^2}}{64}$$

$$\theta_{mn}^{(i)} = \arctan\left(\frac{u_i}{v_i}\right), \ \text{and} \ \phi_{mn}^{(i)} = \arctan\left[\frac{Im(F(u_i, v_i))}{Re(F(u_i, v_i))}\right],$$

$a_{mn}^{(i)}$, $f_{mn}^{(i)}$, $\theta_{mn}^{(i)}$, and $\phi_{mn}^{(i)}$ represent the amplitude, frequency, direction, and phase, respectively.

3. Ridge continuity map: The 2-dimensional sine waves, w_1 and w_2, in two adjacent blocks are continuous if they satisfy the following conditions [21]:

$$\min\{|\theta_1, \theta_2|, \pi - |\theta_1, \theta_2|\} \leq T_\theta,$$

$$\left|\frac{1}{f_1} - \frac{1}{f_2}\right| \leq T_f, \ \text{and}$$

$$\frac{1}{16} \sum_{(x,y) \in \mathcal{L}} \left|\frac{w_1(x, y)}{a_1} - \frac{w_2(x, y)}{a_2}\right| \leq T_p, \quad (3)$$

where $\mathcal{L}$ denotes the 16 pixels on the border of the two adjacent blocks, and the three thresholds, T_θ, T_f, and T_p, are set to $\frac{\pi}{10}$, 3, and 0.6, respectively. Define an indicator function, $I_c(w_1, w_2)$, as follows:

$$I_c(w_1, w_2) = \begin{cases} 1, & \text{if } w_1 \text{ and } w_2 \text{ are continuous,} \\ 0, & \text{otherwise.} \end{cases} \quad (4)$$

Ridge continuity map is defined by:

$$\widetilde{RC}[m, n] = \sum_{[m^*, n^*] \in \mathcal{N}} \max\{I_c(w_{mn}^{(1)}, w_{m^*n^*}^{(1)}), I_c(w_{mn}^{(1)}, w_{m^*n^*}^{(2)})\}, \quad (5)$$

where $\mathcal{N}$ is the 8-neighborhood blocks of the block $[m, n]$.

4. Ridge clarity map: The ridge clarity of block at $[m, n]$ is defined by:

$$RC[m, n] = a_{mn}^{(1)} \cdot \widetilde{RC}[m, n]. \quad (6)$$

Figure 3 shows the ridge clarity maps and the intermediate steps for two different latents. Well-defined ridge structures present in a latent correspond to the high ridge clarity regions in the **RC** map.

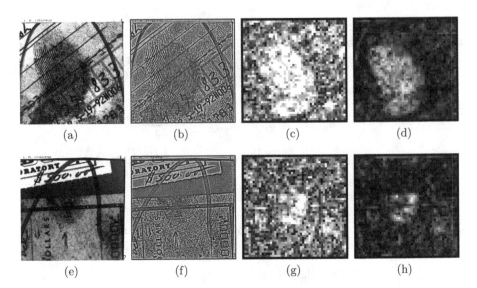

Fig. 3. Ridge clarity maps (**RC**) of two latents in NIST SD27. (a) G051 and (e) G080, (b) and (f) contrast-enhanced latent images, (c) and (g) ridge continuity maps, and (d) and (h) ridge clarity maps (brighter regions indicate higher ridge clarity).

2.2 Minutiae Feature

The most significant features which are directly related to the fingerprint matching performance are the minutiae properties. We investigated a number of different minutiae properties, including the number of minutiae, quality of minutiae based on the **RC** map defined in the Sect. 2.1, and size of the convex hull enclosing the minutiae in the latent. Let N_M, Q_M, and A_M denote the number of minutiae, average quality of minutiae, and size of the convex hull enclosing all the minutiae in a latent.

The average quality of minutiae, Q_M, is obtained from the **RC** map as follows:

$$Q_M = \frac{1}{N_M} \sum_{i=1}^{N_M} \mathbf{RC}[bx_i, by_i], \tag{7}$$

where $[bx_i, by_i]$ is the blockwise position of the i-th minutia.

Two different sets of minutiae are considered: (i) minutiae automatically extracted by an AFIS and (ii) minutiae manually marked by latent examiners. Reliability of the minutiae marked by examiners is significantly higher compared to the minutiae extracted by the AFIS[3] while the consistency of the minutiae markup by the examiners is lower than that of the minutiae extracted by the AFIS. Figure 4 shows the two minutiae sets – minutiae extracted by the AFIS

---

[3] The AFIS used in this study is not a state-of-the-art latent-to-reference print matcher, but instead a state-of-the-art AFIS for reference fingerprint matching. Currently, no AFIS for latent matching is available to us.

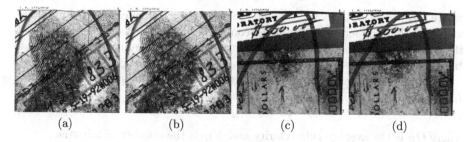

| (a) | (b) | (c) | (d) |

Fig. 4. Minutiae in two latents shown in Fig. 3. (a) Minutiae extracted by an AFIS for the latent in Fig. 3a, (b) minutiae marked by an examiner for the latent in Fig. 3a, (c) minutiae extracted by the AFIS for the latent in Fig. 3e, and (b) minutiae marked by an examiner for the latent in Fig. 3e.

and minutiae marked by examiner – of the two latents in Fig. 3 along with the convex hulls enclosing the minutiae.

2.3 Latent Fingerprint Quality Assessment

To establish the most discriminant features to define latent fingerprint quality, the latent quality assessment is formulated as a 2-class classification problem for ω_{VID} and $\omega_{\overline{VID}}$. To build the "best" performing matcher for latents[4], we fuse a state-of-the-art AFIS for tenprint with the latent fingerprint matcher developed in [22] as follows. The match score of a latent i and a reference print j is obtained by [23]:

$$s_{ij} = r\frac{s_{ij}^A}{\frac{1}{N_R}\sum_{k=1}^{N_R} s_{ik}^A} + (1-r)\frac{s_{ij}^B}{\frac{1}{N_R}\sum_{k=1}^{N_R} s_{ik}^B}, \ 0 \le r \le 1, \tag{8}$$

where s_{ij}^A and s_{ij}^B are the match scores of a latent i and a reference print j from matcher A and B, respectively, N_R is the size of the reference database, and r is a weight which is empirically chosen to obtain the best rank-100 identification accuracy.

We evaluated feature vectors consisting of different combinations of ridge clarity and minutiae features. The following two feature vectors were observed to be the most discriminative:

$$\mathbf{x_1} = (N_M),$$
$$\mathbf{x_2} = (Q_R, N_M, Q_M, A_M),$$

where Q_R is the average ridge clarity in the convex hull of the minutiae in a latent and defined as:

$$Q_R = \frac{1}{|\mathcal{C}|} \sum_{[m,n]\in\mathcal{C}} \mathbf{RC}[m,n], \tag{9}$$

---

[4] Based on the latent matching performance evaluation with the fingerprint matchers available to us, the fusion of the two matchers described in this paper showed the best performance to simulate the performance of a state-of-the-art AFIS for latents.

where $\mathcal{C}$ is the set of blocks that belong to the convex hull enclosing the minutiae and $|\mathcal{C}|$ is the number of blocks in the convex hull. Note that each component of the feature vector is normalized by its minimum and maximum values. A decision tree classifier [24] is used to determine whether a latent belongs to ω_{VID} or $\omega_{\overline{VID}}$.

Based on the above observations, a latent fingerprint image quality measure, $LFIQ$, is defined as:

$$LFIQ = Q_R \cdot N_M, \tag{10}$$

where Q_R is the average ridge clarity and N_M is the number of minutiae.

3   Experimental Results

3.1   Databases

The latent quality measure was evaluated on two latent fingerprint databases: NIST SD27 [14] and WVU latent database [15]. NIST SD27, the only public-domain latent database, contains 258 latents obtained from operational case-work. Although all the latents in this database are labeled as belonging to one of three quality levels ('Good', 'Bad', and 'Ugly'), we follow a formal definition of value determination by latent examiners (i.e., VID, VEO, and NV) which was reported in [10]. The numbers of VID, VEO, and NV latents in NIST SD27 are 210, 41, and 7, respectively.

The WVU database contains 449 latents collected in a laboratory environment. These latents come with value determination and feature markups. The numbers of VID, VEO, and NV latents in the WVU database are 370, 74, and 5, respectively.

As a reference database, the mated rolled fingerprints of the 707 latents (258 from NIST SD27 and 449 from WVU database) are combined with 4,291 additional rolled prints from the WVU database and 27,000 rolled prints of the first impressions in NIST SD14 [25]. In total, the size of the reference database is 31,998.

3.2   Classification Accuracy of Latent Value Determination

The performance of the classifiers using feature vectors, x_1 and x_2 defined in Sect. 2.3, to determine whether a given latent is VID or not-VID was evaluated. Two different sources of minutiae set are used to construct feature vectors: (i) minutiae extracted by an AFIS and (ii) minutiae marked by examiners. A 10-fold cross validation is conducted for evaluation: two latent databases are evenly partitioned into 10 sets, and one set from each database is selected at random without replacement to form a fold. Average classification accuracies along with standard deviations are reported in Tables 2 and 4. Target class label for ω_{VID} and $\omega_{\overline{VID}}$ can be assigned by either (i) latent examiners or (ii) AFIS.

Table 1. Confusion matrix of ω_{VID} versus $\omega_{\overline{VID}}$ classification from value determination by examiners. $\hat{\omega}_{VID}$ and $\hat{\omega}_{\overline{VID}}$ are the predicted class labels. Feature vectors are defined based on (a) minutiae extracted by AFIS and (b) minutiae marked by examiners.

(a)

Feature	$\mathbf{x_1}$		$\mathbf{x_2}$	
	$\hat{\omega}_{VID}$	$\hat{\omega}_{\overline{VID}}$	$\hat{\omega}_{VID}$	$\hat{\omega}_{\overline{VID}}$
ω_{VID}	565	14	496	83
$\omega_{\overline{VID}}$	128	0	91	37

(b)

Feature	$\mathbf{x_1}$		$\mathbf{x_2}$	
	$\hat{\omega}_{VID}$	$\hat{\omega}_{\overline{VID}}$	$\hat{\omega}_{VID}$	$\hat{\omega}_{\overline{VID}}$
ω_{VID}	564	15	523	56
$\omega_{\overline{VID}}$	69	59	64	64

Table 2. Classification accuracy (standard deviation) for ω_{VID} and $\omega_{\overline{VID}}$ from value determination by examiners. Feature vectors are defined based on (a) minutiae extracted by AFIS and (b) minutiae marked by examiners.

Feature	(a)		(b)	
	$\mathbf{x_1}$	$\mathbf{x_2}$	$\mathbf{x_1}$	$\mathbf{x_2}$
ω_{VID} classification accuracy	98 % (2 %)	86 % (4 %)	97 % (3 %)	90 % (5 %)
$\omega_{\overline{VID}}$ classification accuracy	0 % (0 %)	29 % (19 %)	46 % (12 %)	50 % (10 %)
Total classification accuracy	80 % (1 %)	75 % (4 %)	88 % (2 %)	83 % (4 %)

Value Determination by Examiners. Value determination by latent examiners is one of VID, VEO, and NV. All latents determined as VID by examiners comprise ω_{VID} while $\omega_{\overline{VID}}$ consists of VEO and NV latents determined by examiners. Tables 1 and 2 show the confusion matrices and classification accuracies with standard deviations of predicting value determination by examiners.

Value Determination by AFIS. Value determination by AFIS is based on the matching performance of a specific AFIS: a latent belongs to ω_{VID} if its mate in the reference database is retrieved within the top rank-100; otherwise, it belongs to $\omega_{\overline{VID}}$. Tables 3 and 4 show the confusion matrices and classification accuracies with standard deviations of predicting value determination by the AFIS.

Based on these classification results, we make the following observations:

- Feature vectors from the minutiae marked by examiners show better performance than those from the minutiae extracted by the AFIS due to the high reliability of the markup features.
- Value determination by examiners shows higher classification accuracy than value determination by AFIS. This is because the value determination by examiners is done by looking at only latent images so that the quality and the sufficiency of features in the latents are closely related to the value determination. On the other hand, the value determination by an AFIS also depends on the quality of mated reference prints. This emphasizes the need for considering

Table 3. Confusion matrix for ω_{VID} versus $\omega_{\overline{VID}}$ classification from value determination by AFIS. $\hat{\omega}_{VID}$ and $\hat{\omega}_{\overline{VID}}$ are the predicted class labels. Feature vectors are defined based on (a) minutiae extracted by AFIS and (b) minutiae marked by examiners.

(a)					(b)				
Feature	$\mathbf{x_1}$		$\mathbf{x_2}$		Feature	$\mathbf{x_1}$		$\mathbf{x_2}$	
	$\hat{\omega}_{VID}$	$\hat{\omega}_{\overline{VID}}$	$\hat{\omega}_{VID}$	$\hat{\omega}_{\overline{VID}}$		$\hat{\omega}_{VID}$	$\hat{\omega}_{\overline{VID}}$	$\hat{\omega}_{VID}$	$\hat{\omega}_{\overline{VID}}$
ω_{VID}	162	157	195	124	ω_{VID}	456	34	391	99
$\omega_{\overline{VID}}$	126	262	125	263	$\omega_{\overline{VID}}$	117	100	107	110

Table 4. Classification accuracy (standard deviation) for ω_{VID} and $\omega_{\overline{VID}}$ from value determination by AFIS. Feature vectors are defined based on (a) minutiae extracted by AFIS and (b) minutiae marked by examiners.

	(a)		(b)	
Feature	$\mathbf{x_1}$	$\mathbf{x_2}$	$\mathbf{x_1}$	$\mathbf{x_2}$
ω_{VID} classification accuracy	51 % (12 %)	61 % (7 %)	93 % (4 %)	80 % (5 %)
$\omega_{\overline{VID}}$ classification accuracy	67 % (11 %)	68 % (8 %)	46 % (13 %)	51 % (9 %)
Total classification accuracy	60 % (4 %)	65 % (4 %)	79 % (6 %)	71 % (3 %)

the quality of the mates as an independent factor when developing a latent fingerprint quality measure.

- Feature vector $\mathbf{x_1}$ generally shows better performance than feature vector $\mathbf{x_2}$ to predict latent values, except for value determination by AFIS with minutiae extracted by the AFIS. When the reliability of feature extraction is low, the ancillary information on fingerprint ridge quality helps to design a better latent quality measure.

3.3   Prediction of Latent Identification Performance by LFIQ

To evaluate the proposed latent quality measure, $LFIQ$, as a predictor of latent identification performance, we consider rank-100 identification rate when the latents with low quality scores are rejected. Fig. 5 shows the rank-100 identification rate as a function of the rejection rate based on $LFIQ$ when two different minutiae sets (one from examiners and the other from AFIS) are used. Based on these plots, we make the following observations:

- Quality measure based on the minutiae marked by examiners shows better performance than the quality measure based on the minutiae extracted by the AFIS. This implies that, if highly reliable feature extractors are available, the quality estimation using relatively simple features such as ridge clarity and the number of minutiae will suffice in predicting the latent matching performance.

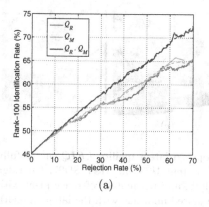
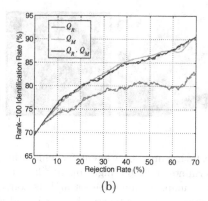

(a)   (b)

Fig. 5. Rank-100 identification rate versus rejection rate when the minutiae are obtained by (a) an AFIS and (b) latent examiners (solid lines). Dotted lines are the approximation with cubic functions.

- For minutiae extracted by an AFIS, the quality measure $LFIQ$ which combines Q_R and N_M shows the best performance compared to either Q_R or N_M alone.
- For minutiae marked by examiners, however, N_M alone shows about the same performance as $LFIQ$, which implies that the amount of information that minutiae contain (i.e., the number of minutiae in the latent) is sufficient to predict the matching performance when the extracted minutiae are highly reliable.

Figure 6 shows an example where the proposed quality measure $LFIQ$ successfully predicts the latent identification performance. Figure 7 shows a latent and its mated reference print of good quality, but the latent identification performance is poor due to the large number of missing minutiae and spurious minutiae extracted by the AFIS in the latent even in the high quality ridge region.

As a comparison to the proposed LFIQ, NIST Fingerprint Image Quality (NFIQ)[5] [26] was used to assess the quality of the latents in the two latent databases. When setting the rejection criterion as 'NFIQ = 5', the rank-100 identification rate of the accepted latents with minutiae extracted by the AFIS was 66 % at a rejection rate of 80 %. At the same rejection rate, the rank-100 identification rate of the accepted latents by NFIQ with minutiae marked by examiners was 80 %. The proposed latent quality measure, $LFIQ$, on the other hand, was able to achieve the same rank-100 identification rate at significantly lower rejection rates as follows: (i) rank-100 identification rate of 66 % can be achieved, with minutiae extracted by the AFIS, by rejecting 53 % of poor quality latents identified by the proposed $LFIQ$; (ii) rank-100 identification rate of 80 %

---

[5] NFIQ assigns one of five discrete quality levels ranging from 1 to 5 to a reference print; '1' refers to the highest quality, and '5' indicates the lowest quality. Note that NFIQ was not designed for latent fingerprint quality assessment.

(a)   (b)   (c)   (d)

Fig. 6. Example of a latent for which the proposed latent quality $LFIQ$ successfully determines it to be 'high' quality latent. (a) Latent U237 in NIST SD27, (b) ridge clarity map, (c) minutiae set and its convex hull, and (d) mated reference print with minutiae extracted by an AFIS (red) and the mated minutiae with the latent (green). Note that while this latent has a high $LFIQ$ value (corresponding to the rejection rate of 83 %) and the mated print is retrieved at rank-1, the value determination by examiners for this latent was not-VID.

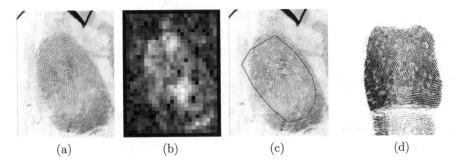

(a)   (b)   (c)   (d)

Fig. 7. Example of a latent where the proposed latent quality measure $LFIQ$ determines it to be a 'high' quality latent, but the retrieval rank of the mated reference print is poor (ranked at 4,658). (a) Latent W944F08B_N in WVU database, (b) ridge clarity map, (c) minutiae set and its convex hull, and (d) mated reference print with minutiae extracted by an AFIS. Note that while this latent has a high $LFIQ$ value (corresponding to the rejection rate of 88 %) and the value determination by examiners is also VID, the matching performance is poor due to the large number of false minutiae extracted by the AFIS in the latent.

can be achieved, with minutiae marked by examiners, by rejecting 21 % of poor quality latents identified by the proposed $LFIQ$.

4   Conclusions and Future Work

Towards the goal of designing a "lights-out" latent fingerprint matching system, we proposed a latent fingerprint quality measure. We first defined the value of a latent based on its rank-100 identification rate to directly relate the latent quality to the matching performance. A set of features based on latent fingerprint ridge clarity and minutiae properties was evaluated by posing the latent value determination problem as a 2-class classification problem (i.e., VID versus not-VID). Based on the classification accuracy, the most salient features were selected to define a latent quality measure as a product of the average ridge clarity in the convex hull enclosing the minutiae and the number of minutiae in the latent. The proposed latent quality measure improves the rank-100 identification rate of an AFIS by effectively rejecting poor quality latents.

Based on the preliminary study of the proposed LFIQ, we identify the following topics that are worthy of further consideration:

- Defining a latent quality measure with a more discriminative feature set representing the reliability of minutiae extracted by an AFIS to predict its matching performance.
- Developing a latent quality measure involving Level-3 features.

Acknowledgments. We would like to thank Austin Hicklin of Noblis for providing us the value determination by examiners of latents in NIST SD27. This research was partially supported by a grant from the NSF Center of Identification Technology Research (CITeR). This paper was presented at the International Workshop on Computational Forensics, Tsukuba, Japan, November 11, 2012. Readers who are interested in the improved algorithm for assessing latent fingerprint quality are directed to [27].

References

1. Maltoni, D., Maio, D., Jain, A.K., Prabhakar, S.: Handbook of Fingerprint Recognition, 2nd edn. Springer-Verlag, Heidelberg (2009)
2. The Federal Bureau of Investigation (FBI). Integrated Automated Fingerprint Identification System (IAFIS). http://www.fbi.gov/about-us/cjis/fingerprints_biometrics/iafis/iafis
3. Wilson, C., et al.: Fingerprint Vendor Technology Evaluation 2003: Summary of Results and Analysis Report. NISTIR 7123 (2004)
4. Ashbaugh, D.R.: Quantitative-Qualitative Friction Ridge Analysis: An Introduction to Basic and Advanced Ridgeology. CRC Press, Boca Raton (1999)
5. Science Working Group on Friction Ridge Analysis, Study and Technology (SWG-FAST): Standards for Examining Friction Ridge Impressions and Resulting Conclusions (Latent/Tenprint) (2011)
6. Office of the Inspector General, Oversight and Review Division: A Review of the FBI's Handling of the Brandon Mayfield Case (2006)
7. Office of the Inspector General, Oversight and Review Division: A Review of the FBI's Progress in Responding to the Recommendations in the Office of the Inspector General Report on the Fingerprint Misidentification in the Brandon Mayfield Case (2011)
8. National Research Council: Strengthening Forensic Science in the United States: A Path Forward (2009)
9. National Institute of Standards and Technology (NIST) and National Institute of Justice (NIJ): Latent Print Examination and Human Factors: Improving the Practice through a Systems Approach (2012)
10. Hicklin, R.A., et al.: Latent fingerprint quality: a survey of examiners. J. Forensic Identif. **61**(4), 385–419 (2011)

11. Ulery, B.T., Hicklin, R.A., Buscaglia, J., Roberts, M.A.: Accuracy and reliability of forensic latent fingerprint decisions. Proc. Natl. Acad. Sci. **108**(19), 7733–7738 (2011)
12. Ulery, B.T., Hicklin, R.A., Buscaglia, J., Roberts, M.A.: Repeatability and reproducibility of decisions by latent fingerprint examiners. PLoS ONE **7**(3), e32800 (2012)
13. Indovina, M., Dvornychenko, V., Hicklin, R.A., Kiebuzinski, G.I.: Evaluation of Latent Fingerprint Technologies: Extended Feature Sets [Evaluation #2]. NISTIR 7859 (2012)
14. NIST Special Database 27: Fingerprint Minutiae from Latent and Matching Tenprint Images. www.nist.gov/srd/nistsd27.htm
15. West Virginia University Latent Fingerprint Database: http://www.csee.wvu.edu/ross/
16. Indovina, M., Dvornychenko, V., Tabassi, E., Quinn, G., Grother, P., Meagher, S., Garris, M.: ELFT Phase II - An Evaluation of Automated Latent Fingerprint Identification Technologies. NISTIR 7577 (2009)
17. Jain, A.K., Feng, J.: Latent fingerprint matching. IEEE Trans. Pattern Anal. Mach. Intell. **33**(1), 88–100 (2011)
18. Yoshida, A., Hara, M.: Fingerprint image quality metrics that guarantees matching accuracy. In: Biometric Quality Workshop (2006)
19. NIST: Latent Print AFIS Interoperability Working Group. www.nist.gov/oles/afis_interoperability.cfm
20. Fronthaler, H., Kollreider, K., Bigun, J.: Local features for enhancement and minutiae extraction in fingerprints. IEEE Trans. Image Process. **17**(3), 354–363 (2008)
21. Jain, A.K., Feng, J.: Latent palmprint matching. IEEE Trans. Pattern Anal. Mach. Intell. **31**(6), 1032–1047 (2009)
22. Paulino, A.A., Feng, J., Jain, A.K.: Latent fingerprint matching using descriptor-based hough transform. IEEE Trans. Inf. Forensics Secur. **8**(1), 31–45 (2013)
23. Dvornychenko, V.N.: Evaluation of fusion methods for latent fingerprint matchers. In: Proceedings of 5th International Conference on Biometrics (ICB), pp. 182–188 (2012)
24. Breiman, L., Friedman, J., Olshen, R., Stone, C.: Classification and Regression Trees. Chapman and Hall/CRC, Boca Raton (1984)
25. NIST Special Database 14: NIST Mated Fingerprint Card Pairs 2 (MFCP2). http://www.nist.gov/srd/nistsd14.cfm
26. Tabassi, E., Wilson, C., Watson, C.: Fingerprint Image Quality. NISTIR 7151 (2004)
27. Yoon, S., Cao, K., Liu, E., Jain, A.K.: LFIQ: Latent fingerprint image quality. In: Proceedings of 6th Biometrics: Theory, Applications and Systems (BTAS) (2013)

A Study of Identification Performance of Facial Regions from CCTV Images

Tauseef Ali[1]([⊠]), Pedro Tome[2], Julian Fierrez[2], Ruben Vera-Rodriguez[2],
Luuk J. Spreeuwers[1], and Raymond N.J. Veldhuis[1]

[1] Faculty of EEMCS, University of Twente,
P.O. Box 217, 7500 AE Enschede, The Netherlands
{t.ali,L.J.Spreeuwers,R.N.J.Veldhuis}@ewi.utwente.nl
[2] Biometric Recognition Group - ATVS, Escuela Politecnica Superior - Universidad
Autonoma de Madrid, Avda. Francisco Tomas y Valiente, 11 - Campus de
Cantoblanco, 28049 Madrid, Spain
{pedro.tome,julian.fierrez,ruben.vera}@uam.es

Abstract. This paper focuses on automatic face identification for forensic applications. Forensic examiners compare different parts of the face
image obtained from a closed-circuit television (CCTV) image with a
database of mug shots or good quality image(s) taken from the suspect. In
this work we study and compare the discriminative capabilities of different facial regions (also referred to as facial features) such as eye, eyebrow,
mouth, etc. It is useful because it can statistically support the current
practice of forensic facial comparison. It is also of interest to biometrics
as a more robust general-purpose face recognition system can be built
by fusing the similarity scores obtained from the comparison of different
individual parts of the face. For experiments with automatic systems,
we simulate a very challenging recognition scenario by using a database
of 130 subjects each having only one gallery image. Gallery images are
frontal mug shots while probe set consist of low quality CCTV camera
images. Face images in gallery and probe sets are first segmented using
eye locations and recognition experiments are performed for the different
face regions considered. We also study and evaluate an improved recognition approach based on AdaBoost algorithm with Linear Discriminant
Analysis (LDA) as a week learner and compare its performance with the
baseline Eigenface method for automatic facial feature recognition.

1 Introduction

The difficulty of automatic face recognition mainly depends on the type of facial
images we want to compare. A lot of research has been carried out to perform
automatic face recognition and as a result several systems are available [1–6].
Problems such as different facial expressions, illumination conditions and poses
have been studied and to certain extent some solutions have been proposed
[2,7,8]. A relatively less investigated problem is the automatic face recognition
from low quality images taken using CCTV camera. To date, there is no automatic system available which can reliably compare CCTV images with high

© Springer International Publishing Switzerland 2015
U. Garain and F. Shafait (Eds.): IWCF 2012 and 2014, LNCS 8915, pp. 83–91, 2015.
DOI: 10.1007/978-3-319-20125-2_8

quality images in mug shot database or image(s) taken from the suspect. This task is manually performed by forensic examiners where instead of following a holistic approach they use a "feature-based" approach. Each part such as nose, eyes, mouth, etc. is compared separately and a conclusion is reached by observing similarities and differences. Finally conclusions based on the different facial features along with the relative importance of each is used to state an opinion in the form of a ratio of how likely is that the two images being compared are obtained from the same person to the ratio of how likely is that the two images being compared are obtained from different persons [8,9].

The task of facial feature comparison is very challenging when one or both images under consideration are taken using CCTV camera because of the low quality. An automatic system comparing individual facial features is highly desirable as it will not only make the manual comparison of forensic examiners faster but will also help standardize this process. It is not possible with current state-of-the art recognition technologies to replace the manual comparison process in forensic face recognition; however, an automatic system can reduce, to a great extent, the manual effort. This can be, for instance, displaying top 10 candidate matches from a database of thousands of images based on a facial feature extracted from a criminal face image taken at a crime scene from a CCTV camera. Individual facial feature recognition is also important in cases such as having partial occlusion of the face and when only one facial feature is visible. In such cases even state-of-the art commercial face recognition systems such as [6] fail to work. Studies like the one presented in this paper are also necessary to scientifically support and help to establish procedures to assign relative weights to the opinions that can be inferred from different parts of the face.

In this paper we study the recognition performance of different facial features using two automatic recognition systems. The first system is the baseline Eigenface approach [4] while the second system is based on AdaBoost algorithm where we use LDA as a weak learner. The remaining of this paper is organized as follows: Sect. 2 reviews the protocol followed by forensic examiners to carry out the facial comparison which is the main motivation for this work. Section 3 describes the database, evaluation protocol and the segmentation of face images. Section 4 briefly describes the improved boosting-based LDA approach. Experimental results based on the Eigenface method and the boosting approach are presented in Sect. 5. Finally, in Sect. 6 we draw conclusions and mention future research directions.

2   Forensic Examiners' Facial Comparison

In this section we briefly review the forensic experts way of facial comparison which is the main motivation behind our work. The discussion is based on the guidelines set forward by the workgroup on face comparison at Netherlands Forensic Institute (NFI) [10,11] which is a member of European Network of Forensic Science Institutes [12]. The facial comparison is based on morphological-anthropological facial features. In most cases the pictures are obtained or processed to be in the same posture. The comparison mainly focuses on:

- Shape of mouth, eyes, nose, ears, eyebrows, etc.
- Relative distance among different relevant facial features
- Contour of cheek- and chin-lines
- Lines, moles, wrinkles, scars, etc. in the face

When comparing faces manually, it should be noted that differences can be invisible due to underexposure, overexposure, resolution too low, out-of-focus and distortions in imaging process, specifically when considering information from surveillance camera. Furthermore, similar facial features can result in different depictions due to the camera position regarding the head, insufficient resolution, difference in focusing of two images, and distortion in imaging process.

Due to the aforementioned effects, which usually make the comparison process difficult, the anthropological facial features are visually compared and classified as: similar in details, similar, no observation, different, different in details. Apparent similarities and differences are further evaluated by classifying facial features as: *weakly discriminative, moderately discriminative,* and *strongly discriminative.* A conclusion based on this comparison process is a form of support for either the prosecutions or defense hypothesis and can be stated as no support, limited support, moderate support, strong support, and very strong support. The process is subjective to great extent and the conclusion of one expert can be different than other. The final result is based on the combination of the comparison results of different individual features. This is in contrast to automatic biometric face recognition systems where the whole face image is usually considered as a single entity [2,4].

3   Database Description and Face Segmentation

We use SCFace database [13] in our experiments which consists of 130 subjects each having one frontal mug shot image and 5 surveillance camera images. This database presents novel and challenging tests for automatic face recognition systems due to the very low quality images taken by surveillance cameras. A few examples of mug shot and surveillance camera images used in our experiments are shown in Fig. 1. There are five different surveillance cameras used each with three different distances from the subjects. For simplicity in our experiments we consider only one surveillance camera with the closest distance to the subjects.

All of the frontal mug shot and surveillance camera images are segmented using the ground truth locations of the eyes. Segmentation of the face image into different parts is based on standard facial proportions [14]. An example of the set of segments into which a face image is divided is shown in Fig. 2. As shown in Fig. 2, pixels outside the region of interest are masked by setting them to zero. Given a probe patch of a facial feature extracted from a surveillance camera image, it is matched with each of the 130 patches extracted from the frontal mug shot images.

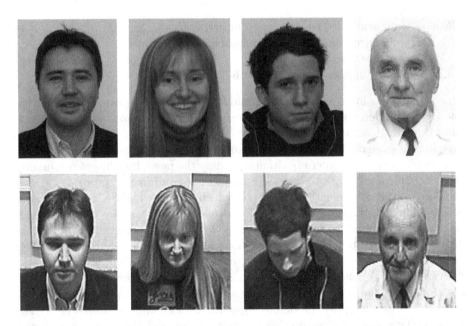

Fig. 1. A few sample gallery (first row) and probe images (second row) used in our experiments.

4   Facial Feature Recognition

To handle the complex nature of individual facial feature recognition from low quality CCTV images we use LDA [15] as a weak learner in Adaboost.M2 [16] for feature[1] extraction while classification is performed using simple Euclidean distance. The performance of traditional LDA-based approach [3] is improved by incorporating it in the boosting framework. Since both LDA and AdaBoost are well known algorithms we only provide a brief description of our employed recognition system highlighting the way LDA is integrated in AdaBoost.M2. Each round of boosting generates a new LDA subspace particularly focusing on examples which are misclassified in previous LDA subspace. The final feature extractor module is an ensemble of several specific LDA solutions. In order to incorporate LDA in boosting framework, slight modifications are introduced in the way the within-class and the between-class scatter matrices are constructed at the end of each boosting iteration by incorporating the weight associated with each sample. Please refer to [5] for a detailed description of using LDA as a weak leaner in AdaBoost algorithm.

---

[1] Here the term "feature" refers to a vector of values describing the characteristics of an image patch. This is the common use of the term "feature" in pattern recognition. In order to avoid ambiguity we always use the term "facial features" for referring to the parts of the face such as eye, eyebrow, nose, etc.

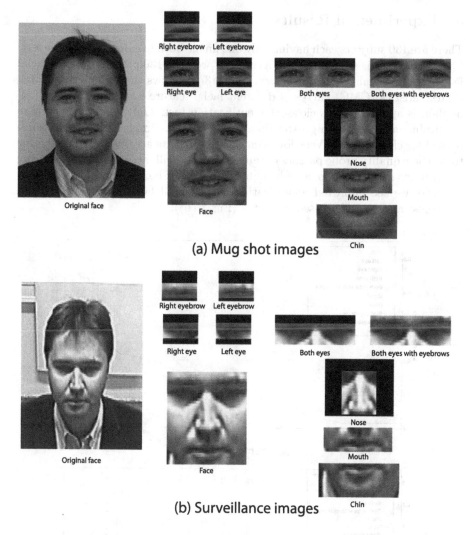

Fig. 2. (a) Mug shot images (b) Surveillance camera images.

This kind of ensemble based approach takes advantage of both LDA and boosting and outperforms simple LDA based systems in complex face recognition tasks. This is particularly important where a small number of training samples for each subject are available (1 image patch per facial feature in this case) compared to the number of dimensions of the samples i.e., the small-sample-size problem [17] and when non-linear variations are present in facial images. Our employed face recognition system is more robust when performing recognition of low resolution face images. This result is also verified by the authors in [5] where they use similar approach for face recognition.

5   Experimental Results

There are 130 subjects each having only one image both in gallery and probe sets. Each face image is segmented and as a result we have 130 patches for each facial feature both in gallery and probe set. Figure 3 (a) shows the Cumulative Match Characteristics (CMC) curves of different facial feature when the Eigenface [4] method is applied to this close-set identification task. Only components whose eigenvalues are equal to or greater than 1 are retained. Simple Euclidean distance is used for classification. Very low identification results are observed mainly due to very low quality probe patches obtained from surveillance camera images, only one training sample, and relatively high size of gallery. For the same identification scenario, we see improved identification rates for all facial features using the AdaBoost approach discussed in Sect. 4 (Fig. 3 (b)).

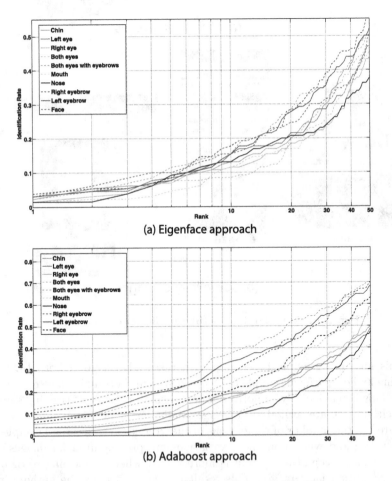

(a) Eigenface approach

(b) Adaboost approach

Fig. 3. Identification performance of different facial features.

Table 1. Rank 1 identification rate (%) (EB stands for eyebrow).

	Left eye	Right eye	Left EB	Right EB	Mouth	Nose	Eyes with EB	Eyes	Chin	Face
Eigenface approach	2.31	1.54	3.08	3.85	1.54	1.54	3.08	2.31	2.31	3.84
Adaboost approach	3.85	5.39	7.69	10.77	3.85	1.54	12.31	8.46	2.31	6.15

Table 2. Rank 10 identification rate (%) (EB stands for eyebrow).

	Left eye	Right eye	Left EB	Right EB	Mouth	Nose	Eyes with EB	Eyes	Chin	Face
Eigenface approach	11.54	11.54	15.38	17.69	11.54	13.08	15.38	8.46	13.08	15.38
Adaboost approach	19.23	16.92	33.85	28.46	10.77	7.69	37.69	23.85	17.69	20.77

Tables 1–2 list the rank 1 and rank 10 identification rate of each facial feature. It can be concluded that different automatic systems might rank different facial feature differently with respect to their discriminative capabilities. It is important to note that since the segmentation process is based on eyes location, the eye regions are expected to be better aligned than other regions. However, it is a standard practice in automatic face recognition to locate eyes positions and normalize face based on eyes positions.

Besides identification performance, it is also important to consider performance in verification scenario. In forensic facial comparison, a simple verification situation happens when an image from a suspect is compared with an image obtained from a crime scene. This is a one-to-one comparison for which different evaluation metrics such as Area under Receiver Operating Characteristics (ROC) curve (verification rate vs. false acceptance rate) and Equal Error Rate (EER) are used. In our experiments we use area under the ROC to summarize the verification performance of both systems for different facial features. Higher value of area under the ROC implies better verification performance of a system and vice versa. Table 3 summarizes results of verification experiments using the

Table 3. Verification performance using percentage of area under ROC (EB stands for eyebrow).

	Left eye	Right eye	Left EB	Right EB	Mouth	Nose	Eyes with EB	Eyes	Chin	Head
Eigenfaces approach	57	56	61	63	55	53	60	56	60	59
Adaboost approach	63	66	75	77	55	57	79	69	61	72

Table 4. Ranking facial feature based on verification performance.

Eigenface method	Adaboost approach
Right eyebrow	Both eyes with eyebrow
Left eyebrow	Right eyebrow
Both eyes with eyebrows	Left eyebrow
Chin	Face
Face	Eyes
Left eye	Right eye
Eyes	Left eye
Right eye	Chin
Mouth	Nose
Nose	Mouth

area under ROC curve metric. In Table 4 we rank facial feature according to their verification performance using each method.

6   Conclusions and Future Work

Comparing individual facial features of two or more faces is a common practice that forensic examiners carry out during their investigation of a crime when there are facial images from a crime scene. In this paper we presented preliminary experiments to compare and evaluate the discriminative capabilities of different facial features. We studied a boosting based LDA approach and compared its performance with the standard Eigenface method for individual facial feature recognition. The studied method has shown improved performance, however, still it is far from the point where it can be used in real applications. It is however important to study and understand the recognition performance of different facial features by recognition algorithms. This can lead to future research such as building more robust face recognition systems by the weighted sum of all facial features recognition results. Also it is more important in cases where crime scene images are partially occluded or only a few facial features are visible. Our future research will include improving the recognition performance as well as combining evidence from different facial feature comparison to single evidence for forensic face recognition.

Acknowledgments. This work is carried out during the secondment of the first author at ATVS, Autonomous University of Madrid. The research is funded by the European commission as a Marie-Curie ITN-project (FP7-PEOPLE-ITN-2008) under grant agreement number 238803 and the Spanish Direccion General de la Guardia Civil (DGGC). The authors would like to thank Nicomedes Exposito, Francisco J. Vega, Patricio Leston and Pedro A. Martinez for their valuable comments.

References

1. Abatea, A.F., Nappi, M., Riccioa, D., Sabatino, G.: 2D and 3D face recognition: a survey. Pattern Recogn. Lett. **28**, 1885–1906 (2007)
2. Zhao, W., Chellappa, R., Phillips, P.J., Rosenfeld, A.: Face recognition: a literature survey. ACM Comput. Survey. **35**, 399–458 (2003)
3. Belhumeur, P.N., Hespanha, J.P., Kriegman, D.J.: Eigenfaces vs. fisherfaces: recognition using class specific linear projection. IEEE Trans. on Pattern Anal. Mach. Intell. **19**, 711–720 (1997)
4. Turk, M., Pentland, A.: Eigenfaces for recognition. J. Cogn. Neurosci. **3**, 72–86 (1991)
5. Lu, J., Plataniotis, K.N., Venetsanopoulos, A.N.: Boosting linear discriminant analysis for face recognition. Proc. IEEE Int. Conf. Image Process. **1**, 657–660 (2003)
6. http://www.cognitec-systems.de/FaceVACS-SDK.19.0.html
7. Kong, S.G., Heo, J., Abidi, B.R., Paik, J., Abidi, M.A.: Recent advances in visual and infrared face recognition-a review. Comput. Vis. Image Underst. **97**, 103–135 (2005)
8. Ali, T., Spreeuwers, L.J., Veldhuis, R.N.J.: Forensic face recognition: a survey. In: Face Recognition: Methods, Applications and Technology, Computer Science, Technology and Applications. Nova Publishers, 9 (2012). ISBN 978-1-61942-663-4
9. Ali, T., Spreeuwers, L.J., Veldhuis, R.N.J.: Towards automatic forensic face recognition. In: Manaf, A.A., Zeki, A., Zamani, M., Chuprat, S., El-Qawasmeh, E. (eds.) ICIEIS 2011. CCIS, pp. 47–55. Springer, Heidelberg (2011)
10. Netherlands Forensic Institute. http://www.forensicinstitute.nl
11. General method of facial comparison, Addendum 1, internal document, Netherlands Forensic Institute
12. European Network of Forensic Science Institutes, http://www.enfsi.eu/
13. Grgic, M., Delac, K., Grgic, S.: SCface - surveillance cameras face database. Multimedia Tools Appl. J. **51**, 863–879 (2011)
14. Tome, P., Blazquez, L.: Face regions segmentation based on facial proportions. Technical report, ATVS - Biometric Recognition Group. Universidad Autonoma de Madrid (2012)
15. Duda, R.O., Hart, P.E., Stork, D.H.: Pattern Classification, 2nd edn. Wiley Interscience, Hoboken (2000). ISBN 0-471-05669-3, MR 1802993
16. Freund, Y., Schapire, R.E.: A decision-theoretic generalization of on-line learning and an application to boosting. J. Comput. Syst. Sci. **55**, 119–139 (1997)
17. Raudys, S.J., Jain, A.K.: Small sample size effects in statistical pattern recognition: recommendations for practitioners. IEEE Trans. Pattern Anal. Mach. Intell. **13**, 252–264 (1991)

Document Image Inspection

Inverse of Low Resolution Line Halftone Images for Document Inspection

Biswajit Halder[1(✉)], Utpal Garain[2], Rajkumar Darbar[3], and Abhoy Ch. Mondal[1]

[1] Department of Computer Science, University of Burdwan, Bardhaman, West Bengal, India
biswajithalder88@gmail.com, abhoy_mondal@yahoo.co.in
[2] Indian Statistical Institute, Kolkata, India
utpal@isical.ac.in
[3] School of Information Technology, Indian Institute of Technology, Kharagpur, India
rajdarbar.r@gmail.com

Abstract. In this paper, a new inverse half toning method has been proposed for reconstructing low resolution line halftone images. This reconstruction is done in order to authenticate an image in question. The reconstructed image is compared with its original image in terms of standard image quality metrics such as peak signal to noise ratio (PSNR) and structural similarity index measure (SSIM). The existing inverse halftone methods have rarely considered line halftone images which are normally of low resolution and the quality of the inverse halftone largely depends on the characteristics like frequency or shape of halftone dots. Our proposed inverse halftone technique consists of two parts: at first, the resolution (in lines per inch, lpi) of an input image is estimated and a low level image from the binary line halftone image is constructed. In the second phase, gray level continuous image is generated from the low level description and the lpi information. The method is based on learning based pattern classification techniques namely, neural nets. A comparative study shows that the proposed method outperforms many existing inverse halftone techniques while dealing with line halftone images.

Keywords: Line half-tone · Inverse halftoning · RBF-NN · Image quality

1 Introduction

Halftone images are essential part of printed materials [1–3]. In printing pictures in books, a continuous tone original picture is first converted into a halftone (HT) one which finally gets printed in the book. Inverse halftone (IHT) is the method that attempts to generate the original picture from a given halftone image. IHT is important for several purposes. For instance, if we want to compare an original image with the one which has been actually printed by other printers. It may happen that the original copy of the image is not available at all and in this

U. Garain and F. Shafait (Eds.): IWCF 2012 and 2014, LNCS 8915, pp. 95–103, 2015.
DOI: 10.1007/978-3-319-20125-2_9

situation, IHT may help to regenerate the original picture from its HT image available in printed form. Reprinting of old books for which the original pictures are not available, IHT plays an important role. In today's world, IHT is an important tool for copyright authentication.

There are two types dots by which halftone images are composed of: (i) dispersed dot and (ii) clustered dot. Dispersed dots are of fixed size and dot diameter are not directly related to the dot frequency. The number of dots in a region defines the basis of tonal levels. The clustered dot occurs when the halftone dots are of variable sizes. In this scheme, the dot diameter is proportional to the dot frequency. Dispersed dots are used in limited case digital printing (e.g. laser jet printers, photocopiers, etc.) whereas clustered dots are used in large scale printing (e.g. offset printing, lithography, silkscreen printing, etc.)

In literature, various types of IHT techniques are available [4,5]. Almost all of these techniques considered dispersed dot halftone images which are largely relevant for digitally printed materials. The effectiveness of these methods for clustered dot halftone images is not well studied. Some works have reported results on both dispersed as well as clustered dots where dealing with dispersed dots is mostly stressed upon. This dominant trend, i.e. dealing with the dispersed dots as observed in the existing IHT methods maybe because of the easy availability of digital printers under lab environment. Original pictures are converted into corresponding their halftone versions which are then printed using digital printers. As the digital printers are used, dispersed dots came into discussion. However, for large scale printing offset/silk screen printers instead of digital ones are used. Therefore, IHT methods working on clustered dots are important in many practical situations. Moreover, dispersed dot halftone images are generally of higher resolution (around 150 lines per inch or lpi and more) than that of clustered dot based halftone images (as low as 50 lpi to as high as 150 lpi). Consequently, efficiency of most of the existing IHT methods on low resolution halftone images is also not well explored. This paper attempts to fill this gap by considering design of an efficient IHT method working on clustered dot halftone images.

The clustered dots can be of different shapes. The line halftone dots are one of them and mostly used by the printing houses. Line half tone images are commonly used in printed books, old manuscripts, magazines etc. including many security documents like certificates, bank checks, currency notes, legal deeds and so on. In security documents, line halftone images are normally used as background design that serves as a protection against counterfeiting. Such design involves micro print-line patterns, guilloches patterns, latent image pattern, relief line pattern etc. Most of these patterns are produced from continuous tone image. The design details of such patterns are not clear with the naked eye but become clear with magnification. Characteristics of these line patterns are line thickness, line density and ink colour. Fine-line design features are changed in the event of a photocopying attack. For example, when a forger attempts to copy the page, the design will appear blurred and display a pattern spread. Generally, a document examiner inspects this deformation with a magnifier [6–8]. The document in question is inspected using different light sources, i.e. transmitted light, oblique light, etc. This inspection is grossly manual and therefore, time consuming. For quick decision-making and for better visual inspection, a sophisticated machine-assisted technique is called for. This paper is aimed at developing an inverse half toning technique (IHT) for authenticating line HT images. The method attempts to formulate a statistical measure in order to judge the quality of the image in question against the original image. We have considered line halftone image at three different resolutions namely, 60, 70, and 80 lpi which are commonly used in practice.

Another significant contribution of this study is to use learning based pattern classification technique for designing the IHT method. The existing methods rarely exploit this technique rather make use of static template or edge analysis based pattern matching. Many techniques borrow idea from digital signal processing. Pattern classification based inverse halftoning has also been attempted in few works [9,10]. These methods do not consider resolution of an input image separately and therefore, inverse halftoning is done based on a overall learning over images of many resolutions. Our method brings novelty by finding the lpi information so that generation of inverse halftone becomes more precise. Secondly, empirically we observe that use of more than one neural net gives better quality inverse halftone than the one given by only one neural net. First neural net generates an approximate low level image (k-level, where $2 < k < 256$) which is taken by the second neural net as input and produces the final gray tone image. Lastly, we have presented a comparative study to show the effectiveness of our proposed method over several existing IHT methods when applied on line halftone images.

2   The Proposed Inverse Transform Method

The main of the inverse transform method is to take a line halftone (HT) image as input and produce a high quality gray-scale image corresponding to the input. A radial basis function neural net (RBF-NN) is the core of this transform method. The reason for using RBF-NN as the neural network lies in the fact that the inverse transform is a complex non-linear process and for doing this, RBF-NN shows better performance for universal non-linear approximation over the other neural nets (e.g. MLP-NN) [9].

The reconstruction function is given by

$$C = \sum_{h}^{n} w_h \cdot \phi(||x - t_h||) + B \tag{1}$$

where n is the total number of input samples applied for output neuron C which corresponds to the intensity level of a pixel (i, j) in the output image, w_h is the synaptic weight connecting hidden neuron h to output neuron, B is a bias of the output neuron and the activation function $\phi(\cdot)$ is defined as

$$\phi(||x - t_h||) = \exp\left\{\frac{-(||x - t_h||^2}{2\sigma_h^2}\right\} \tag{2}$$

where the set of centres $\{t_h|h = 1, 2, \ldots, n\}$ are m^2-dimensional vectors to be determined, x is the m^2 dimensional pattern obtained by placing a $m \times m$ template around the (i, j) pixel of the input image, and σ_h is the variance of Gaussian function. The gradient descent is used for error-correction learning process.

Two different architectures are used to achieve this transform.

Architecture 1. A single RBF-NN is used that takes the binary HT image as input, predicts lpi of the input image and generates the gray image as output. This is somewhat similar to what has been used in previous works for inverse halftoning of dithered halftone images [9], but these works do not compute lpi information.

Architecture 2. This architecture consists of two levels of RBF-NNs as shown in Fig. 1. The first level takes the input image, I_{HT} and predicts the lpi information for the given image. In addition, the first level produces a low level (k-level) image, I_k. The lpi information helps to choose a particular NN on the second level. If we consider three different lpi based HT images (I_{HT}) then three different RBF-NNs corresponding to three specific lpi values are present on the second level. Depending upon the lpi detected by the first level RBF-NN, the intermediate k-level image (I_k) is passed to the particular RBF-NN on the second level. The RBF-NN of the second level produces the final gray scale image (I_G).

The values of m and k have definite impact on the quality of the inverse halftone and therefore, several alternatives have been tried. In our experiment, three different values of m namely, 3, 5 and 7 and three different values for k namely, 4, 8 and 16 are used. Variation in m will give different pixel templates based on which prediction of lpi information and the intensity level of a pixel in the output image is predicted. Variation in k defines the intermediate approximated image at different intensity levels.

3   Experimental Protocol

3.1   Dataset

In this experiment, five standard digital grayscale images namely, (i) *Peppers*, (ii) *Mandrill*, (iii) *Barbara*, (iv) *Atlas hand* and (v) *Lena eye* which have no background have been considered. Line HT images are generated using a commercial software namely Adobe Photoshop Software 7.0. All the images are processed at 100 dpi resolutions with specified screen angle namely, $45°$ and dot frequencies of 60, 70 and 80 lpi. Printing is done through single color offset printing machine (black ink used here). Printed images are digitized by flatbed HP scanner (Scan-Jet 8250) with same resolution (i.e. 100 dpi). Binary images are obtained by using Otsu thresholding method.

HT binary images of the first three images (i.e. *Peppers*, *Mandrill* and *Barbara*) have been considered for training the RBF-NNs and remaining two images (i.e. *Lena eye* and *Atlas hand*) have been considered for testing. For architecture-1, i.e. use of only one RBF-NN, about 500,000 (500K) binary

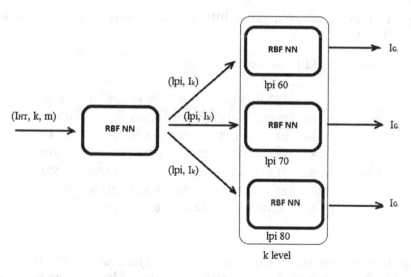

Fig. 1. Block diagram of Architecture 2

feature vectors tagged with lpi information and gray value are generated from the training halftone images. For architecture-2, i.e., two-level RBF-NN, the first-level RBF-NN is trained with feature vectors tagged with lpi, k-level value and gray level. The k-level values are generated by down-sampling the original gray images. The gray level tag is not required by the first-level RBF-NN, but it is used by the second RBF-NN.

3.2 Evaluation Strategy

Two methods namely, peak-signal-to-noise ratio (PSNR)and structural similarity index measure (SSIM) [11] often used for measuring image quality are applied for judging the efficiency of the proposed inverse halftoning method as well as comparing its performance with some of the well cited previous studies. PSNR value is inversely proportional with the mean square error (MSE). The value of SSIM is computed combining correlation, luminance and contrast. Its range lies in $[0, 1]$. If SSIM be 1 then both images are maximally correlated.

3.3 Results and Discussions

The performance of the inverse transform methods are presented on two pictures namely *Atlas hand* and *Lena eye* which are halftoned at three different resolutions: 60, 70 and 80 lpi. The performance of the architecture-1 is presented first in Table 1.

Note that for the *Atlas hand* PSNR values of around 27-28 and SSIM value of around 0.8 is achieved which is slightly better than what is obtained by the same architecture but without using lpi information [9]. Without using lpi information

Table 1. Performance of a single RBF-NN based Inverse Transform Method (Architecture-1)

Image	LPI	Context Pattern ($m \times m$)					
		3 × 3		5 × 5		7 × 7	
		PSNR	SSIM	PSNR	SSIM	PSNR	SSIM
Atlas hand	60	25.052	0.859	*27.805*	*0.901*	27.200	0.891
	70	24.868	0.873	*27.283*	*0.896*	27.240	0.890
	80	18.010	0.710	27.010	0.789	*28.040*	*0.810*
Lena eye	60	21.673	0.565	18.273	0.505	*21.797*	*0.571*
	70	21.585	0.557	*23.903*	*0.641*	23.660	0.636
	80	20.735	0.514	*23.956*	*0.624*	23.656	0.623

(i.e. if the training of the neural is done without lpi information) PSNR value of around 24-25 is obtained. The same trend is supported by the *Lena eye* image. This shows lpi information better guides the inverse halftoning process. Context pattern based on which features are extracted around a pixel has definite effect and the result shows that 5 × 5 context produces best average case result. We can further note that similar inverse halftoning methods [9,10] produced image giving PSNR of around 30-31 when the halftones are based on dispersed dots and printed digitally. The reason is the resolution which is far more (around 150 lpi) for dispersed dot based halftones than it is in line halftones.

Next the performance of the two-stage RBF-NN is reported in Table 2. Here a k-level is approximated image is generated first which is then converted into gray tone. Quality of inverse halftone image has been investigated at different values of k. It is to be noted that for all cases, this 2-level RBF-NN architecture gives better performance than single RBF-NN. Though the amount of improvement looks small in terms of PSNR and SSIM values but these improvements are statistically significant for all the three resolutions, $p < 0.05$ by a two-tail t-test. Figures 2 and 3 show the inverse halftone images at different resolution levels. Results for 5 × 5 context pattern are shown in these figures.

From the Tables 1 and 2, one more observation maybe noted. In these tables, SSIM values varies from 0.5 to 0.9 whereas PSNR varies from 18 to 29 (dB). It is observed that when SSIM increases from 0.2 to 0.8, PSNR increases linearly or nearly following a straight line. However, when SSIM rises to 0.8 or higher, PSNR increases rapidly. This observation is supported by the findings in [11].

Next, we compare the performance of our method against the largely cited inverse halftoning methods [12–15] which have been shown performing well on dispersed halftone images. We checked their performance on line halftone images and results are reported in Table 3. The comparison shows that the proposed method outperforms the other methods often by significant margin based on both the metrics, i.e., PSNR and SSIM and for all the three resolutions.

Table 2. Performance of two-stage RBF-NN based Inverse Transform Method (Architecture-2)

Image	LPI	k	Context Pattern ($m \times m$)					
			3 × 3		5 × 5		7 × 7	
			PSNR	SSIM	PSNR	SSIM	PSNR	SSIM
Atlas hand	60	4	24.875	0.866	27.553	0.899	27.400	0.896
		8	25.526	0.877	27.812	0.890	*27.900*	*0.903*
		16	24.874	0.873	27.843	0.901	27.700	0.893
	70	4	24.884	0.870	26.778	0.889	28.705	0.891
		8	25.005	0.870	26.870	0.879	27.690	0.876
		16	24.936	0.873	27.071	0.893	*29.670*	*0.909*
	80	4	18.370	0.750	27.572	0.809	28.670	0.887
		8	18.887	0.768	27.670	0.890	*28.900*	*0.894*
		16	18.910	0.784	27.550	0.886	28.400	0.865
Lena eye	60	4	21.108	0.528	23.188	0.610	23.437	0.597
		8	22.875	0.582	23.753	0.613	*24.387*	0.622
		16	22.295	0.588	24.026	*0.631*	23.921	0.619
	70	4	21.021	0.521	23.514	0.615	24.893	0.688
		8	22.388	0.578	23.798	0.625	*26.368*	*0.807*
		16	22.972	0.598	24.145	0.644	24.184	0.642
	80	4	21.219	0.518	23.735	0.601	23.904	0.616
		8	22.060	0.561	25.050	0.623	*25.066*	*0.682*
		16	22.590	0.573	24.046	0.619	24.289	0.634

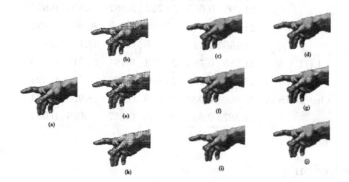

Fig. 2. Inverse Halftoning of *Atlas hand*: (a) original gray image, (b), (e), (h): line halftone document images at 60, 70 and 80 lpi; (c), (f), (i): inverse halftone images at 60, 70, 80 lpi by using single RBF-NN architecture-1; (d), (g), (j): inverse halftone images at 60, 70, 80 lpi by using two-stage RBF-NN architecture-2.

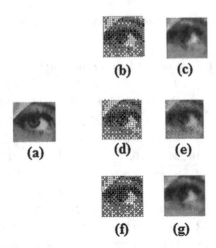

Fig. 3. Inverse Halftoning of *Lena eye*: (a) original gray image, (b), (d), (f): line halftone document images at 60, 70 and 80 lpi; (c), (e), (g): inverse halftone images at 60, 70, 80 lpi by using two-stage RBF-NN architecture-2.

Table 3. Performance Comparison: the first row for each method corresponds to the image *Atlas hand* and the second corresponds to the image *Lena eye*

IHT Method	60 LPI		70 LPI		80 LPI	
	PSNR	SSIM	PSNR	SSIM	PSNR	SSIM
LPA-ICI [12]	25.502	0.782	26.005	0.845	26.001	0.845
	24.190	0.631	24.364	0.650	24.232	0.636
WInHD [13]	25.589	0.862	25.596	0.862	25.592	0.862
	24.306	0.655	24.722	0.687	24.370	0.657
MAP [14]	26.996	0.892	26.999	0.892	26.995	0.892
	24.136	0.621	24.455	0.634	24.170	0.617
LUT [15]	24.885	0.780	25.213	0.781	25.211	0.780
	23.341	0.621	23.806	0.630	23.428	0.624
Our Method	27.900	0.903	29.670	0.909	28.900	0.894
	24.387	0.631	26.368	0.857	25.066	0.682

4 Conclusion

Though line halftone technique is largely used in practice for large scale printing but there was little research on inverse halftoning of line halftone images. This study presents a neural net based inverse halftoning method for line halftones. Experimental results show that the proposed method works well for the line halftones compared to the several existing methods. As line halftones are generally of low resolution images, inverse halftone images give slightly less PSNR and SSIM value compared to the those obtained for dispersed dot (higher resolution) based halftones. The present study can be extended in several directions. At first, improvement of inverse halftone images is definitely an area where more research is needed. It is shown here that a two-stage neural net performs better than a single stage architecture. This can be further extended to investigate whether a series of neural net could produce better quality inverse halftone.

As the current work is motivated by the practical need of generating original gray tone image in situation where the original image is not available or the printed halftone is in question of copyrighting issue, performance evaluation on a much larger dataset is required to bring out the potential of the present approach in practical scenario. Once established its efficiency on a larger dataset the present method could of good assistance for the forensic scientists, printing engineers and even for restoration of many historical documents.

References

1. Lau, D.L., Arce, G.R.: Modern Digital Halftoning. Marcel Dekker, New York (2001)
2. Knuth, D.E.: Digital halftones by dot diffusion. Published ACM Trans. Graph. (TOG) **6**(4), 245–273 (1987)
3. Analoui, M., Allebach, J.P.: Model based halftoning using direct binary search In: Proceedings SPIE Human Vision, Visual Digital Display III, vol. 1666, pp. 96–108, San Jose, CA (1992)
4. Kite, T.D., Damera-Venkata, N., Evans, B.L., Bovik, A.C.: A fast, high-quality inverse halftoning algorithm for error diffused halftones. IEEE Trans. Image Process. **9**(9), 1583–1592 (2000)
5. Chung, K.L., Wu, S.T.: Inverse halftoning algorithm using edge-based lookup table approach. IEEE Trans. Image Process. **14**(10), 1583–1589 (2005)
6. Reserve Bank of India, High Level RBI Group Suggests Steps to Check Menace of Fake Notes, Press release: 2009–2010/232 (2009)
7. Procedure Manuals, prepared by Directorate of Forensic Science, Ministry of Home Affairs, Government of India. http://www.dfs.gov.in
8. Counterfeit Banknotes, report of the parliamentary office of science and technology, UK (1996). www.parliament.uk/briefing-papers/POST-PN-77.pdf
9. Huang, W.B., Su, A.W.Y., Kuo, Y.H.: Neural network based method for image halftoning and inverse halftoning. Expert Syst. Appl. **34**(4), 2491–2501 (2008)
10. Chang, P.C., Yu, C.S.: Neural net classification and LMS reconstruction to halftone images. In: Proceedings SPIE Visual Communications and Image Processing, vol. 3309, pp. 592–602 (1998)
11. Hore, A., Ziou, D.: Image quality metrics: PSNR vs. SSIM. In: Proceedings IEEE International Conference of Pattern Recognition, pp. 2366–2369 (2010)
12. Foi, A., Katkovnik, V., Egiazarian, K., Astola, J.: Inverse halftoning based on the anisotropic LPA-ICI deconvolution. In: Proceedings of the International TICSP Workshop Spectral Method Multirate Signal Processing (SMMSP), pp. 49-56, Vienna (2004)
13. Neelamani, R., Nowak, R., Baraniuk, R.: WInHD: wavelet-based inverse halftoning via deconvolution. IEEE Trans. Image Proc. **6**(12), 1673–1687 (2002)
14. Stevenson, R.: Inverse halftoning via MAP estimation. IEEE Trans. Image Proc. **6**, 574–583 (1997)
15. Mese, M., Vaidyanathan, P.P.: Look-up table (LUT) method for inverse halftoning. IEEE Trans. Image Proc. **10**(10), 1566–1578 (2001)

When Document Security Brings New Challenges to Document Analysis

Sébastien Eskenazi(✉), Petra Gomez-Krämer, and Jean-Marc Ogier

Laboratoire L3i, Université de La Rochelle, La Rochelle, France
{sebastien.eskenazi,petra.gomez,jean-marc.ogier}@univ-lr.fr

Abstract. It is very easy to ensure the authenticity of a digital document or of a paper document. However this security is seriously weakened when this document crosses the border between the material and the digital world. This paper presents the beginning of our work towards the creation of a document signature that would solve this security issue. Our primary finding is that current state of the art document analysis algorithms need to be re-evaluated under the criterion of robustness as we have done for OCR processing.

Keywords: Hybrid security · Text hashing · OCR hashing · Document analysis robustness

1 Introduction

With the ever increasing digitization of our world, people and companies now have to ensure the authenticity of many documents. For instance, an easy way to get a fraudulent identity card is not to forge one but to obtain a real one with fraudulent documents such as a fake electricity bill and a fake birth certificate [1]. Some of these documents are in a paper format and some are in a digital format. Ensuring the security of these two kinds of documents and of documents that can change format is called hybrid security. So far there is no other choice but to use two authentication systems: one for the paper documents and one for the digital documents. Even though watermarks or fingerprints can bridge the gap between the paper and the digital world they do not ensure the authenticity of the content of the document. They only ensure the authenticity of its support i.e. the file or the paper material [2].

The digital world has a very efficient tool to ensure the authenticity of a file: a hash key [3]. It cannot be used as-is on a paper document because of the noise of the scanning process which would always produce different files. We have the idea of extracting the content of the document and to hash this content instead of the raw scan of the document. This raises the immediate question of the content we want to extract. Is it just the text or does it also include the images, the handwritten signatures, or even a combination of those? And with which precision do we want to extract it? Is it plain text or do we also want to have the font, the font size and the emphasis? While investigating

© Springer International Publishing Switzerland 2015
U. Garain and F. Shafait (Eds.): IWCF 2012 and 2014, LNCS 8915, pp. 104–116, 2015.
DOI: 10.1007/978-3-319-20125-2_10

this question, our first experiments prove that most document analysis tasks need to be thought again under a completely new paradigm in this community: robustness. It appears that current content extraction algorithms produce very different results with only a slight amount of noise. This makes it impossible to produce a reproducible signature. We started studying this robustness with the base algorithm of our signature: OCR. We plan to study the other necessary algorithms after we obtained a suitable OCR.

This paper is organized as follows. In Sect. 2, we introduce the general problem of hybrid signature and the performance objectives. Section 3 presents the workflow we intend to build to solve it and the issue of robustness. Then, we present our analysis for the task of OCR analysis in Sect. 4. Finally, Sect. 5 concludes our work.

2   Hybrid Signature

Before presenting the hybrid signature itself we will present the hash algorithms on which it is based.

2.1   Digital Hash Algorithms

A digital hash algorithm computes a digest for a message. A very good overview of digital hash algorithms can be found in [3].

The first kind of hash algorithm was cryptographic hashing. It was made in order to be able to control the integrity of the message content without having to read the entirety of the message. This was useful at the beginning of the Internet because of network transmission errors. Cryptographic hash algorithms are now mostly used for security applications and content retrieval. They have several features. The first one is that any small change in the message will change the digest with a very high probability. This is reflected in the collision probability, which is the probability of two different messages having the same digest. Another important feature of hash algorithms is the inability to recover the original message from its digest (hence the name "cryptographic"). The main consequence of this requirement is that any smallest change will completely change the digest. This allows the authentication of a confidential message without having to compromise the confidentiality of the message. The current standard cryptographic hash algorithm is SHA-256 as defined in the Federal Information Processing Standard FIPS PUB 180-4 [4] and FIPS PUB 186-4 [5]. A security analysis of SHA-256 can be found in [6].

The next kind of digital algorithm is fuzzy hash algorithms. Contrarily to cryptographic hashes, a small change in the message will only change a portion of the digest. This allows the retrieval of different messages that have similar message parts, but that are not completely identical (hence the name "fuzzy"). For this reason, the content of the message is not as protected as in a cryptographic hash algorithm. The most common fuzzy hash algorithm is ssdeep [7]. Fuzzy hash algorithms are also called perceptual hash algorithms especially in

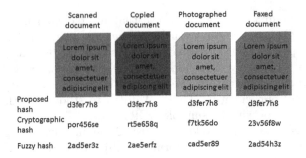

	Scanned document	Copied document	Photographed document	Faxed document
Proposed hash	d3fer7h8	d3fer7h8	d3fer7h8	d3fer7h8
Cryptographic hash	por456se	rt5e658q	f7tk56do	23v56f8w
Fuzzy hash	2ad5er3z	2ae5erfz	cad5er89	2ad54h3z

Fig. 1. Comparison of proposed, cryptographic and fuzzy digests on several copies of the same document and a fraudulent version of it. The cryptographic digests have nothing in common while the fuzzy ones all contain small variations making it impossible to identify which document is fraudulent.

the image processing community as the fuzzy hash is related to the content of the message and to the way a human perceives it. They are widely used for message retrieval, where the message can be of any kind such as an image [8], a text [9] or even raw bits of data on a hard drive [10]. A security analysis of perceptual hash algorithms can be found in [11].

Figure 1 shows the differences between these different hash algorithms and the proposed one.

2.2   Hybrid Security Algorithms

Villán et al. [12] elaborated two hashing algorithms. The first one is based on the combination of an OCR software (Abbyy Finereader) and a cryptographic hash (SHA-180). The second one is based on a random tiling hash, which computes the average luminance value on 1024 random rectangles for each word. They used an Arial font with a font size of 10 and no emphasis. The text was simple English text. While the first algorithm performs rather well with only two errors out of 64, the random tiling algorithm cannot differentiate one character from a similar one such as "o" and "e".

Tan et al. [13] developed a perceptual text hasing algorithm, which is very interesting as it is based on the skeleton features of each character. It has the drawback of removing all punctuation from the text.

The most recent work on hybrid security was made in two projects: the ANR Estampille [2,14] and the European project SIGNED [15].

The Estampille project aimed at developing a 2D-barcode that could be used as a fingerprint. The barcode is printed with extreme precision in a specific printing process. This fingerprint is supposed to be impossible to be reproduced or to be copied without detection. The latest results actually prove that having a dozen copies of an authentic fingerprint is enough to forge one. This does not include the fact that the document content is not included in the fingerprint. Thus once a forged fingerprint is made, it is possible to render any document authentic-like.

The SIGNED project was more ambitious and corresponds to what we can call a "hybrid signature". The goal of the project was to produce a digest of a document that allows the detection of any modification. It is based on a fuzzy hash algorithm, which has the disadvantage of breaching the possible confidentiality of the document, but this also allows for the localization of the modification. The document is analyzed at the signal level. They cut the document in tiles and use a Discrete Haar Wavelet Transform [16] on each of these tiles. For a document scanned at 600dpi, the tiles have a size of 64 by 64 pixels. Then a cryptographic hash is applied on each tile and all the digests are concatenated to create a fuzzy digest. The fuzzy digest is then printed on the document. During the verification process the digest of the scan is computed and compared with the one that is printed on it. A distance is computed between these two digests and if it is too large the document is considered to be fraudulent.

The results of the SIGNED project had to meet six performance indicators:

1. Probability of missed detection and false alarm
   (a) Probability of false alarm (PFA) below 0.001
   (b) Probability of missed detection (PMD) below 0.001 with $PFA < 0.001$
       – for the replacement of digits in Arial 8, 10 and 12
       – for the replacement of dots by commas in Arial 10 and 12
2. Collision probability below 0.001
3. Minimum area size to detect a manipulation: 42×42 pixels at 600dpi
4. Throughput below 5 seconds per page
5. Size of the document digest below 4 kB
6. Compatibility with current scanners and printers

A false alarm occurs when a document is detected as fraudulent while it is not and a missed detection is the contrary. The minimum area size means that a manipulation has to be bigger than a square of 42 by 42 pixels to be detected.

The project met all these requirements except for:

– The PMD for the replacement of dots by commas that required a bigger font than Arial such as Verdana
– The minimum area size that is of 64×64 pixels at 600dpi
– The throughput that was not achieved for the verification phase (no figure was given)
– The size of the document digest that was between 4.8 and 170 kB depending on the required precision

The performance indicators were given by the industrial partners of the project and as such represent a reasonable goal to reach. We can also notice that if we want to use OCR processing the minimum area size performance indicator is not relevant anymore.

3 Proposed Solution

Since a hash algorithm cannot be applied directly on a document image because of the variability and the acquisition noise, our idea is to extract the content from the document image, to format this content properly and to apply the hash algorithm on it. This will drastically reduce the amount of data to hash and will allow to hash only the significant (semantic) content of the image. The interest of extracting the content is that this is exactly what is not supposed to – and what we do not want to – change. This will eliminate the noise and so the variability of the data, and will allow the use of a cryptographic hash. Thus, we can expect this technique to be applicable also in the case of a camera captured document.

As the notion of "semantic" can have several meanings we will attempt to define it now. Usually a hash algorithm is applied directly on the raw data, the bits of information. We intend to apply it on the content extracted from the raw data. Hence we consider a semantic hash on the contrary to a normal hash. We do not take into account the level of abstraction of the content on which we apply the hash. For instance, applying a hash algorithm on a sequence of characters without any understanding of their division in words still makes a semantic hash. What matters is that the data on which is the hash algorithm applied to is the one that contains only the information that is meaningful for a human (and in our case that is not supposed to change).

3.1 Signature Workflow

Figure 2 shows the basic workflow for the signature computation. There are three main phases: the preliminary phase (orange) extracts the different elements such as text, images, tables and diagrams from the document image. The second phase (gray) extracts the content of each of these elements. The last phase (green) reconstructs the document and computes its digest.

The first step of the preliminary phase removes any geometric distortions such as skew and warp. We then proceed with the segmentation phase and the tagging of each segmented element according to its content (text, image, table, etc.).

During the second phase, the elements are analyzed by a content extraction algorithm. The algorithm is specific for each element tag such as an OCR for the text.

Finally all the extracted contents are used to rebuild the document according to the segmented and analyzed data. We apply SHA-256 to compute the document hash.

3.2 The Issue of Robustness

The objectives require a false positive rate below one in a thousand and the same for a missed detection.

The case of missed detection is not very important, except for some specific cases. For instance, in the case of undersegmentation, missed detections are mainly related to the precision of each content extraction algorithm. Should one algorithm not be good enough, we can either try to improve it, not use it and consider that the corresponding information is not secured or consider that the corresponding information is secured with a degraded level of security. Another solution is to only

954f7d96502b5c5fe2e98a5045bca7f5

Fig. 2. The workflow of the signature computation.

consider certain types of document images for which we have the desired accuracy. The precision of most document analysis algorithms is the most frequent criteria used to evaluate them. So the precision is usually quite good.

The case of false positives is very different. To prevent a false positive, we need to ensure that an algorithm will produce the same results for reasonably similar images of the same document and/or with some additional noise. This is the robustness of the algorithm and it is usually not analyzed. The issue with robustness goes even further than that: with a missed detection we accept a document that has a necessarily small modification (otherwise we would not miss it), while with a false positive we reject an entire document that is completely fine. From a practical point of view, if the rate of false positives is too high, there will be too many rejected documents. This means that either the document verification process is useless or it will require a lot of manpower to hand-verify each rejected document. False positives can be created at every step of the signature process: the segmentation, the content extraction and the document reconstruction can all produce false positives that will have a direct impact on the signature.

This shows how critical it is to ensure the robustness of the algorithms used to compute the document signature. Unfortunately this robustness has hardly been studied. We did this work for OCR and present it in the next section.

4   Study of OCR Capabilities

We will first describe in detail our test dataset, our test protocol and our results of the OCR analysis. Finally we will discuss possible OCR improvements.

4.1   Dataset

Considering the quite stringent requirement for the OCR accuracy, we chose to use clean, text-only, typewritten documents. Tesseract can analyze documents

Table 1. Scanning resolution for each scanner, one "X" per scan

Scanner	150 dpi	300 dpi	600 dpi
Konica Minolta Bizhub 223		X	XX
Fujitsu fi-6800	XXX	X	
Konica Minolta Bizhub C364e		X	X

with a single or double column layout, so we tested it with a combination of these. We used only and all the characters that it can recognize.

The dataset is made of 22 pages of text with the following characteristics:

- 1 page of a scientific article with a single column header and a double column body
- 3 pages of scientific articles with a double column layout
- 2 pages of programming code with a single column layout
- 4 pages of a novel with a single column layout
- 2 pages of legal texts with a single column layout
- 4 pages of invoices with a single column layout
- 4 pages of payslips with a single column layout
- 2 pages of birth extract with a single column layout

We created several variants of these 22 text pages by combining:

- 6 fonts : Arial, Calibri, Courier, Times New Roman, Trebuchet and Verdana
- 3 font sizes : 8, 10 and 12 points
- 4 emphases : normal, bold, italic and the combination of bold and italic

This makes 1584 documents. We printed these documents with three printers (a Konica Minolta Bizhub 223, a Sharp MX M904 and a Sharp MX M850) and scanned them with three scanners and at different resolutions between 150dpi and 600dpi as shown in Table 1. This makes a dataset of 42768 document images. Figure 3 shows an example of the images contained in the dataset.

4.2   Test Protocol

Most of the security algorithms are publicly available. For this reason we chose to use Tesseract [17] which is open-source. We used Tesseract version 3.02 with the default English training. We ran it on every image of the data set and used the ISRI evaluation tool [18] to compute the accuracy of the OCR and to analyze its errors. We also computed a hash digest of each OCR output file with SHA-256. We used these digests to compute the probability of false positives.

Computation of PFA. We will explain in the following the computation method for the probability of false positives. We consider a set of n documents. What a document exactly is will be defined for each computation. For each document there are m_i different digests, $i \in [1, n]$. Each digest is present s_{ij} times,

Fig. 3. An example of three document images of the dataset

$j \in [1, m_i]$. This creates a pseudo matrix S_{ij} containing all the s_{ij} values. For any i, m_i is the number of non null values on the ith row and the number of images is the sum of all the values contained in the matrix.

The signature verification process can be modeled by the successive draw without replacement of two digests among all the digests available for the document. The draw is without replacement as we consider it impossible to produce twice exactly the same image. A false positive happens when the two digests that are drawn are not the same. Hence the probability of a false positive for the ith document is given by:

$$P_i = 1 - \sum_{j=1}^{m_i} \left(\frac{s_{ij}}{\sum_{k=1}^{m_i} s_{ij}} \times \frac{s_{ij} - 1}{\sum_{k=1}^{m_i} s_{ij} - 1} \right) . \tag{1}$$

The global false positive probability is the mean of the probabilities for each document.

Post Processing. After some preliminary tests we noticed that it is unreasonable to require the OCR to distinguish some characters such as a capital "i" and a lower case "l" or a capital "o" and a zero. Tesseract regularily mistakes on for the other and it would be the same for a human. For this reason we added an alphabet reduction as post processing step. Table 2 summarizes the alphabet reduction.

4.3 Results

We evaluate the results of our proposed method in terms of precision, probability of false positives and collision probability, which are detailed in the following. Table 3 sums up most of our results.

Table 2. Alphabet reduction

Character	Replacement
Empty line	Removed
Tabulation and space	Removed
—(long hyphen)	- (short hyphen)
','(left and right apostrophes)	' (centered apostrophe)
",","(left and right quotes, double apostrophe)	" (centered quote)
I, l, 1 (capital i, 12th letter of the alphabet, number 1)	|(vertical bar)
O (capital o)	0 (zero)
fi (ligature)	fi (two letters f and i)
fi (ligature)	fl (two letters f and l)

Precision. The OCR precision ranges from 14.2 % to 100 % with an average of 96.79 %. The worst results are obtained for the pages of code as tesseract does not handle well the code text syntax. The other low precision results are due to segmentation errors.

The precision increases seriously when using a resolution of 300dpi rather than 150dpi as it increases from 91.92 % to 99.25 %. The improvement is much less significant when using 600dpi instead of 300dpi with a precision reaching 99.37 %.

The font size and emphasis also play an important role. The average precision is 92.57 %, 98.62 % and 99.20 % respectively for a font size of 8, 10 and 12 points. The use of italic worsens the accuracy results as, by instance, the vertical bars "|" can be misrecognized as division bars"/".

The choice of the font has a similar effect. Courier and Times New Roman get the worst results and the best ones are obtained for Verdana. This is explained by the fact that Courier characters have a very special shape, Times New Roman is the smallest font and Verdana the biggest.

Even though the accuracy results are not perfect they allow for us to meet the probability of missed detection criteria.

False Positives. The probability of false positives is quite different. As the OCR extracts only the text without taking into account the font, font size or emphasis we can consider that our dataset as 1944 copies of 22 document pages. A document is then only defined by its textual content. This produces a probability of false positives of 94 %!!

We then decided to consider a document as being defined by its textual content, the font, font size, font emphasis and scanning resolution. Our dataset is then composed of 9 copies of 4752 documents. This produces a probability of false positives of 90 %.

This is where increasing the scanning resolution has a real interest as the probability of false positives decreases from 99 % to 79 % and to 73 % for a resolution of 150, 300 and 600dpi respectively. The other influencing factors are the same as for the probability. This is understandable as the less errors there are, the less variation possibilities there are and the lower the false positive probability. However one could imagine that the same errors could be done every time thus reducing the false positive probability. This is not the case.

The best case scenario is when we consider a scanning resolution of 600dpi, a font size of 10 or 12 points, no italic emphasis and any font but Courier and Times New Roman. This allows us to reach a probability of false positives of 57 % and even 53 %, if we do not take into account the pages of code. The OCR precision reaches 99.67 % and 99.76 % in these two cases respectively.

We can see that the issue of robustness has not been resolved at all. If we consider a text of 2000 characters and we want to have less than one different OCR text out of one thousand copies of the text; this means an error rate of one in two million.

Collision Probability. The collision probability is the probability of having two different documents producing the same digest. It can be due to three factors: the OCR, the alphabet reduction and the hashing algorithm.

The OCR introduces a collision probability when it recognize two different characters as the same. This probability can be considered equal to its error rate which is about 0.002.

The alphabet reduction introduces a collision when two different characters are replaced by the same character. However the alphabet reduction was made so that only characters that a human could mistake for one another are replaced. This means that it does not actually create collisions except for reference numbers combining letters and numbers and for the replacement of capital "i" by an "l". We applied the alphabet reduction algorithm on the Aspell English dictionary in order to see how many similar words it would produce. As expected the only collisions were due to the replacement of a capital "i" by an "l". If we take the font case into account we obtain a collision probability of 0.0002.

Finally SHA-256 has a negligible collision probability usually below tens of orders of magnitude below the OCR and alphabet reduction collision probabilities. No collision has been found so far for SHA-256 [6].

Hence, the most critical part is the OCR precision which brings the collision probability up to 0.002. It should not require much work to bring it below 0.001.

Other Performance Criteria. All the other performance criteria are met. The probabilities of missed detections are equal to the OCR error rate, which is below 0.1 % in the case of digits, commas, and dots. The minimum area size is not relevant for an OCR algorithm. The throughput is about 3 seconds on average which is well below 5 seconds. SHA-256 produces a digest whose size is 256 bits, which is well below the 4kB limit. Finally, our system was tested with three printers and three scanners which proves its compatibility with current scanners and printers.

Table 3. Average values of the results of the OCR testing

Criteria	General case				Best case scenario
	150 dpi	300 dpi	600 dpi	All resolutions	
Precision	91.92 %	99.25 %	99.37 %	96.79 %	99.76 %
Probability of false positive	99 %	79 %	73 %	84 %	53 %
Collision probability	8.1 %	0.7 %	0.6 %	3.2 %	0.2 %

4.4   Possible Improvements

Kae et al. [19] created a document specific OCR for each document. They ran Tesseract on the document to detect a set of reliable characters. Then they used SIFT as a character descriptor and an SVM classifier to OCRize the document. Unfortunately this requires training the classifier for each document and prevents the algorithm from performing in real time, which is necessary for our application. They used a test set of 10 documents and reduced Tesseract's error rate by 20 %.

Reynaert [20,21] created a lexicon of word variants to compensate for OCR errors. He applied a space reduction similar to our alphabet reduction and searched for the word in the lexicon in order to find its correct form. This allows for the correction of any errors within a Levenstein distance of 2 e.g. a maximum of two edition operations. The algorithm called TICCL can detect between 55 % and 89 % of OCR errors on a corpus of Dutch newspapers.

Finally, Niklas [22] combines the work of Reynaert with a new word hashing algorithm called OCR-Key. He achieves an error reduction rate between 39 % and 75 % on a corpus made of several issues of The Times newspaper between 1835 and 1985. However for these last two works, the use of a lexicon is inapplicable for names or reference numbers combining letters and numbers especially those occurring in invoices, playslips etc.

We also started preliminary testing with Abbyy Finereader which is considered to be more robust than Tesseract by the document analysis community. We expect an improvement between one and two orders of magnitude for the error rate.

5   Conclusion

We presented our beginning work on securing a hybrid document by creating a document signature based on its content. The issue of robustness is the most critical and needs to be studied for every task involved in the computation of the document signature. This could also be a criteria not to include some document features in the signature. If the extraction algorithm for a document feature is not robust enough, the probability of false positives will be too high and hence should not be included until it has been improved.

We found that the robustness of Tesseract is quite low. While an accuray of 99.76 % is quite good; a probability of false positives of 53 % is not acceptable. The objective is to have it below 0.1 %. Moreover, these figures are obtained in a constrained best case scenario. The scanning resolution has to be at least 600dpi and the font size no less than 10 points. There can be no italic emphasis and no small fonts such as Courier or Times New Roman. The content of the document must also respect some sort of human readability e.g. it cannot be programming code. Another finding is that increasing the scanning resolution from 300dpi to 600dpi does not improve the accuracy much but it significantly reduces the probability of false positives. The collision probability at 0.002 is nearly acceptable and the other performance criteria are satisfied.

One can also wonder about the robustness of segmentation algorithms and of the retranscription of the document structure. Any quantization or randomness will most likely lead to a fragile and/or not reproducible algorithm.

We have shown that the current state of the art does not perform sufficiently well on a seemingly easy task when studied under the angle of robustness. This issue of robustness is of great interest as it could lead to a new document security technology. Considering the work at hand any help or collaboration from the document analysis and security community would be welcome.

References

1. Smith, A.: Identity fraud: a study. Technical Report July, Economic and Domestic Secretariat Cabinet Office (2002)
2. Baras, C., Cayre, F.: Vers un modèle de canal réaliste pour l'analyse de la sécurité du processus d'authentification par code matriciel 2D. In: XXIVème Colloque GRETSI, pp. 2–5 (2013)
3. Zauner, C.: Implementation and benchmarking of perceptual image hash functions. Ph.D. thesis, University of Applied Sciences Hagenberg (2010)
4. Bryson, J., Gallagher, P.: Secure Hash Standard (SHS) (2012)
5. Kerry, C.F., Gallagher, P.: Digital Signature Standard (DSS) (2013)
6. Gilbert, H., Handschuh, H.: Security analysis of SHA-256 and sisters. In: Matsui, Mitsuru, Zuccherato, Robert J. (eds.) SAC 2003. LNCS, vol. 3006. Springer, Heidelberg (2004)
7. Kornblum, J.: Identifying almost identical files using context triggered piecewise hashing. Digital Invest. **3**, 91–97 (2006)
8. Hadmi, A., Puech, W., Said, B.A.E., Ouahman, A.A.: Perceptual image hashing. In: Das Gupta, M. (ed.) Watermarking - Volume 2. InTech, pp. 17–42 (2012)
9. Belazzougui, D., Navarro, G., Valenzuela, D.: Improved compressed indexes for full-text document retrieval. J. Discrete Algorithms **18**, 3–13 (2013)
10. Winter, C., Schneider, M., Yannikos, Y.: F2S2: Fast forensic similarity search through indexing piecewise hash signatures. Digital Invest. **XXX**, 1–11 (2013)
11. Koval, O., Voloshynovskiy, S., Beekhof, F., Pun, T.: Security analysis of robust perceptual hashing. In: Delp III, E.J., Wong, P.W., Dittmann, J., Memon, N.D. (eds.) Proceedings of SPIE 6819, Security, Forensics, Steganography, and Watermarking of Multimedia Contents X, SPIE, pp. 1–10, February 2008

12. Villán, R., Voloshynovskiy, S., Koval, O., Deguillaume, F., Pun, T.: Tamper-proofing of electronic and printed text documents via robust hashing and data-hiding. In: Delp III, E.J., Wong, P.W. (eds.) Proceedings of Security, Steganography, and Watermarking of Multimedia Contents IX, pp. 65051T–65051T-12, February 2007

13. Tan, L., Sun, X., Zhou, Z., Zhang, W.: Perceptual text image hashing based on shape recognition. Adv. Inf. Sci. Serv. Sci. (AISS) **3**(8), 1–7 (2011)

14. Baras, C., Cayre, F.: 2D bar-codes for authentication: a security approach. In: Proceedings of 20th European Signal Processing Conference (EUSIPCO), pp. 1760–1766. IEEE Computer Society Press (2012)

15. Malvido Garcià, A.: Secure Imprint Generated for Paper Documents (SIGNED). Technical Report, December 2010, Bit Oceans (2013)

16. Haar, A.: On the theory of orthogonal function systems. Math. Ann. **69**(3), 331–371 (1910)

17. Google: Tesseract (2013)

18. Rice, S., Jenkins, F., Nartker, T.: The fifth annual test of OCR accuracy. Technical Report April, Information Science Research Institute (1996)

19. Kae, A., Huang, G., Doersch, C., Learned-Miller, E.: Improving state-of-the-art OCR through high-precision document specific modeling. In: Proceedings of IEEE Conference on Computer Vision and Pattern Recognition (CVPR), pp. 1935–1942. IEEE Computer Society Press (2010)

20. Reynaert, M.: Non-interactive OCR Post-correction for Giga-scale digitization projects. In: Gelbukh, A. (ed.) CICLing 2008. LNCS, vol. 4919, pp. 617–630. Springer, Heidelberg (2008)

21. Reynaert, M.W.C.: Character confusion versus focus word-based correction of spelling and OCR variants in corpora. Int. J. Doc. Anal. Recogn. (IJDAR) **14**(2), 173–187 (2010)

22. Niklas, K.: Unsupervised post-correction of OCR errors. Ph.D. thesis, Leibniz Universität Hannover (2010)

Stamp Verification for Automated Document Authentication

Barbora Micenková[1](✉), Joost van Beusekom[2], and Faisal Shafait[2]

[1] Aarhus University, Aarhus, Denmark
Barbora@cs.au.dk
[2] German Research Center for Artificial Intelligence (DFKI),
Kaiserslautern, Germany
{Joost.van_Beusekom,Faisal.Shafait}@dfki.de

Abstract. Stamps, along with signatures, can be considered as the most widely used extrinsic security feature in paper documents. In contrast to signatures, however, for stamps little work has been done to automatically verify their authenticity. In this paper, an approach for verification of color stamps is presented. We focus on photocopied stamps as non-genuine stamps. Our previously presented stamp detection method is improved and extended to verify that the stamp is genuine and not a copy. Using a variety of features, a classifier is trained that allows successful separation between genuine stamps and copied stamps. Sensitivity and specificity of up to 95 % could be obtained on a data set that is publicly available.

1   Introduction

Stamps are still widely used in everyday paper-based business correspondence. They can be frequently found on invoices and official documents. The widespread use of high-quality color copiers, however, has made it feasible to generate forged documents with stamp images that can be easily mistaken for genuine stamps.

A trend that is aggravating the problem is, that more and more companies are scanning all their incoming mail in order to automate their processing as far as possible. An implicit first line inspection [1] formerly done by employees who visually checked the documents is disappearing. However, in state-of-the-art document digitization systems, as they are used in many companies nowadays, absolutely no verification of authenticity of the document is done. Thus, even simple forgeries can easily be accepted as genuine documents, as long as the system is able to read and understand its content.

To cope with these problems, automatic authentication tools are needed to substitute the former first line inspection done by employees. Several approaches exist in literature that use *intrinsic features* (features that originated in a normal document generation process) for authentication of the document source. These approaches follow the idea of comparing an incoming ("questioned") document with genuine documents from the same source that are already in the database. If the features differ significantly, the incoming document is considered as suspicious, and further examination by an expert can be initiated.

U. Garain and F. Shafait (Eds.): IWCF 2012 and 2014, LNCS 8915, pp. 117–129, 2015.
DOI: 10.1007/978-3-319-20125-2_11

Apart from using *intrinsic features*, also *extrinsic features* (features that are added solely to allow authentication of the document) can be analyzed, as e.g. signatures, counterfeit protection system (CPS) codes and stamps. For signatures (e.g. [2]) and CPS codes [3], automatic approaches have been presented in literature. For stamps, however, no automatic approach for ensuring their genuineness has been presented so far, to the best of our knowledge.

In order to verify the genuineness of a stamp, the stamp first has to be extracted from a document image. The question that arises is, how a stamp can be automatically identified and, in what ways it differs from other elements in the document image, e.g. logos. Specific positions, shapes and colors have already previously been used to detect stamps. However, considering documents with e.g. logos or other graphical content, these features alone will not lead to good stamp detection. Other features have to be added that better describe the essence of a stamp imprint, namely the very specific way of imprinting a stamp. It becomes clear, that stamp detection and stamp verification are two closely related and partially overlapping problems.

Therefore, our previously presented method for stamp detection [4] is improved and extended to enable also stamp verification. A two stage approach is followed: first, stamps are detected and extracted based on the approach presented in [4]. The resulting stamp candidates are then subjected to a second classifier trained to discriminate between genuine stamps and copied stamps.

An overview of the system is given in Fig. 1. Using color space transformations and k-means clustering, the scanned color image is split according to colors. Using the XY-cut algorithm [5], the separated colors are segmented into stamp candidates. Finally, different features are extracted which are then used to classify the candidates into genuine stamps and non-stamp objects (laser-printed or photocopied). The detection and verification parts can also be separated if the application scenario requires it.

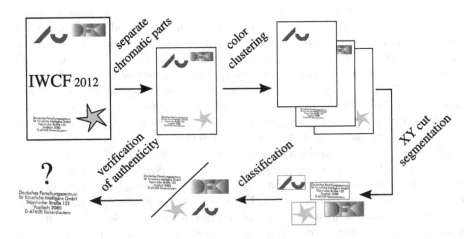

Fig. 1. An overview of the stamp detection and verification system.

The remaining sections of the work are organized as follows: Sect. 2 gives an overview of the advances in stamp detection and verification. Section 3 describes our overall approach. Evaluation and results are presented in Sects. 4 and 5. The paper concludes with Sect. 6.

2   Related Work

Concerning the main goal of the proposed work, **stamp verification** or revealing of photocopied stamps, no relevant literature could be found by the authors among standard document image processing publications. However, some work has been done in related fields.

Concerning **stamp detection**, or localization of stamps in document images, a reliable general solution has also not been given yet [6]. As prior knowledge of the structure (shape or color) of the stamp is helpful to localize it in images, previous research has been focused on detection of stamps of a particular type. The approaches selected by various authors can be divided into three groups:

(1) **Color analysis approaches:** these methods assume that the stamp is of a predefined color. Objects of this color are then detected by the methods and returned as stamps. Examples are [7–9], that use color clustering in the RGB color space to detect stamps of a specific color. Forczmański et al. [6] presented a method that uses color clustering in the YC_bC_r color space to detect red and blue stamps.

(2) **Shape information approaches:** these approaches typically assume that the stamp has a known, fixed shape, e.g. oval or rectangular. In [10], Chen, Liu et al. detect seals on Chinese bank checks with a region-growing algorithm. They suppose the seal to be the only object in the cheque to have an outer frame. Zhu et al. [11] presented a method that uses Hough Transform [12] to search for circular and elliptical candidates for stamps. A recent approach from Ahmed et al. [13] can detect previously unseen shapes provided a training set with stamp and non-stamp examples is supplied. In order to distinguish new stamps in documents, they use a keypoint detector and extract part-based and geometrical features.

(3) **Symbol spotting approaches:** if the images of the stamps are known beforehand, symbol spotting techniques can be used for stamp recognition. Symbol spotting is a way how to efficiently localize symbols in images, without need of previous segmentation of the image [14]. These techniques are more suitable for stamp retrieval than for general detection as they are initiated with a query image selected by user (QBE – *query by example*). The query is used to find similar symbols in the database. Examples of such approaches can be found in [15]. Symbol spotting approaches could be used to distinguish between known stamps and forged stamps with the same content but different layout. For copied stamps, however, symbol spotting techniques will fail to classify them as non-genuine stamps.

Printing technique recognition can also be considered as a related field since stamps are a special form of printing. Inkjet versus laser print classification [16,17], inkjet versus laser versus photocopy [18] or laser versus photocopy [19] are a few examples of such methods. However, to the best of the authors' knowledge, no method has been presented so far for detecting stamps based on their printing technique features.

A relevant method proposed by Berger et al. [20] can separate overlapping objects of a very similar color (e.g. stamp and signature) by means of support vector machines. However, it is not applicable in our settings, since small areas belonging to each object have to be chosen manually.

3   Method Description

In this paper we consider stamps to be single-color objects. Therefore, the basic idea of how to detect them in an image is to group components having the same color and being close to each other at the same time. Special cases of multiple-color stamps (such as in Fig. 7) are detected as multiple stamps and then merged.

With such an approach we can determine *candidate* segments. Each stamp in the image forms one candidate segment. If there are color logos or pictures present in the image, they (or their single-color parts) are also identified as candidate segments. In the next step, the challenge is to classify which segments represent genuine stamps and which correspond to printed objects such as copied stamps or logos (Sects. 3.2 and 3.3). Segmentation by color clustering and extraction of candidate segments has been described in our previous work [4]. Therefore, only a short revision will be given in Sect. 3.1.

3.1   Segmentation

The RGB color model is not convenient for image segmentation because of high correlation among the channels [21]. To process color stamps, it is desirable to first separate out background, black text and other approximately achromatic (white, black and grey) parts of the image. For this purpose, YC_bC_r color space is useful because it separates information about luminance (Y) and chrominance (C_b, C_r). C_b corresponds to blue and C_r to red difference.

To separate out pixels close to grey levels, projection on C_bC_r plane is made and each pixel value is treated as a polar vector (r, θ), where $r = \sqrt{C_b^2 + C_r^2}$ and $\theta = atan2(C_b, C_r)$, $\theta \in [0, 2\pi)$. A threshold T is fixed and all vectors with magnitude $r > T$ are marked as chromatic. These are used for color clustering.

Color Clustering is needed for separation of components of different colors. From 3D scatter plots in YC_bC_r color space it can be observed that clusters corresponding to inks always have elongated shapes and that they stretch from the background cluster. A good separation can be done by projecting the pixel vectors onto C_bC_r plane and taking just the polar vector θ as the discriminative property. The angle values are quantized into 360 bins and a histogram is created. The k-means clustering algorithm is then run on the (1D) angle histogram space which is very fast. Number of clusters is estimated by an approximate calculation of number of peaks in the histogram.

The result of color clustering are k binary mask images of the same size as the original. Black pixels denote parts of the original image having similar color and belonging to one color cluster.

Candidate Segments have to be extracted out of the mask images. Since there can be more objects of the same color on the page, the mask images have to be segmented. However, one stamp is usually composed of several connected components, therefore connected components labeling is not suitable for this task. Instead, the XY-Cut algorithm [5] is used. It recursively partitions the page until it returns minimum bounding boxes for the candidate segments.

3.2 Feature Extraction

To differentiate stamp candidates from printed objects such as logos, color texts and potentially also copied stamps, classification must be performed. From each identified candidate segment, features are extracted. The features relate to geometrical properties of the segment, its color hue and the quality of the print.

Geometrical and color features for stamp detection were described in our previous work [4]. Briefly, it is width-to-height ratio, area of the minimum bounding box, pixel density within the bounding box, rotation and standard deviation of hue. Rotation is computed in case that some text-lines are detected.

Standard deviation of hue can be well exploited also to distinguish between genuine and copied stamps. Variation of hue within the imprint is significantly greater for copied stamps than for genuine ones. An illustration is given in Fig. 2. Besides, we propose new features related to the quality of the print since stamp imprints have several remarkable properties.

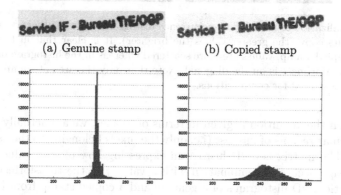

(a) Genuine stamp   (b) Copied stamp

Fig. 2. Histograms reveal that the variation in hue is greater for the copied stamp.

Uniformity of Area. Stamp imprints can be perceived as uniform, having no distinct texture, as opposed to laser-printed or photocopied objects. Printers (and copiers) cause frequent alternations in intensities – a pattern which is well visible in large single-color areas after magnification.

Lampert et al. [16] worked on recognition of source of a printed text (inkjet, laser printer or copier). They used a technique similar to co-occurrence matrices [22] but they computed them from two different images. The first was the original image and the second a certain transformation of the original. We adopted this technique for feature extraction and selected Gaussian smoothing for transformation of the input image.

Co-occurrence matrix $H(i,j)$ of a grayscale image $f(x,y)$ and its smoothed version $s(x,y)$ can be mathematically defined as

$$H(i,j) = \frac{1}{MN} \sum_{m=1}^{M} \sum_{n=1}^{N} \begin{cases} 1 & \text{if } f(m,n) = i \text{ and } s(m,n) = j, \\ 0 & \text{otherwise.} \end{cases} \quad (1)$$

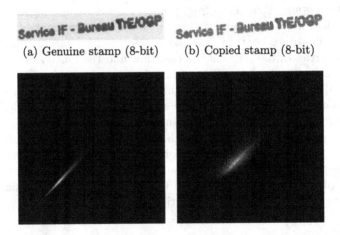

(a) Genuine stamp (8-bit)   (b) Copied stamp (8-bit)

Fig. 3. Visualization of modified co-occurrence histograms of two subjects – a genuine stamp and its copy (the greater values the brighter). It is clear that in the 2D histogram of copied stamp, values are more scattered whereas in the histogram of genuine stamp, the major mass is on the diagonal. Note that only the area of stamps without background was used for computations.

Although the definition is given in terms of images, we are actually working with particular regions of interest (i.e. only the pixels belonging to the candidate segment). The matrix is a 2D histogram expressing how often a value i in the original image occurs in combination with a value j in the transformed image. For illustration, 2D histograms of a genuine and a copied stamp from Fig. 2 are visualized in Fig. 3.

The histogram itself is too big and sparse to give us itself a meaningful information about the texture. Therefore a subset of four so called Haralick features [22] is extracted from it: **contrast, correlation, energy** and **homogeneity**. Please find the formulas in [16].

Sharpness of Edges. Edge sharpness is the degree of intensity change at a particular region in the image and it can be measured by gradients. Comparing gradient maps of genuine stamp imprints and copied or laser-printed text characters, it can be observed that genuine stamp imprints are characterized by slightly higher gradient values. It is caused by the fact that stamps tend to have more blurred and smooth edges. An example of gradient maps of a genuine and a copied stamp is given in Fig. 4.

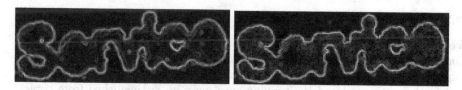

Fig. 4. Magnitude gradient images of genuine (left) and copied (right) stamp. Gradient values at the edges of copied stamp are slightly higher than for genuine stamp.

The gradient of an intensity function f at each coordinates (x, y) is a 2D vector $\nabla \mathbf{f} = (G_x, G_y)$ where G_x and G_y are derivatives in the horizontal and vertical direction. The gradient vector points in the direction of the largest intensity increase. The magnitude of this vector is given by

$$\nabla f = \left[\left(\frac{\partial f}{\partial x} \right)^2 + \left(\frac{\partial f}{\partial y} \right)^2 \right]^{1/2}. \tag{2}$$

To obtain approximate gradient images, the original image must be converted to grayscale and then convolved e.g. with Prewitt filter. To extract statistical information needed for classification, the magnitude gradient image ∇f is computed and subsequently its histogram $\nabla H(i)$, $i = 0, \ldots, 255$ is constructed.

Schreyer et al. [23] analyzed gradient histograms of text characters to differentiate the printing technique (laser print, inkjet print or photocopy). According to the study, the greatest variance among different printing techniques can be observed in the histogram in intervals $[1, 40]$ and $[80, 120]$.

As statistical features for classification, the **mean, standard deviation** and **maximum** are derived from the appropriate intervals of the histogram.

Roughness of Edges. Due to the ink diffusion effect, stamp edges are rough as opposed to edges of laser-printed characters.

Schulze et al. [24] have shown that edge roughness features are useful for recognition of the source of printed text. A method how to measure edge roughness is to compare a binarized image to its smoothed version and then derive features via distance mapping.

Distance mapping [25] requires the input image as well as the smoothed input image to be binarized. Then, the distance map is initialized with values from I_{bin}^{smooth} and then distances of all foreground pixels of I_{bin} are propagated to the nearest background pixel of I_{bin}^{smooth}. Denoting background pixels by 0, for each entry (x,y) of the distance map we get:

$$D(x,y) = \min\{d : d = \sqrt{(x-m)^2 + (y-n)^2}, I_{bin}^{smooth}(m,n) = 0, \forall m,n\}. \quad (3)$$

Only edge pixels of I_b are of interest and so their distances are extracted from the map and a histogram is created. Statistical measures such as **mean, standard deviation** and **maximal and relative distance** are then derived.

3.3 Classification

For both tasks, detection and verification of authenticity, classification is performed. In the first stage we want to differentiate between stamps and other objects in the page. In the second stage, only segments determined as stamps are further processed and the genuine ones must be distinguished from copies. The schema of two-stage classification is given in Fig. 5.

Before actual classification, candidates whose geometrical features exceed fixed thresholds are removed. The features are: width-to-height ratio, area and number of pixels within the bounding box and pixel density. The thresholds are set loose enough to eliminate only extreme candidates.

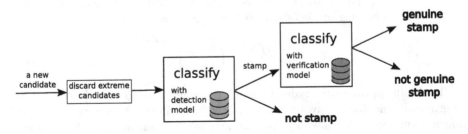

Fig. 5. Two-stage classification for joint stamp detection and verification.

Training of the full system is then also performed in two phases (see Fig. 6). A model for detection and a model for verification are trained separately. There are altogether 13 features used for detection: rotation, standard deviation of hue and all print-related features. Our experiments with verification indicated that the edge roughness features (4 features) do not improve the classification result. Also rotation is naturally not relevant for verification (1 feature), and so the remaining 8 features are used.

It has to be noted, that in the first stage where stamps are separated from non-stamp candidates, very obvious stamp copies might be already revealed because their properties are close to properties of other printed objects such as logos.

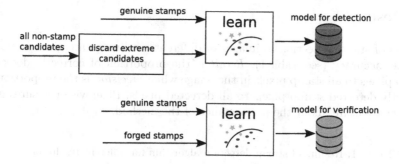

Fig. 6. Training for the two-stage classification.

Different classifiers have been tested for the two stages: Multi-Layer Percep-
trons, Random Forests, Bayes Networks and Support Vector Machines (SVM).
It showed that the best results were achieved using an SVM classifier.

4   Evaluation

We evaluated both classification stages, detection and verification, separately.
In [4] we published a data set of 400 document pages for evaluation of stamp
detection algorithms. This data set contains stamped invoices with color logos
and texts. Stamps are often overlapped with text or other objects. It was generated by printing automatically generated invoices, stamping them manually
and scanning them in color with a resolution of 600dpi. To limit the effort of
ground-truth labeling, the lower resolutions were obtained by downscaling.

To evaluate the performance of verification, we created and published a new
data set[1] of copied documents. A total of 14 invoices were selected randomly
from our data set and their copies were made on 5 different models of Ricoh
Aficio copy machines. We obtained 70 images with 78 copied stamps altogether.

To discover the ideal settings for SVM classifiers, a grid search was used to
find the parameters which gained the best accuracy. The settings differed a bit
for different resolutions of the images but we always used ν-SVC classifier with
radial-basis function, $\nu \in [0.08, 0.12]$, and $\gamma = \frac{1}{numberOfFeatures}$.

Stamp detection was evaluated on the 400-page data set scanned at different
resolutions by cross-validation with leave-one-out method. In each round, one
document page (not a segment) was left out. Altogether training was performed
on around 1000 candidate segments, from which 290 were genuine stamps.

Stamp verification was evaluated by 10-fold cross validation on all available
genuine stamps and 78 copied stamps.

---

[1] The data set is available at http://madm.dfki.de/downloads-ds-staver.

5   Results

Results of stamp detection in images of different resolutions are given in terms of pixel accuracy (see Table 1). *Recall* is the proportion of correctly detected stamp pixels to all stamp pixels in the image while *precision* is the proportion of correctly detected stamp pixels to all detected pixels. Pixel-wise measures give us a clear picture about the performance of the method.

Table 1. Results of stamp detection algorithm for different resolutions.

	200 dpi	300 dpi	400 dpi	600 dpi
Recall	0.89	0.89	0.89	0.89
Precision	0.90	0.90	0.92	0.90

It is not meaningful to give the results of stamp authentication as pixel-wise accuracies since already segmented (genuine or copied) stamps are expected as input. We will express the results in terms of sensitivity and specificity. *Sensitivity* is the proportion of correctly classified copied stamps to all stamps and *specificity* is the proportion of correctly classified genuine stamps to all stamps (Table 2).

Table 2. Results of stamp authentication (classification between genuine and forged stamps) for different resolutions.

	200 dpi	300 dpi	400 dpi	600 dpi
Sensitivity	0.90	0.92	0.93	0.95
Specificity	0.96	0.91	0.96	0.96

(a) Original stamp   (b) Candidates found   (c) Result

Fig. 7. A two-color stamp is split into two segments during the process and then merged again on output of the stamp detection algorithm.

Note that detection as well as verification of authenticity perform well even for images of low resolution which makes it possible to use them in common office environments. With increasing resolution, more copied stamps are revealed while stamp detection gives stable results for all resolutions. There are also some unanticipated deviations in the values which were probably caused by inappropriate settings of variables dependant on resolution (e.g. radius of masks).

6   Conclusion

In the paper we presented a first automatic approach to verification of authenticity of stamps in documents by assuring that they are not photocopies. Having a questioned stamp on input, sensitivity and specificity of 95 % have been achieved on the data set that we created and made publicly available.

Besides, we improved the accuracy of our previously published method on stamp detection by extracting new features that attempt to describe the quality of the print of the candidate segments. We exploited the fact that both tasks, stamp detection and verification of authenticity, have a similar nature because in both cases we intend to differentiate objects printed from a different source.

Combining both methods we have proposed a two-stage approach which can be used as a part of a system for automatic athentication of the document source. New incoming documents can be compared to genuine documents from the same source that are already stored in the database, and a missing or photocopied stamp indicates a forgery. To verify the content or the shape of the questioned stamp, symbol recognition or image registration methods could be used.

The assumption that stamps are single-color objects does not limit us from detecting multiple-color stamps at all (though they are rare). The stamp is split into single-color parts which are then detected separately. In a next step they are merged again. An example of one stamp from our data set is given in Fig. 7.

The presented method works with color parts of documents, therefore detection and verification of authenticity of black stamps is so far not possible. However, segmentation of the achromatic part of the image might also lead to a proper extraction of candidates and then the color-independent features could be used for classification. Such an extension to the method is presumed, but has not been tested yet[2].

References

1. van Renesse, R.: Paper based document security - a review. In: European Conference on Security and Detection, London, UK, pp. 75–80 (1997)
2. Pu, D., Ball, G.R., Srihari, S.N.: A machine learning approach to off-line signature verification using Bayesian inference. In: Geradts, Z.J.M.H., Franke, K.Y., Veenman, C.J. (eds.) IWCF 2009. LNCS, vol. 5718, pp. 125–136. Springer, Heidelberg (2009)

[2] This project was partially funded by the Rheinland-Palatinate Foundation for Innovation, project AnDruDok (961-38 6261 / 1039).

3. van Beusekom, J., Shafait, F., Breuel, T.M.: Automatic authentication of color laser print-outs using machine identification codes. Pattern Anal. Appl. **16**(4), 663–678 (2013)

4. Micenková, B., van Beusekom, J.: Stamp detection in color document images. In: Proceedings of the 11th International Conference on Document Analysis and Recognition, Beijing, China, September 2011

5. Nagy, G., Seth, S.C.: Hierarchical representation of optically scanned documents. In: Proceedings of the 7th International Conference on Pattern Recognition, Montreal, Canada, pp. 347–349. July 1984

6. Forczmański, P., Frejlichowski, D.: Robust stamps detection and classification by means of general shape analysis. In: Proceedings of the International Conference on Computer Vision and Graphics, Warsaw, Poland, pp. 360–367. September 2010

7. Ueda, K.: Extraction of signature and seal imprint from bankchecks by using color information. In: Proceedings of the 3rd International Conference on Document Analysis and Recognition, Montreal, Canada, vol. 2, pp. 665–668. August 1995

8. Cai, L., Mei, L.: A robust registration and detection method for color seal verification. In: Procedings of the International Conference on Intelligent Computing, Hefei, China, pp. 97–106. August 2005

9. Soria-Frisch, A.: The fuzzy integral for color seal segmentation on document images. In: Proceedings of the 13th International Conference on Image Processing, Barcelona, Spain, pp. 157–160. September 2003

10. Chen, L., Liu, T., Chen, J., Zhu, J., Deng, J., Ma, S.: Location algorithm for seal imprints on Chinese bank-checks based on region growing. Optoelectron. Lett. **2**(2), 155–157 (2006)

11. Zhu, G., Jaeger, S., Doermann, D.: A robust stamp detection framework on degraded documents. In: Proceedings of SPIE Document Recognition and Retrieval XIII, San Jose, CA, USA, vol. 6067, pp. 1–9. January 2006

12. Tsuji, S., Matsumoto, F.: Detection of ellipses by a modified Hough transformation. IEEE Trans. Comput. **27**(8), 777–781 (1978)

13. Ahmed, S., Shafait, F., Liwicki, M., Dengel, A.: A generic method for stamp segmentation using part-based features. In: Proceedings of 12th International Conference on Document Analysis and Recognition, pp. 708–712 (2013)

14. Delalandre, M., Valveny, E., Lladós, J.: Performance evaluation of symbol recognition and spotting systems: An overview. In: Proceedings of the 8th IAPR Workshop on Document Analysis Systems, Nara, Japan, pp. 497–505. September 2008

15. Roy, P.P., Pal, U., Lladós, J.: Seal object detection in document images using GHT of local component shapes. In: Proceedings of the 25th ACM Symposium on Applied Computing, March 2010

16. Lampert, C.H., Mei, L., Breuel, T.M.: Printing technique classification for document counterfeit detection. In: Proceedings of the International Conference on Computational Intelligence and Security, Ghuangzhou, China, pp. 639–644. November 2006

17. Gebhardt, J., Goldstein, M., Shafait, F., Dengel, A.: Document authentication using printing technique features and unsupervised anomaly detection. In: Proceedings of the 12th International Conference on Document Analysis and Recognition, pp. 479–483. IEEE (2013)

18. Schulze, C., Schreyer, M., Stahl, A., Breuel, T.M.: Using DCT features for printing technique and copy detection. In: Proceedings of the 5th International Conference on Digital Forensics, Orlando, FL, USA, pp. 95–106. January 2009

19. Tchan, J.: The development of an image analysis system that can detect fraudulent alterations made to printed images. In: Proceedings of SPIE Optical Security and Counterfeit Deterrence Techniques V, San Jose, CA, USA, vol. 5310, pp. 151–159. January 2004

20. Berger, C.E., Koeijer, J.A., Glas, W., Madhuizen, H.T.: Color separation in forensic image processing. J. Forensic Sci. **51**(1), 100–102 (2006)

21. Cheng, H.D., Jiang, X.H., Sun, Y., Wang, J.: Color image segmentation: advances and prospects. Pattern Recognit. **34**(12), 2259–2281 (2001)

22. Haralick, R.M., Shanmugan, K., Dinstein, I.: Textural features for image classification. IEEE Trans. Syst. Man Cybern. **3**(6), 610–621 (1973)

23. Schreyer, M.: Intelligent printing technique recognition and photocopy detection for forensic document examination. In: Proceedings of Informatiktage 2009, Bonn, Germany, vol. S-8, pp.39–42 (2009)

24. Schulze, C., Schereyer, M., Stahl, A., Breuel, T.M.: Evaluation of graylevel-features for printing technique classification in high-throughput document management systems. In: Srihari, S.N., Franke, K. (eds.) IWCF 2008. LNCS, vol. 5158, pp. 35–46. Springer, Heidelberg (2008)

25. Rosenfeld, A., Pfaltz, J.L.: Distance functions on digital pictures. Pattern Recogn. **1**(1), 33–61 (1968)

Lessons Learned from Automatic Forgery Detection in over 100,000 Invoices

Joost van Beusekom, Armin Stahl, and Faisal Shafait[✉]

German Research Center for Artificial Intelligence (DFKI),
Kaiserslautern, Germany
j_v_b@gmx.net, {Armin.Stahl,Faisal.Shafait}@dfki.de

Abstract. Digitization and automatic processing of incoming paper mail is a crucial component of document management systems and is widely adopted in medium and large enterprises. Besides several advantages of this automated processing, it complicates the first line inspection of incoming documents which are often of vital financial or legal relevance. We have developed a number of different techniques to allow automatic detection of forged or manipulated documents over the last years. In this paper, we present an analysis of the application of our methods on a large real-world dataset of invoices to identify the weaknesses of our existing methods and propose some promising directions of future work in the field.

1   Introduction

Even though many traditional paper-based business processes are more and more transferred to pure electronic processing, paper documents still play a vital role in many business scenarios. Since a manipulation or forgery of such documents may lead to significant financial loss or legal problems, an appropriate inspection of incoming documents is often crucial. A typical example is the processing and reimbursement of invoices in insurance companies.

However, the degree of automation in document processing pipelines has dramatically increased in the last decade: data that was previously transferred manually from thousands of documents the day is now being extracted and processed automatically. Due to the automatic processing, observations during manual processing like "that signature looks strange", or "this part was written using a different pen" or even "the layout of this invoice normally looks different" cannot be made anymore. This complicates the identification of questionable documents additionally or even makes it impossible in practice.

To address these issues, some research has been done to pursue the goal of adding automatic authentication methods to replace the formerly manually done first line inspection in document digitization and processing systems. In the context of documents, "authentication" is defined by J. Hails [1] as "... *showing that writing is what it is claimed to be*". In the scenario of incoming invoice processing, this can be further restricted to "*showing that the writing originates*

© Springer International Publishing Switzerland 2015
U. Garain and F. Shafait (Eds.): IWCF 2012 and 2014, LNCS 8915, pp. 130–142, 2015.
DOI: 10.1007/978-3-319-20125-2_12

from where it claims to be from". Thus, if an invoice claims to come from source X, we want to check if this is really the case or not.

Although this will cover already many forgery scenarios, from the definition it becomes clear that not all scenarios are being covered; e.g. if someone uses the hard- and software from source X to generate a forged invoice, or if only small modifications are made directly on the genuine document (like changing a 1 to a 7 to increase the total amount of the invoice).

In this paper, the results and conclusions of an extended test of our previously developed authentication methods on real-world data, and the implication for the ultimate goal of developing an automated system, are presented. This paper does not claim to present new methods, the methods presented here have been published before and are only briefly introduced to better understand the results. The main contribution of this paper is that the authors evaluated authentication techniques on a large real-world data set of invoices. To the author's best knowledge, there is no other work in the domain of document authentication having done an evaluation on such a large and diverse data set. It should be clarified, that these methods are tested independently, no integrated system is yet available, combining the outcomes of the different methods.

The remaining sections of the paper are organized as follows: in Sect. 2 the automatic methods for forgery detection or verification are shortly introduced. In Sect. 3, the evaluation setup is described. The results of the analysis and the conclusions are discussed in Sects. 4 and 5 respectively.

2   Methods

The main idea behind all the presented methods is the following: the incoming documents can be clustered into groups of documents claiming to be from the same source. This can be done, e.g. using optical character recognition (OCR) to read the address of the sender. It is also assumed that many more genuine documents are present in each group than forgeries. The last assumption is that there are some features in a cluster of documents that are similar for genuine documents but that are different for forgeries.

Since the main focus of this paper lies on the results and conclusions of the real-world experiment, the features will be presented here only in a short, high-level manner. Text-line alignment and orientation is presented in Sect. 2.1. Examination of the counterfeit protection system codes from color laser printers and color copiers is presented in Sect. 2.2. Examination of the scanning distortion measurement for detecting possible manipulations is presented in Sect. 2.3. More detailed information about each method can be found in previous publications. References can be found in the concerning sections.

2.1   Text-Line Examination

The idea of this approach is to measure text-line rotation angles and the text-line alignment and to identify text-lines that have an angle that is too far off from

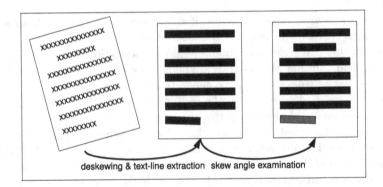

Fig. 1. Visualization of the text-line skew examination: the binarized document is deskewed. The text-lines are examined if their skew angles are abnormally high or not.

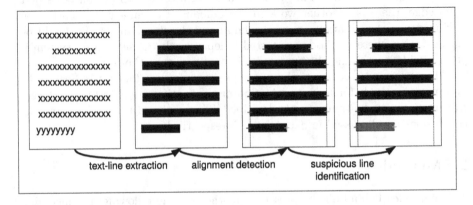

Fig. 2. Visualization of the text-line alignment examination: the text-lines are extracted from the binarized document image. Then the left and right alignment lines are computed. Finally, each text-line is examined whether it shows normal alignment or not.

the normal rotation angle or that show an abnormal alignment. The method is described in detail in [2] and in [3].

An overview of the text-line rotation evaluation method can be found in Fig. 1. First, the document is deskewed [4]. Then, the text-line rotation angles are compared to a previously defined model. If a value differs too much from the model, the corresponding text-line is considered as a suspicious one.

For the alignment of text-lines, a visualization can be found in Fig. 2. After extraction of the text-lines, the left and right vertical alignment lines (margin line) are computed. The distances of the start and end point of the text-lines to the respective alignment lines are used as features to decide if the text-line has a suspicious distance to either of the alignment lines or not.

2.2   Counterfeit Protection System Codes

The image based analysis of counterfeit protection system codes for document authentication has been presented in our previous papers [5] and in [6]. The idea is to use the tiny yellow dots that are generated by many color laser printers to authenticate the document by visually comparing the patterns. This is done by comparing the *prototype patterns* of two documents against each other.

First, the horizontal and vertical size of the prototype pattern are computed by computing the horizontal and vertical pattern separating distance (HPS and VPS distance). Figure 3 gives a rough idea how this step works. Using the so computed width and height, a prototype pattern can be computed from one of the two images whose patterns should be compared. This prototype pattern indicates with what frequency every single dot in the pattern appears in the document. This pattern is then matched to the second image. If a significant difference in frequency of a single dot is detected, the patterns are returned as different. An example of two prototype patterns is given in Fig. 4.

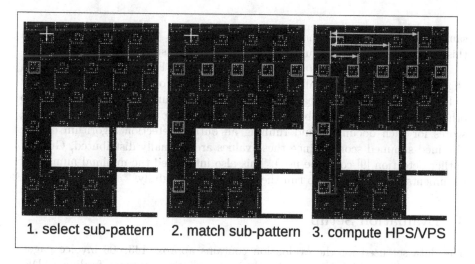

1. select sub-pattern   2. match sub-pattern   3. compute HPS/VPS

Fig. 3. Computation of HPS and VPS distances: first, a sub pattern is selected. This is matched at different positions in the same column or row respectively. The computed translation parameters in x and y direction are used to extract the HPS and VPS distance of the pattern.

2.3   Distortion Measurement

In this approach, we try to measure the scanning distortions that would be introduced to the forged document through scanning the document (thus, also through the copy process). Details about this method can be found in [7,8].

The main idea of this method is that repeating parts of documents, e.g. headers and footers, should be identical among documents originating from the

Fig. 4. Examples of extracted prototypes. The darker the cross is the higher its frequency of occurring in a match.

same source and thus, it should be possible to align these pixel-accurately. If this is not the case, the documents are considered as suspicious.

First, all the documents are pair-wisely aligned. From this, a matrix with alignment qualities (also called *matching scores*) is obtained that shows how well each document fits to each other. Distorted documents will fit less well to other documents. This can be detected by computing the sum of the matching scores for each document and running an outlier detection algorithm on the obtained summed scores. Since these values are normally distributed, Grubbs' outlier detection [9] could be used. This also influenced the minimal number of documents that is needed to run the method meaningfully.

3   Evaluation Setup

The data set used for the evaluation contains approx. 143, 000 invoice pages. These were scanned using a high-volume automatic document feeding (ADF) scanner using a resolution of 400 dpi and 24 bit color depth. We only considered the first page of every invoice, since in most cases, a forgery attempt will have influence on the first page, even though the main forged part my be found on some other page of the invoice. Unfortunately, the automatic method for detecting the first page did not work at a 100 % accuracy, leading to false alarms by the forgery detection methods. This cases showed up during manual inspection of the automatic results and where recorded as clustering errors.

The data is unlabeled, meaning that we have no information if there are any forgeries or not. A problem with the missing labels is that we are not able to evaluate quantitatively how good or how bad the methods work. Also, no exact information is available about the composition of the data set: from our observations we can conclude the following:

- The vast majority of the documents are machine printed. Only a few consist in majority of handwritten parts. However, signatures are frequent.
- The quality of paper varies greatly: from high-quality watermarked paper to low-quality carbon copies of invoices, nearly every type of paper can be found.
- The quality and type of printing varies considerably: from low-quality ink jet, over middle-quality laser to high quality color laser print-outs. While printing technique itself might be usable as a clue for forgery [10], in some cases multiple printers of different types are used to generate various invoices from one source.

The first pages were clustered according to their source by using OCR and a specialized software. On these clusters, the above methods were executed. Cases where one of the methods threw an alarm were inspected manually. It should be noted here that neither the expert knowledge of a forensic document examiner nor the necessary equipment for doing an in-depth analysis of the documents was available for the manual inspection. However, we know from our customer that forgeries have been detected in the past, mostly by chance, and that these forgeries were of a quite amateurish nature. Also, press releases from other companies having a similar business suggest, that forgeries are to be expected in the invoice dataset that was provided by our customer.

Manual inspection consisted of verification of the cluster's consistency. The digital images and the intermediate debug images of the methods were analyzed. In most cases these could provide an explanation for the detected observation.

In case of doubt, the paper documents were used to verify the results. This was done by one of the authors only, leading to a relative high consistency in the decision making process. Since none of the authors are forensic document experts, we do not claim that from a forensic point of view our analysis meets the requirements of valid forensic analysis. However, since in many cases semantic information was available we were able to reject the hypothesis of forgery in many cases. Also, there were numerous cases where other invoices from the same source, but from different clients were available that showed the same peculiarities. This was also used to reject forgery hypothesis, since we do not assume our customer's clients to cooperate in order to perform fraud.

Only if no reasonable and likely explanation for the observation could be found, the concerned document is labeled as suspicious. This will be finally returned to the client for further investigation on their side.

Due to the missing knowledge about the genuineness or forged nature of the documents, the only outcome of the analysis is either a false positive (an alarm was triggered, although with all available information, a more likely non-fraudulent explanation could be found) or a suspicious document, that might still be a false alarm.

3.1 Test Setup for Text-Line Analysis

For this setup, the text-lines were extracted from the documents and documents that showed large variations of text-line rotation angles compared to a previously learned model were analyzed manually.

3.2   Test Setup for CPS Codes

Two different setups were defined: first, the horizontal and vertical pattern separating distances (HPS and VPS distances) [11] were extracted from each image and a clustering was done based on these distances. Then, the clusters were manually analyzed to see whether the distance clusters actually show CPS codes or if they only represent some noise dots that were mistaken for CPS patterns.

Second, for each document source clusters containing documents with CPS codes, all the CPS codes of the documents were compared pair-wisely against each other. Manual inspection of all the clusters containing differences in CPS codes was done. These differences might be:

- **differing CPS codes:** both documents contain CPS patterns, but they differ in their visual appearance.
- **codes vs. no codes:** one document has CPS codes, the other has not.
- **match:** both documents show the same CPS code.

3.3   Test Setup for the Distortion Measurement

Since Grubb's outlier detection works only reasonably on at least 7 or more values, only the clusters with at least 7 documents were considered in this step. The documents were aligned pair-wisely, the summed matching scores were computed and Grubb's outlier detection was used to detect if there is any outlier or not. If so, the cluster is reported and manual inspection of the results is done. Multiple outliers are detected by removing a detected outlier from the set and rerunning Grubb's method. This process is repeated until either no outlier is detected or the number of remaining samples is equal to 6.

4   Results

Since no ground-truth is available, the results that are presented here base on manual verification and also partially on estimations based on manual inspection.

4.1   Results for the Text-Line Examination

Condensing it to a single sentence: this method in its current form, is not practically useful for forgery detection in real-world invoices. The main reason for this being, that there are too many sources that lead to variations in text-line rotation angle, not to talk of the left and right alignment.

These sources are:

- **pre-printed stationeries** often show variations in the rotation angle of the pre-printed parts in comparison to the actual content part. These are most likely due to the imperfections of the paper paths of the printers that allow the paper to be rotated slightly.

- **unusual layouts and tables** will make the text-line extraction algorithm fail. These unusual layouts show situations that were not expected to be seen in real-world data, as e.g. text-lines with multiple font and font-sizes in one single line. Tables present another problem for the text-line verification approach: the text-line extraction method will find some text-lines where it should not find any and vice-versa.
- **paper cut apart** and pasted together again: while opening the envelopes, some documents are being cut. To allow automatic processing, these are pasted together again by the scanner operator. The rotation angle of the pasted part will diverge from the remaining document part.

On other document types, where long and regular text-lines are more frequent (e.g. contracts and wills), this method might still be useful.

4.2   Results for the CPS Code Verification

The main result of the first evaluation setup was that Tweedy's [11] classification seems still to be up-to-date. No new VPS distances could be found.

The second conclusion is that there were an important number of false detections: CPS points were detected although there were none (e.g. black-and-white print-out) or at least, no regular or repeating pattern could be detected. This problem was solved by adding thresholds on the number of minimally extracted yellow dots: if this number is too small, the extracted dots are considered do be only noise.

The third conclusion is that only an estimated 0.5 % of the invoice documents show CPS dots. This is most likely due to the fact that in this business-related scenario, for financial reasons, most documents are printed in black and white only, thus using either a black and white only printer or using the non-color mode of color laser printers, that in some cases also avoids the appearance of CPS dots on the paper.

The comparison of the CPS codes inside a document cluster lead to some false alarms. In total, 403 clusters containing at least one document with CPS codes were analyzed. These clusters contained a total of 1,181 documents.

In Table 1 the results of the manual verification of the 403 clusters is given.
The meaning of the different result cases are as follows:

- **Correct match** is when all documents in the cluster have the same pattern.
- **Cluster errors** are a frequent source of error for all cluster-based methods, meaning that at least one document in the cluster is from a different source. These are due to the limited resources that were available for tuning the clustering method and manually correcting the results. These errors, however, can be easily removed in a production system, since human operators do correction of the system's clustering results.
- **Method errors** occur due to different problems as e.g. noise, logos or other elements that can eventually lead to yellow dots in the document image. This results in most cases in a imaginary pattern that just consists of noise dots.

Table 1. Results of the verification of the CPS comparison results. In total 403 clusters containing 1,181 files were analyzed

Result	Absolute	Relative [%]
Correct match	156	38.7
Cluster error	127	31.5
Method error	46	11.4
Printer / layout	38	9.4
Suspicious	25	6.2
Copy	6	1.5
Other	5	1.2

In some other cases, a prototype pattern was extracted, but due to noise, it showed differences to the pattern of a clean document image. One reason for these errors are sparse CPS patterns, the reason for these patterns to appear not yet being known.

– **Printer / layout** means that either two or more different printers were consistently used for one document source. In this case, the documents of one cluster could be clustered into different groups with identical patterns. In some cases, the layout of the document was changed by adding some color text or logo, that, most likely, lead to a color print-out instead of a black and white print-out. These clusters thus contained documents both with and without CPS codes.

– **Suspicious** is used when no likely normal explanation could be found on the basis of the data at hand, e.g. when only one single document uses different CPS patterns. These documents are further analyzed by the client. It is reasonable to assume that most of these cases can be reclassified to known cases when background information or other documents are taken into account.

– **Copy** means that one document in the cluster was copied using a color laser copier. Other copy artifacts could be found that vote in favor of this hypothesis, e.g. prints of stamping or staple holes.

– **Other** includes patterns of Xerox printers, where date and time is included into the pattern. This leads to false alarms, since every print-out will show a different time stamp. In some cases the stationeries seem to have been printed using different color laser printers instead of offset print. Also, in a few cases, colored scanner artifacts lead to mis-detection of yellow dots.

4.3   Results for the Distortion Measurement

In total, 2,215 clusters containing 6 or more pages (24,124 pages for all of these clusters) were created. On 88 of these clusters, an outlier was returned by the method. These clusters contained 715 pages. These 88 clusters were verified manually.

An overview over the different, most frequent cases that lead to an outlier being detected can be found in Table 2.

Table 2. Results of the distortion measurement verification. In total 88 clusters containing 715 pages were analyzed

Result	Absolute	Relative [%]
Cluster error	29	32.9
Suspicious	15	17.0
Method error	14	15.9
Layout	8	9.1
Skew	7	7.9
Copy	5	5.7
Document Type	4	4.5
Other	5	1.2

The manual inspection of the results showed, that the main reasons of errors are the following:

- **Cluster errors**, just as for the CPS pattern comparison, are a frequent source of error for all cluster-based methods, meaning that at least one document in the cluster is from a different source.
- **Suspicious** is used when no likely normal explanation could be found on the basis of the data at hand, e.g. if for one document no measurable and visible distortions could be noticed, no sign of a copy could be detected and the document is the only one differing from the source. These documents are further analyzed by the client. It is reasonable to assume that most of these cases can be reclassified to cases when enough background information or further documents are taken into consideration.
- **Method errors** occur due to different problems as e.g. improper matching, noise, improper pre-processing (e.g. problems with binarization) or threshold selection for outlier detection.
- **Layout** stands for varying layouts over time. Document sources tend to change their layout more often than initially expected. This will lead to bad matching, thus to lower matching scores and eventually to an outlier alarm.
- **Skew** was removed before aligning the document images. In some cases the skew of the scanned image was too high. The document could not be unskewed correctly. Thus, the document could not be matched accurately and it would be detected as an outlier.
- **Copy** denoted cases where enough other information could be gathered that increased the likelihood of being a normal copy. Although the data set should not contain copies, the distortion measurement gave some alarms due to copies of most likely genuine documents.

- **Document types** need to be separated for this approach. An invoice should e.g. not be mixed with a formal letter, even if they come from the same source. Although most of the documents were from the same class, some could be found that were of a different class and thus raised a false alarm.
- **Other** includes all other kinds of errors: outliers to the top (e.g. when two exactly identical documents were inside one cluster, e.g. if one invoice was printed twice by the invoice source with exactly the same content); documents that were cut apart and pasted together; stationeries that showed a lot of positional displacement of the main document content and the stationery content and also in rare cases distortions introduced by scanning when the paper was transported in an non-uniform way through the scanner.

5   Conclusions

After processing over 140,000 document pages with the previously mentioned methods and after laborious manual verification of the results, several important conclusions can be drawn concerning the development of automatic document authentication systems.

The main conclusion is that the methods, despite from working reasonably well under laboratory conditions, show weaknesses on real world data. The main problem is that some of the basic assumptions made during development and testing the methods did not hold in their entirety in practice: we assumed that one source uses one printer or type of printer, that layout changes do not occur frequently, scanning distortions are not large enough to cause false alarms when aligning two genuine documents, that paper always remains intact, etc.

The reasons for the assumptions not to hold are not going to be solved in a way to make the authentication methods work error-free. Thus, we think that much more resources should be spent in the logic that comes after the authentication methods: this should bring together all possible information from the analysis methods as well as background information to make a decision whether a document should be finally marked as suspicious or not.

One such an extension would be the **combination of method outcomes**: this would not only be useful in increasing the confidence of forgery detection, but it could also be used in other ways: if e.g. the CPS codes match, other processing steps that could lead to false alarms can be skipped.

Another extension is the allowance of different document **sub-sources** inside one source: the multiple printers and layouts of one company would need to be clustered into different sub-sources. Then the authentication step of an incoming document would be done on the sub-source level.

The most important extension, however, is a **time-relative modeling** of the invoice source: changes in layout, printer hard- and software or stationeries should be visible in most cases if a chronological time-line model of the documents would be available. Then, e.g. a change in layout would not trigger alarm immediately, but only if after a certain amount of time, no layout of the same type is seen by the system. The same procedure could be used for varying printer settings (e.g. black and white print versus color print) and changing printers.

Concerning the research in the area, the following conclusions were drawn: there is missing **understanding of the many factors that influence the document generation**: where do sparse patterns originate from, what influence have software and printer on the visual appearance of the document on the paper, what is the influence of the scanner on the digital image and thus on the results of the image, etc. Some of these questions might have already been discussed in the forensics community, however, they are not explored in the computer science community so far.

Most important for further research is the **availability of real-world data** – genuine as well as forged documents. This would give the possibility to evaluate the methods against real data and not against "what computer scientists think the real data and forgeries could look like". This would also help to get an impression about which forgery methods are being used. However, information security and copyright issues are major obstacles in creating a public data repository for such purpose. As an alternative, researchers should publish their home-brew, synthetic data sets to allow other researchers to compare their methods against and to bring more new ideas into this research area.

Acknowledgment. This project was partially funded by the Rheinland-Palatinate Foundation for Innovation, project AnDruDok (961-38 6261 / 1039).

References

1. Hails, J.: Criminal Evidence. p. 150, Thomson Learning, Boston (2004)
2. van Beusekom, J., Shafait, F., Breuel, T.: Automatic line orientation measurement for questioned document examination. In: Geradts, Z.J.M.H., Franke, K.Y., Veenman, C.J. (eds.) IWCF 2009. LNCS, vol. 5718, pp. 165–173. Springer, Heidelberg (2009)
3. van Beusekom, J., Shafait, F., Breuel, T.M.: Text-line examination for document forgery detection. Int. J. Doc. Anal. Recogn. **16**(2), 189–207 (2013)
4. van Beusekom, J., Shafait, F., Breuel, T.M.: Combined orientation and skew detection using geometric text-line modeling. Int. J. Doc. Anal. Recogn. **13**(2), 79–92 (2010)
5. van Beusekom, J., Schreyer, M., Breuel, T.M.: Automatic counterfeit protection system code classification. In: Proceedings of SPIE Media Forensics and Security XII, San Jose, CA, USA, January 2010
6. van Beusekom, J., Shafait, F., Breuel, T.M.: Automatic authentication of color laser print-outs using machine identification codes. Pattern Anal. Appl. **16**(4), 663–678 (2013)
7. van Beusekom, J., Shafait, F.: Distortion measurement for automatic document verification. In: Proceedings of the 11th International Conference on Document Analysis and Recognition, Beijing, China, September 2011
8. Ahmed, A., Shafait, F.: Forgery detection based on intrinsic document contents. In: Proceedings of the 11th IAPR Workshop on Document Analysis Systems, Tours, France, pp. 252–256. April 2014
9. Grubbs, F.E.: Procedures for detecting outlying observations in samples. Technometrics **11**, 1–21 (1969)

10. Elkasrawi, S., Shafait, F.: Printer identification using supervised learning for document forgery detection. In: Proceedings of the 11th IAPR Workshop on Document Analysis Systems, Tours, France, pp. 146–150. April 2014
11. Tweedy, J.S.: Class characteristics of counterfeit protection system codes of color laser copiers. J. Am. Soc. Questioned Doc. Examiners 4(2), 53–66 (2001)

Applications

Introducing and Analysis of the Windows 8 Event Log for Forensic Purposes

Javad Talebi[1], Ali Dehghantanha[2(✉)], and Ramlan Mahmoud[1]

[1] Faculty of Computer Science and Information Technology,
University Putra Malaysia, Seri Kembangan, Malaysia
javad@cyberdefenceteam.com, ramlan@fsktm.upm.edu.my
[2] School of Computing, Science and Engineering,
University of Salford, Manchester, UK
A.Dehghantanha@salford.ac.uk

Abstract. All operating systems are employing some sort of logging mechanism to track and note users activities and Microsoft Windows is not an exception. Log Analysis is one of the important parts of Windows forensics process. The Windows event log system introducing in Windows NT was released with a new feature for Microsoft Windows family and since then went through several major changes and updates. The event log experienced major updated in Windows 8. This paper first introduces Windows 8 event log format and then proceeds with explaining methods for analyzing the logs for digital investigation and incident handling. The main contributions of this paper are introducing Windows8 logging service and forensic examination of it.

Keywords: Windows event logging · Windows forensic · Digital investigation

1 Introduction

Digital forensics which also introduces as computer forensics is the procedure of preparing, acquiring, preserving, examining and analyzing and also reporting of digital data. The aim of this procedure is to acquire admissible and legal evidences existing in digital media [1]. Nowadays, digital forensics techniques are used in a variety of situations, such as evidence collection for lawful actions and internal disciplinary proceedings, and investigating malware incidents [2].

Previous researches in digital forensics examined various aspects of digital forensics namely, privacy and security issues [4, 6], framework, conceptual and architectural matters [7, 11], investigation of malware defense and detection techniques [9, 10] and challenges and opportunities for future research [3, 5, 8].

However, the focus of this paper is only on analyzing Windows log data for forensics purposes. In this context, log forensics plays an important role in extracting digital evidences from computers and other electronic devices. The logs generated from the various activities of the system are one of the most common sources of evidences that an investigator should analyze and consider [12].Windows event logs record crucial information that can be used as an important forensics evidence of attacks and operations of a system [13]. From digital forensic investigator point of view, having

© Springer International Publishing Switzerland 2015
U. Garain and F. Shafait (Eds.): IWCF 2012 and 2014, LNCS 8915, pp. 145–162, 2015.
DOI: 10.1007/978-3-319-20125-2_13

logs from all system events during the incident provides a detailed step by step account of system activities and assist in the process of forensics analysis and event reconstruction [14]. Since Windows Vista, Microsoft operating system has been equipped with event logging function under Event Tracing for Windows (ETW) or Event Logging features [15]. Windows 8 Event Viewer offers a remarkable event log service to investigate and examine important messages in the logs. In addition to the System and Application logs, user may find Hardware Events and installed programs activities in Windows Event Viewer as well.

Since analyzing log data is certainly good place to start windows forensic process, the main contribution of this study is describing of Windows logging system and analyzing related files. The investigation of log data should be rigorous and credible.

This research explores Microsoft's EVTX log format and the structure of an event log file. This article also explains the history of Windows system log service, key elements of the new log file format and latest Windows event logging features and functions. This paper is organized as follow:

Section 2 gives a brief introduction to Windows event log services' history. The structure of a Windows event log service is documented in Sect. 3. Section 4 explains log file format and Sect. 5 offers key concepts of log file structure and important parts of an event file. Finally, Sect. 6 looks at forensic analysis of the Windows 8 event logs and presents an investigation case that processes extracted data from event log file using Event Viewer to look for any unauthorized use of Windows machine.

2 Windows Event Log Services History

The ability to store the events happened on a computer system is a part of the Windows security package. It was originally built to find out the problems of the operating system as a diagnostic tool which provides the user with the capability of controlling what type of events should be monitored.

The Microsoft Windows NT 3.5 was released with a new event logging service in 1994, a new feature for Microsoft Windows family of operating systems at that time. NT only logs local processes services and these logs are not accessible remotely. There were three types of logs namely System, Application and Security. The NT event log is composed of a header, a description of the event (based on the event type), and additional optional data. Most security logs only include header and a description. Log messages consist of constant part and variable part. Constant part of the message would be sent to a message table which is a resource of a proper executable file. Then, the event log service registers this file as an event source. Now, rather than a string the index and the source along with the variable data will be passed to the logging service. All of that information then is stored, in a binary format, by the logging services to prevent storage of redundant information [15]. Constant and variable parts of a message get bound together at the time of viewing.

In Windows' world, starting with Microsoft Windows Vista and Windows Server 2008, Microsoft has completely changed its event log format and introduced the new EVTX log format.

Although traditional event log system was used for more than a decade from NT 3.5 to Windows Server 2003, several issues were found in the event log service. One of the main problems of the NT event log service was that it needed the whole file to be mapped into shared memory. Large files occupy valuable address spaces in an area that can be used for inter-process communication in the shared memory.

Microsoft Windows Vista log file format stores event log records as a stream of binary XML files. This new log file format forms a small file header followed by a series of chunks. Over the boundary between two chunks no event record will extend. In fact, for every event log, only the file header and the current chunk have to be mapped into memory. This new event logging considerably affects system resources usage.

Using a new application programming interface is needed to access data in the new EVTX files that is not available in older Windows operating systems. Also, the structure and data within the fields in the EVTX log records have changed notably [15].

2.1 Microsoft Windows 8

Several additional features and functions were introduced for Event Tracing in Windows 8 compared to older Windows operating systemand many new Logs and Sources were added to its core Event Logging system.

The infrastructure that underlies Windows 8 event logging has been completely revamped in Windows Vista. Although such as this service is existed in Vista and XP, Windows 7 and now Windows 8 have developed the interface and extended the range of logs that can be interrogated.

The Windows 8 Event Viewer makes available a marvelous interface to investigate critical and error messages in the logs. Information about each event offers to an XML schema, and the XML representing a given event can be accessed.

The Windows 8 Event Log service is run as NT AUTHORITY\LocalService in a shared process of svchost.exe. Using this Log service can examine not only the System and Application logs, but also Hardware Events and records of activity from IE and other programs.

3 Windows Event Log Service

The Windows Event Log service is capable of monitoring generated events during its operation. It captures log data generated by installed applications, services and system processes and puts them into event log channels which are intermediate locations and finally records them to an event log file. Applications such as Microsoft's Event Viewer would use these log channels to display events happened on the system.

3.1 Windows Event

In Microsoft operating systems, a large amount of information about the occurrence of various types of events is preserved and presented in Windows event logs. Also, Microsoft introduces the event log as a service that logs event messages happened by programs and the operating system.

A number of these events are derived from usual activities of the target systems whereas others are issued when failures and errors affect local or remote systems. As a brief aside, Windows event logging is employed by computer systems to capture the occurrence of important events including system alerts, error reports and diagnostic messages.

When an error happens, the system administrator should specify the cause of error, try to recover any lost data, and prevent the error from occurring again. The operating system applications and other system services record significant events, such as low-memory situations or accesses to disk. Then, system administrators use these event logs to discover causes of the error and determine the context in which it happened. In fact, by regularly viewing Windows event logs, system administrators are able to determine issues (such as a failing hard disk) before they cause problem.

Windows event log is not only useful in diagnosing problems, but also can be employed in digital forensic cases. Since digital forensics is the science of retrieving digital evidence, event Log reports contain information that can be useful in Windows forensics investigations [17].

3.2   Event Types

Five types of events are logged by Windows logging system. All of the events have well-defined common information, and also it is possible optionally include event-specific data. The application specifies the type of event when it reports an event. An event type should be of a single type. In event viewer each type of the event logs would be displayed indifferent icons. Five types of event used in event logging are as follow:

- *Error*: Some significant problems such as loss of data or loss of functionality are indicated by this event. For example, an Error event is reported if during system start up a service fails to load.
- *Warning*: This event is used to indicate a possible future problem. Indeed, if an event denotes system issues that are recoverable, it can generally be classified as a Warning event. For instance, a Warning event is logged when disk space is low.
- *Information*: Describes an event that is expected under normal operation. In fact, the successful operation of an application, driver, or service is denoted by an information event. For example, when a network driver loads successfully, an Information event is logged.
- *Success Audit*: An event that records the successful completion of an audited security event. For example, a Success Audit event is logged when a user logs on to the computer.
- *Failure Audit*: This event loges an audited security event that was not completed successfully. For example, a Failure Audit may be logged when a user cannot access a network drive [18].

3.3 Windows Log Files Directory

In Windows8, all computers' event logs are normally found in:
C:\Windows\System32\winevt\Logs\as shown in Fig. 1.

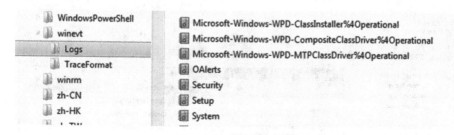

Fig. 1. Windows log files directory

Simply exporting and viewing them in whatever preferred event log viewer is all that is necessary.Some important log files of many Windows Event Logs [19] are listed in Table 1:

Table 1. Event log files

Filename	Description
Application.evtx	Application events
Security.evtx	Security events
Setup.evtx	Setup events
System.evtx	System events
Microsoft-Windows-Forwarding %4Operational.evtx	Forwarded Events log
OSession.evtx	Office sessions events
Internet Explorer.evtx	Internet Explorer events.

3.4 Windows Event Viewer

As soon as Windows is started, it begins to trace what it is happening, and continues to record log files continuously that may provide valuable data when something goes wrong.

Event Viewer presents an interesting and easy interface to look those logs as shown in Fig. 2.

In fact, the Event Viewer is a Microsoft Management Console (MMC) that helps to browse and manage event log files used for monitoring the issues and health of systems and troubleshooting problems when they arise. Event Viewer enables users to view events from multiple event logs, record helpful event filters as custom views that can be used later and also is able to schedule a task to run in response to an event.

Windows Event Viewer is one of the advanced features of Windows. This tool enables the user to view all information especially on all important events occurred within Windows operated machine in detail. This will be very helpful and useful in troubleshooting both errors and problems.

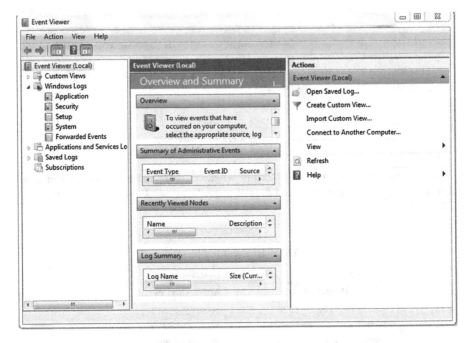

Fig. 2. Event viewer main screen

A large number of files in an .evtx file format will be saved under the Saved Logs even if the original .evt or .evtx files are deleted. You will need to have administrator privileges to view all these logs [20].

3.5   Event Tracing for Windows (ETW)

Since Windows Vista, Microsoft has introduced a new event logging model that unified both the Event Tracing for Windows (ETW) and Windows Event Log API. Event Tracing for Windows (ETW) is a logging and tracing mechanism provided by the operating system. ETW can help administrators to find out what is happening in their internal Windows systems, Microsoft applications and third-party applications, and trace any problems they might find.

ETW enables application programmers to start and stop event tracing sessions, instrument an application to offer trace events, and consume trace events. According to the diagram in Fig. 3, it is observed that the event tracing session is divided into three main components including Controllers, Providers and Consumers.

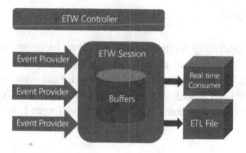

Fig. 3. Event tracing components for windows (source: http://blogs.technet.com/)

Controllers define the start and stop of an event tracing session with the size and location of the log file. This will enable the Provider to log and generate the event. Consumer is an application that has the ability to select one or more event tracing session as its source of event. It can also request and receive events stored in the log file and from session in real time. While processing event, it is an event that will be delivered to consumer based on the specified time frame requested by the consumer.

Some features and functions which have been added to the Event Tracing on Windows 8 and Windows Server 2012 are namely functions that provide event payload parsing, perform operations on a registration object, query event tracing session settings, provide trace provider browsing, and process a reclogged trace file [21].

3.6   What Information Appears in Event Logs (Event Viewer)?

Windows Event logs are specific files that store information of significant events related to software or hardware on your computer. When system or applications encounter an error a warning or information can be logged into these files as an event. This is a standard method to create logs, view, customize, clear and set the properties for your application events. The event logs can be traced for any trouble shooting problem and also can save important information into logs [22].

There are various logs types available in Windows Vista as follow:

- **Application (program) events**: Events which provide application level information such as error, warning, or information depend on the severity of the event. The event can be logged from program, driver, or service. An error event indicates significant problem, such as loss of data. A warning describes a possible future problem, and an information event indicates the successful operation of a service, program or driver.
- **Security-related events**: These events depend on windows security level. If fails to log into Windows or any other authentication issue, it would be logged to this.
- **Setup events**: Some additional logs are viewed here that belong to the computers that are configured as domain controllers.
- **System events**: Services or system service related events are logged here.
- **Forwarded events**: Logged events which are forwarded from other computers.

4 Log File Format

Different Windows Operating Systems have different locations of storing Windows Event Log and also differences in naming the log files. In addition in Windows 8 the number of event logs has been significantly increased. Following subsections compare EVT log format with EVTX and also explore EVTX log files. Currently EVTX data stream and format is used as a basis for the Windows Event Logging service.

4.1 EVT Vs EVTX

Different Windows operating systems are storing Event Log files in different location. In addition to difference in location, difference in names of the log files is also another factors and the latest operating system has significantly increased the number of event logs.

EVTX is the Microsoft new log format which has been implemented since Windows Vista operating system. EVTX log format which is also known as the Windows Event Log is equipped with a new Event Viewer and a rewritten Windows Event Log service. The most obvious change in EVTX is the use of channels to store.

The main pre-set channel was divided into two categories, namely Windows logs and Application and Services Logs. Windows Logs contain Application, Security, Setup, System and Forwarded Events channels. Application and Services Logs encompass many individual channels that publish events from single application [23].

4.2 EVTX Event Definition

The EVTX log file format provides expanded log data fields which help applications to precisely record log events and enable administrators to more easily interpret the event logs. EVTX supports various types of sources for logging of events data, and the logs have different event IDs and a great number of fields compared to EVT. Event log records are stored as a stream of binary XML (Extensible Markup Language) in the EVTX file format store events. The structure, number and data within the fields in the EVTX log records have been modified from the EVT format because of the change to XML format.

Some detailed information of the XML schema for event records is documented in the Microsoft Developers Network (MSDN) by Microsoft. As shown in (Fig. 4), the Events element is the top-level container that keeps all of the Event elements in which a single event describes. Also, every record is started with a System element.

```
<Events>
  <Event>
    <System>...</System>
    <EventData>...</EventData>
  </Event>
  <Event>
    ...
  </Event>
</Events>
```

Fig. 4. XML event log file structure

This element is "automatically populated by the system if the event is raised or when it is saved into the log file". Some basic and valuable information is provided by this element such as the name of the computer which it originates, time stamp, the subsystem, the record number and a numbered scribing the event. Furthermore, there may offer each of the following elements: EventData, DebugData, BinaryEventData, Processing ErrorData, Rendering Info and UserData [24].

4.3   EVTX Components

Each event log consists of a header with a fixed size (indicated by the ELF_LOG-FILE_HEADER structure), along with a number of event records (represented by EVENTLOGRECORD structures), and an end-of-filerecord (indicated by the ELF_EOF_RECORD structure).

As soon as the event log is made The ELF_LOGFILE_HEADER structure, the ELF_EOF_RECORD structure is stored in the event log and is updated when an event is written to the log (Fig. 5).

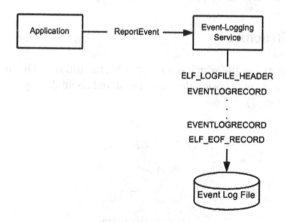

Fig. 5. EVTX components (source: http://msdn.microsoft.com/)

Each time that the ReportEvent function is called by an application to record an entry to the event log, the parameters is passed to the event-logging service. The event-logging service uses this data to store an EVENTLOGRECORD structure to the event log. The Fig. 5 shows this process [25].

4.4   Evtx Data Types

One of the new features of the Windows event logging is that it supports a wide variety of data types (Fig. 6). The Evtx defines the possible data types of a variant data item which are documented in a header file (WinEvt.h) and in the Microsoft Developer Network [26].

```
typedef enum _EVT_VARIANT_TYPE {
    EvtVarTypeNull          = 0,
    EvtVarTypeString        = 1,
    EvtVarTypeAnsiString    = 2,
    EvtVarTypeSByte         = 3,
    EvtVarTypeByte          = 4,
    EvtVarTypeInt16         = 5,
    EvtVarTypeUInt16        = 6,
    EvtVarTypeInt32         = 7,
    EvtVarTypeUInt32        = 8,
    EvtVarTypeInt64         = 9,
    EvtVarTypeUInt64        = 10,
    EvtVarTypeSingle        = 11,
    EvtVarTypeDouble        = 12,
    EvtVarTypeBoolean       = 13,
    EvtVarTypeBinary        = 14,
    EvtVarTypeGuid          = 15,
    EvtVarTypeSizeT         = 16,
    EvtVarTypeFileTime      = 17,
    EvtVarTypeSysTime       = 18,
    EvtVarTypeSid           = 19,
    EvtVarTypeHexInt32      = 20,
    EvtVarTypeHexInt64      = 21,
    EvtVarTypeEvtHandle     = 32,
    EvtVarTypeEvtXml        = 35
} EVT_VARIANT_TYPE;
```

Fig. 6. Evtx data types (source: http://computer.forensikblog.de/)

5   Log File Structure

The structure of .evtx log file which is a binary file is as follows: The file is started with
a file header in which some basic information is stored about the log file and the chunks
used by the file (Fig. 7).

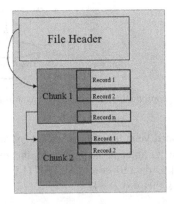

Fig. 7. Log file structure

In deed the event log file consists of some chunks each of which stores the event
records and represents a set of event log entries. Each record points to an event log
entry. The next subsections describe in more detail each of the aforementioned
structures [15].

5.1   File

Some main and valuable information about the log file is presented by the file header (see Table 2).The file header is permanently mapped into memory. It begins with the magic string "ElfChnk" followed by the version which helps for easy identification of the file as a Windows event logging file. The size of file header is 4096 bytes but only 128 bytes are used. The integrity of header by a 32 bit check sum is protected. The number of chunks in the log file is identified by the header.

Table 2. File header

No.	Ofs	Len	Meaning
1	0x00	8	Magic string :ElfFile" 0x00
2	0x10	8	No. of current chunk
3	0x18	8	No. of next record
4	0x20	4	Header space used, constant 0x80
5	0x24	2	Minor version, constant1
6	0x26	2	Major version, constant3
7	0x28	2	Size of header, constant 4096
8	0x2a	2	Chunk count
9	0x78	4	Flag
10	0x7c	4	Check sum

Sometimes, the real size of the file might be much larger than the calculated size using the header information. It seems that the logging service pre-reserves free space in order to hold several chunks according to commonly used log files such as the Application, Security and System logs. Also, the number of the current Chunk is given which is zero-based. If the chunk that is currently in use is not the last one, because of the retention policy, the oldest records are overwritten.

A dirty log is identified by the bit 0 of the flags. When this bit is set it means that the log file was opened and changed although it is possible that some changes have not been reflected in the file header.

If the event logging-service is re-opened a dirty log, it will be scanned by all the chunks and the file header is updated. After that, the flag would be clear and also the check sum would be modified. Moreover, a full log is identified by the bit 1 of the flags when the size of the log file would be its maximum size. Thereafter an event could not be stored to the log file. For a forensic investigator, it means that it is possible that some information of evidential value was not logged [16].

5.2   Chunk

The event log file consists of one or more chunks in which the event records are stored. The size of each chuck is 64 KB. In addition to the file header, only the current chunk is mapped into memory. Each chunk comprises of a small header, hashed tables of strings and XML templates, and a series of event records. The size of the chunk header is 128 bytes. The chunk starts with the magic string "ElfChnk" which helps to identify a chunk.

The starts of the last record and also free space are indicated by the pointers. Again, a 32 bit check sum protects the integrity (see Table 3). Two different counters are employed by the new event logging service using for record numbers. When the size of the file reaches to the maximum, then the event log service renames the file and a new file is created under the old name.

Table 3. Chunk header

No.	Ofs	Len	Meaning
1	0x00	8	Magic string :ElfChnk" 0x00
2	0x08	8	Number of first record in log
3	0x10	8	Number of last record in log
4	0x18	8	Number of first record in file
5	0x20	8	Number of last record in file
6	0x28	4	Size of header
7	0x2c	4	Offset of last record
8	0x30	4	Offset of next record
9	0x7c	4	Check sum

Thereafter, the counter based on the record continues, while the file-based counting would be reset. So far it seems that the only way to reset the log-based counting is to clear the log. Immediately after the chunk header, the string table can be seen.

The event log service has the StringTable and TemplateTable which are used to convert an event log file into a user-readable form. While the log service stores the records into the log file these tables help the service to prevent the redundant definition of string and template objects [15].

5.3   Event Record

A magic string including the two asterisks followed by two null bytes helps for easy identification of the start of the event record.

Table 4. Evtx event record structure

Offset	Type	Meaning
0x00	char[4]	Magic, const 0x2a, 0x2a, 0x00, 0x00
0x04	unit32	Length1
0x08	int64	NumLogRecord
0x10	FILETIME	TimeCreated
Var.	char[]	BinXmlStream
Var.	unit32	Length2

Two length indications which are at the beginning and the end of the event record help the logging service to traverse between the records in both directions. Num-LogRecord indicates the record number. The date and time of the record creation defines by TimeCreated (see Table 4). The BinXmlStream that is a complex stream consists of the logged information containing of XML data in a binary format [15].

6 Digital Forensics and Windows 8 Event Logs Analysis

Log Analysis is one of the important parts of Windows forensics process. During forensics investigation logs are collected based on investigation requirements.

For Windows Forensics, the application, security and system logs are recorded in the event viewer. Moreover, some activities should be avoided to keep logs suitable for investigation as below:

- Rebooting/formatting the infected system before obtaining the logs.
- Cleaning/modifying/carrying out any activity on the infected machine, until the forensic analysis is completed.
- Deleting/modifying any type of logs.
- Carrying out any activity that might modify the logs.
- Hiding anything from Incident Response team.

After collecting the logs, now they have to be analysed. Log analysis can either be done with the help of tools or manually. There are some helpful tools which take raw data as input and present the data in readable format. Some of these log analysis tools support various type of formats of logs. These tools are equipped with some filters which are used according to the needs and goals.

By using these filters, the unwanted data are removed and it helps focus the analysis on the target data until the desired goal is achieved. In fact the combination of the manual analysis and using tools help a Forensic analysis perform in an efficient way [27].

6.1 Examination of the Security Log on the Windows 8 for Evidence of Failed Account Logon Attempts

Security issues like hacks and data thefts are some of the biggest concerns every business is worried about today. According to researches, illegal authentication attempts are the causes of the majority of the hacks and data thefts.

When a user is trying to access a resource on a computer, related Logon event is generated. Indeed, the user should be authenticated before user can logon to a computer. When the authentication (account logon) succeeds, then the user is granted access (logon) to a system, but the authentication fails if the user is denied access to the system. In next section, the security log of the system would be examined in order to check the evidence of the unauthorized activities.

Case Study: Use Event Viewer to Check Unauthorized Use of Windows 8. Event Viewer is basically a log that keeps a set of crucial information for forensic investigator to trace back the event or blueprint an incident. In this research paper, the following part will demonstrate a case study corresponding to log files which can be employed in this scenario. Each of these log files comprises different types of logs which serve the same purpose but different function, for example: Errors, Information, success audit, failure audits and warning in the system. To start off with, the investigator have to study and examine one of the log file in event viewer, which is Security log file comprising events such as valid and invalid logon attempts, in addition to events related to resource exploit, including establishing, opening, or deleting files or other suspicious objects. As mentioned above, only Administrators of the PC can identify what events are logged in the security log. For example, if the user has enabled logon auditing, attempts to log on to the system are logged in the security log.

Method. All systems that were executed concerning this research paper are created using a virtual machine with the specification as shown below.

Virtual Machine: VMware Player

Version: 5.0.1 build-894247

The operating system that was selected and used to accomplish this research experiment is the Microsoft Windows 8, the latest operating system introduced by Microsoft Corporation. Refer to the following details for the specification.

Operating System: Windows 8

Version: Professional

Architecture: 64-bit

The Scenario. In a company, an employee's PC was suspected to have unauthorized access by someone else. The employee has log out from its user account before he left for lunch. The operating system of the employee's PC is Windows 8. The forensic investigators have to trace back the event log to analyze the incident. Event Log service in Windows is routinely start off once the windows machine is activated. All users can view application and system logs. Only administrators can gain access to security logs.

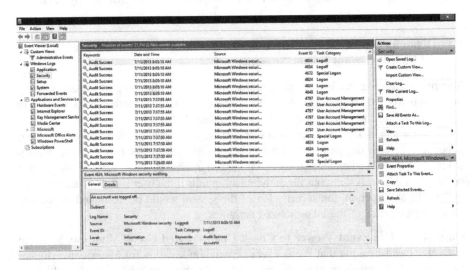

Fig. 8. Illustrate security log, one of the windows log in event viewer

Security logging is turned off by default. The administrator should turn on the security log by default in order to enable to system to perform logging.

One of the first pictures which comprise the audit access of the employee PC is seen in (Fig. 8). As seen from (Fig. 9), there is a group of recorded actions which correspond to user's action on that particular PC. For example, it includes log on and log off to the user account, special log on and user account management.

Keywords	Date and Time	Source	Event ID	Task Category
Audit Success	7/11/2013 8:05:10 AM	Microsoft Windows securi...	4634	Logoff
Audit Success	7/11/2013 8:05:10 AM	Microsoft Windows securi...	4634	Logoff
Audit Success	7/11/2013 8:05:10 AM	Microsoft Windows securi...	4672	Special Logon
Audit Success	7/11/2013 8:05:10 AM	Microsoft Windows securi...	4624	Logon
Audit Success	7/11/2013 8:05:10 AM	Microsoft Windows securi...	4624	Logon
Audit Success	7/11/2013 8:05:10 AM	Microsoft Windows securi...	4648	Logon
Audit Success	7/11/2013 7:37:55 AM	Microsoft Windows securi...	4797	User Account Management
Audit Success	7/11/2013 7:37:55 AM	Microsoft Windows securi...	4797	User Account Management
Audit Success	7/11/2013 7:37:55 AM	Microsoft Windows securi...	4797	User Account Management
Audit Success	7/11/2013 7:37:55 AM	Microsoft Windows securi...	4797	User Account Management
Audit Success	7/11/2013 7:37:55 AM	Microsoft Windows securi...	4797	User Account Management
Audit Success	7/11/2013 7:37:50 AM	Microsoft Windows securi...	4672	Special Logon
Audit Success	7/11/2013 7:37:50 AM	Microsoft Windows securi...	4624	Logon
Audit Success	7/11/2013 7:37:50 AM	Microsoft Windows securi...	4624	Logon
Audit Success	7/11/2013 7:37:50 AM	Microsoft Windows securi...	4648	Logon
Audit Success	7/11/2013 7:26:00 AM	Microsoft Windows securi...	4672	Special Logon

Event 4634, Microsoft Windows security auditing.

Fig. 9. Demonstrate a clearer overview of security log file in event viewer

Each action carried out by user bond with Date and Time where to indicate, when the action takes place and with the keywords – Audit Success, which indicates a user who successfully logs in to the system and Audit Fail where it indicates a user who fails to access to the system like entering wrong password, etc. In addition, once an event was chosen, general details of the particular event can be examined as shown in (Fig. 10).

Fig. 10. Shows the general details of a particular selection event in the secu-rity log file viewer

It includes the particulars such as Log Name, Source, Event ID, Level, user etc. It provides general information for the investigator regarding a specific event.

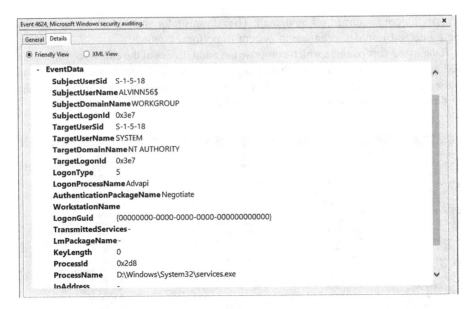

Fig. 11. Illustrate event data which compromise a comprehensive information of a particular event in friendly view security log file viewer

It has been separated to two type of views, which are the Friendly View (Fig. 11) and XML View (Fig. 12). Friendly view is basically filter the information and arrange it in easy navigable format that enable the investigator to examine.

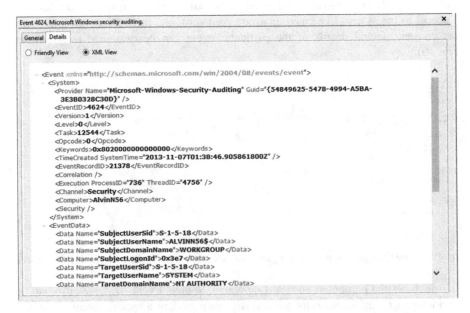

Fig. 12. Illustrate details of the Event data in XML view security log file viewer

In contrary to friendly view, the XML view displays the same event information in friendly view but in different format. The purpose of the XML logging is to deliver machine-readable explanation of automatically performed operations, including when using scripting.

Furthermore, xml enable the script to find a list of files that were actually uploaded/downloaded, when transferring whole directory or files matching a mask with directory listing.

Findings. According to the finding of the security log file in event viewer, all login performed by the employee was authorized whereby there is no sign of intruders login to the PC. All log in and log out events were seamlessly carried out by the employee, and there is no sign of log in activities on the PC during the lunch hour of the employee. Therefore, no person has had access to the system in that particular time upon examining the security log file.

7 Conclusion

The event logs in windows include lots of different information related to the happening of various types of events that have occurred on the system. Indeed, information stored in log files of a computer system is extremely important to collect forensic evidence of investigated processes.The Windows 8 Event Viewer offers a remarkable event log service to investigate and examine important messages in the logs. Log analysis can either be done with the help of tools or manually. In fact, by combining the manual analysis approach and the tools, a Forensic analysis can be done in an efficient way.

References

1. Sharma, H., Sabharwal, N.: Investigating the implications of virtual forensics. In: 2012 International Conference on Advances in Engineering, Science and Management (ICAESM), pp. 617–620. IEEE (2012)
2. Gupta, S.: Windows Logon Forensics. SANS Institute InfoSec Reading Room. https://www.sans.org/reading-room/whitepapers/forensics/windows-logon-forensics-34132
3. Daryabar, F., Dehghantanha, A., Udzir, N.I.: A review on impacts of cloud computing on digital forensics. Int. J. Cyber-Secur. Digit. Forensics (IJCSDF) 2(2), 77–94 (2013)
4. Aminnezhad, A., Dehghantanha, A., Abdullah, M.: A survey on privacy issues in digital forensics. Int. J. Cyber-Secur. Digit. Forensics (IJCSDF) 1(4), 311–323 (2012)
5. Dezfoli, F.N., Dehghantanha, A., Mahmoud, R., Sani, N.F.B.M., Daryabar, F.: Digital forensic trends and future. Int. J. Cyber-Secur. Digit. Forensics (IJCSDF) 2(2), 48–76 (2013)
6. Damshenas, M., Dehghantanha, A., Mahmoud, R., bin Shamsuddin, S.: Forensics investigation challenges in cloud computing environments. In: 2012 International Conference on Cyber Security, Cyber Warfare and Digital Forensic (CyberSec), pp. 190–194. IEEE (2012)
7. Parvez, S., Dehghantanha, A., Broujerdi, H.G.: Framework of digital forensics for the samsung star series phone. In: 2011 3rd International Conference on Electronics Computer Technology (ICECT), vol. 2, pp. 264–267. IEEE (2011)

8. TzeTzuen, Y., Dehghantanha, A., Seddon, A., Mohtasebi, S.H.: Greening digital forensics: opportunities and challenges. In: Das, V.V., Ariwa, E., Rahayu, S.B. (eds.) SPIT 2011. LNICST, vol. 62, pp. 114–119. Springer, Heidelberg (2012)
9. Daryabar, F., Dehghantanha, A., Broujerdi, H.G.: Investigation of malware defence and detection techniques. Int. J. Digit. Inf. Wireless Commun. (IJDIWC) 1(3), 645–650 (2011)
10. Mohtasebi, S.H., Dehghantanha, A., Broujerdi, H.G.: Smartphone forensics: a case study with Nokia E5-00 mobile phone. Int. J. Digit. Inf. Wireless Commun. (IJDIWC) 1(3), 651–655 (2011)
11. Mohtasebi, S.H., Dehghantanha, A.: Towards a unified forensic investigation framework of smartphones. Int. J. Comput. Theory Eng. 5(2), 351–355 (2013)
12. Saleh, M., Arasteh, A.R., Sakha, A., Debbabi, M.: Forensic analysis of logs: modeling and verification. Knowl.-Based Syst. 20(7), 671–682 (2007)
13. Borhan, N., Mahmod, R., Dehghantanha, A.: A framework of TPM, SVM and boot control for securing forensic logs. Int. J. Comput. Appl. 50, 15–19 (2012)
14. Ibrahim, N.M., Al-Nemrat, A., Jahankhani, H., Bashroush, H.: Sufficiency of windows event log as evidence in digital forensics. In: Georgiadis, C.K., Jahankhani, H., Pimenidis, E., Bashroush, R., Al-Nemrat, A. (eds.) ICGS3/e-Democracy 2011. LNICST, vol. 99, pp. 253–262. Springer, Heidelberg (2012)
15. Schuster, A.: Introducing the Microsoft Vista event log file format. Digit. Invest. 4, 65–72 (2007)
16. Guy Thomas.: Microsoft Windows 8 Event Viewer. Computer Performance LTD. http://www.computerperformance.co.uk/win8/windows8-event-viewer.htm
17. Microsoft Corporation, Redmond.: Event Logging. http://msdn.microsoft.com/en-us/library/windows/desktop/aa363632(v=vs.85).aspx
18. Microsoft Corporation, Redmond.: Event Types. http://msdn.microsoft.com/en-us/library/windows/desktop/aa363632(v=vs.85).aspx
19. Fleisher, E.: Windows 8 Forensics: Reset and Refresh Artifacts., cyber arms – computer security. http://www.computerperformance.co.uk/win8/windows8-event-viewer.htm
20. Brengle, M.: Working with the Event Viewer in Windows., 7 tutorials-Help & Howto for windows. http://www.7tutorials.com/basics-about-working-event-viewer-windows
21. InsungPark, Buch, R.: Improve Debugging And Performance Tuning With ETW., MSDN Magazine. http://msdn.microsoft.com/en-us/magazine/cc163437.aspx
22. Microsoft Corporation, Redmond.: What information appears in event logs. http://windows.microsoft.com/en-us/windows/what-information-event-logs-event-viewer#1TC=windows-7
23. TZWorks Limited Liability Company.: Windows Event Log Viewer. TZWorksLLC. https://www.tzworks.net/index.html
24. Microsoft Corporation, Redmond.: Event Logging. http://msdn.microsoft.com/en-us/library/windows/desktop/aa363652(v=vs.85).aspx
25. Microsoft Corporation, Redmond.: Event Log File Format. http://msdn.microsoft.com/en-us/library/windows/desktop/bb309026(v=vs.85).aspx
26. Von Schuster, A.: Evtx Data Types., Computer-Forensik. http://computer.forensikblog.de/en/2007/08/evtx-data-types.html
27. Verma, P.: Basics of Forensics Log Analysis., Information Security Intelligence. http://palizine.plynt.com/issues/2009Oct/forensic-log-analysis/

Automatic Creation of Computer Forensic Test Images

Hannu Visti[✉], Sean Tohill, and Paul Douglas

University of Westminster, London, UK
{h.visti,s.tohill,douglap}@westminster.ac.uk
http://www.westminster.ac.uk

Abstract. This paper investigates the possibilities for the automatic creation of scenario-based test file images for computer forensics testing purposes, and goes on to discuss and review a tool developed for this task. The tool creates NTFS images based on user-selectable data hiding and timeline management. In this paper we document both the creation of the tool and report on its use in a variety of test situations.

Keywords: Computer forensics · NTFS · Data hiding · File system · Timeline management

1 Introduction

Documented computer forensic test images are necessary to improve the learning process, test students and to test and compare computer forensic software. An undocumented image file cannot be used to verify tool performance or student progress; it is entirely possible that the researcher or teacher is not aware of the full contents of the image. The need for documented test material is well documented. Guo [1], for example, says *However, the growth in the field has created a demand for new software (or increased functionality to existing software) and a means to verify that this software is truly forensic, i.e. capable of meeting the requirements of the trier of fact.*

In Computer Forensic education, test material is needed for both practice and assessed tests. Hands-on excercises have been found to increase interest in the topic and enhance learning results [2], while Agarwal and Karahanna argue *Training programs can also be designed to provide potential users with opportunities for cognitive absorption. Game-based training environments are and more likely to result in cognitive absorption, thus amplifying both beliefs about the instrumentality of the technology and its ease of use, as well as enhancing its adoption and diffusion throughout the organization* [3]. Providing students with "interesting" examination cases while preventing plagiarism requires test images that are random representations of a scenario. All such images should bear equal complexity, to make results comparable if used in testing.

Generally, two different approaches exist in obtaining documented test images. One is to rely on the work of others and the other is manual creation. A few documented test images exist, for example http://dftt.sourceforge.net [4] but testing of

© Springer International Publishing Switzerland 2015
U. Garain and F. Shafait (Eds.): IWCF 2012 and 2014, LNCS 8915, pp. 163–175, 2015.
DOI: 10.1007/978-3-319-20125-2_14

highly specialised tools generally requires manual test image creation. Manual creation, while reliable, can be a cumbersome task if hundreds or thousands of images are needed. This paper introduces a versatile and extensible tool to rapidly create a large number of documented file system images based on a *scenario* defined by the user. All created images based on a scenario fulfill the chosen scenario criteria but contain random elements, thus they are different from each other.

2   Background

2.1   Related Work

A tool (Forensig^2) exists to provide automatic test image creation [5]. Forensig^2 is a versatile tool based on a scripting language to allow users to create images inside a virtual machine. This allows virtually unlimited versatility but does not provide a user interface [6,7].

The strength of Forensig^2 is in its method of creating images inside virtual machines. Virtual machine clocks can be set to any date and time and actions to the image are performed by underlying operating system commands. This makes timeline and contents management easy as long as the user is able to execute all actions in a correct order. If the order of actions is incorrect, this could cause *contamination* to the created images.

Data hiding in NTFS has been studied by Huebner *et al.* [8]. This paper documents a piece of software that implements some of their methods as a proof of concept. The purpose of this software is to create a framework to implement various data hiding methods. The framework is intended to be flexible enough that it will allow the addition of further data hiding methods in the future.

2.2   NTFS

NTFS is a proprietary file system developed by Microsoft. The greatest challenge posed by NTFS is the fact that its documentation has never been officially published [9]. Variance between NTFS versions has also been detected [10]. This paper describes only relevant NTFS concepts.

Master File Table. NTFS contains a file named $Mft, which contains a record for every file in the file system. This is called the Master File Table (MFT) Each *MFT record* contains *attributes*, which in turn contain timestamp information, file storage information, permissions information, and so forth. The first 16 entries are considered system files. MFT record number 0 points to $Mft itself. Record 1 ($MftMirr) is a file containing backup storage of the first 16 entries of $Mft.

Attributes. Attributes can be added to NTFS file systems without losing backward compatibility. However, forensic interest focusses on the following attributes:

- $STANDARD_INFORMATION: This attribute contains timestamp information and is mandatory.
- $FILE_NAME: Stores information about file name and size, and another set of timestamp information.
- $DATA: The actual contents of a file, or in the case of large files, a collection of pointers to the actual contents.
- $INDEX_ROOT, $INDEX_ALLOCATION: B-tree indices.

Directory Trees. While every file could be located from $Mft, a sequential search of this file would be inefficient. NTFS stores contents of directories in B-trees, where structures formatted as $FILE_NAME -attributes contain both file name and a set of time stamps.

2.3 Timestamp Management

NTFS has MACE (modified, accessed, created, entry changed) timestamp information stored in three full MACE sets:

1. $Mft record $STANDARD_INFORMATION attribute
2. $Mft record $FILE_NAME attribute
3. Directory entry $FILE_NAME attribute

Timestamp behaviour inside $Mft record has been studied by Bang *et al.* [11]. Depending on Windows version and action performed to the file, changes are made to only $STANDARD_INFORMATION or to both attributes. Directory entry timestamp information follows $Mft record $STANDARD_INFORMATION attribute despite being in $FILE_NAME format.

3 Design

The tool takes instructions from the user in form of database entries, with a provided user interface. Its outputs are created images and information sheets explaining the contents of each created image. This is illustrated in Fig. 1.

3.1 Terminology

The following definitions are used to describe the image creation process:

- **ForGe:** Computer Forensic Test Image Generator - the tool described by this paper.
- **Case:** Top-level entity. A case contains file system selection, the number of images required, image size, file system parameters, root directory timestamps and timeline variance boundaries.
- **Image:** Images are representations of *cases* and created by the tool.
- **Hiding method:** A method of writing a *secret file* to an *image*.

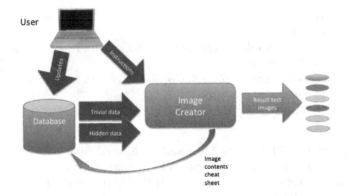

Fig. 1. Inputs and outputs of forensic test image generator

- **Trivial file:** A file without any importance to the *case*. Trivial files are used in file system creation to place files on *images* according to a *trivial strategy*.
- **Trivial strategy:** An instruction related to *case* to place a random selection of *trivial files* in the image.
- **Secret file:** An important file to the *case*.
- **Secret strategy:** An instruction related to *case* to place a single *secret file* using a *hiding method* to an *image*.
- **Action:** A simulated operation performed on a *hidden file*, related to time-line management. For example action "rename" with a timestamp sets the timestamps to correspond to a rename action at the given time.

3.2   Requirements

Top level functionality requirements are outlined in Table 1. The assumption is to build the tool on a Linux platform and use the Linux operating system tools and interfaces where possible.

3.3   Avoiding Contamination

Contamination occurs if a later action modifies or overwrites scenario related information or processes the file system only partially. The following examples illustrate the problem:

1. A file has been placed on the image and its timestamps changed to reflect the scenario. A hiding method then concatenates a secret file to this file. This action changes M and A timestamps to image creation time.
2. A file has been hidden in the file slack of a trivial file. The trivial file is extended, which causes the hidden file to be overwritten.
3. A file has been hidden in the file slack of a trivial file. The trivial file is then deleted. The secret file survives the deletion but if more files are written to the image, these writes can overwrite the hidden file by reusing the now—free clusters.

Table 1. Top-level functional requirements

ID	Requirement	Reason
1	The tool must create working and mountable file systems	As long as file systems are fully functional, it does not limit the choice of forensic tools used to analyse them.
2	The tool must be extensible with new file systems and hiding methods	By creating a framework to manipulate file systems, users can define their own "hiding methods" if those provided are not suitable.
3	A user interface must be provided	A web browser based user interface for database management and application access reduces the expertise needed to operate the tool.
4	The tool must allow the addition of random elements to individual images	If several images are required for external tool evaluation or academic setup, adding the random element to the generator reduces the amount of user work needed.
5	The tool must be designed to be non-sequential in image building. The order of entries and actions configured by the user should not dictate the order in which they are implemented on images	The generator must choose the correct order of implementation to avoid contamination.
6	If an image fails to be created, it must be deleted and the user must be notified	Partial images do not represent the case and must not be allowed to mix with successful images.
7	Successful image contents must be documented and a means of accessing the documentation provided	If exact information of the contents of an image is required, this must be provided in a user-friendly manner. If image generation uses random elements, documenting the actual result for each image is useful if images are used, for example, to assess students.

4. A file has been hidden in empty space. Another file is hidden with the same method. If safeguards are not in place, the second file can overwrite the first file fully or partially.
5. Root directory (MFT entry 5) timestamps are changed. If this change is not reflected in $MftMirr that contains a copy of first 16 file entries, the file system is in an inconsistent state and if mounted, the disk repair process can cause

undesired changes. The same problem occurs if the cluster allocation state is changed and the change is not applied to $MftMirr.

6. When changing timestamps, the three independet timestamp sets are not treated in a coherent manner. File system checks can detect an anomaly and the result might not correspond to the scenario anymore.
7. If new files are written to the file system after deletions have been made, metadata information in $Mft or directory indices can be overwritten.
8. If the last file written to the file system is deleted, NTFS implementations can shrink the size of $Mft file. If this happens, there is no reliable way to locate the MFT entry of the deleted file anymore in case its timestamps should need to be modified.

This list is not exhaustive. Contamination avoidance is a key topic in application design. Instead of treating the user scenario input as a serial course of actions, the image creator needs to understand consequences of performing these actions, and schedule actions accordingly. It is thus essential to know if a data hiding method modifies a mounted file system through operating system commands or writes to raw disk space directly. More volatile actions should be performed after persistent actions.

Modifying timestamp information requires raw disk access. Timestamps cannot be modified using operating system commands without contaminating the result. System calls exist to modify information, depending on NTFS implementation. However, modifying timestamp information is an action in itself, causing an update to "entry changed" attribute. The reliable method of modifying timestamps is to make changes to unmounted file systems. Existing tools, for example Timestomp, also tend to ignore the third set of timestamps located in directory entries [12].

The following order of actions creates a coherent NTFS file system that represents the scenario:

1. Create an empty file system
2. Mount the file system
3. Process trivial strategies: create directories and copy files
4. Process secret strategies that write to a mounted file system using operating system tools or programming language library functions
5. Unmount the file system
6. Process secret strategies that require raw file access, for example those using slack space or unallocated space
7. Mount the file system
8. Write a placeholder file to the file system to ensure the file written last is never deleted
9. Process all file deletions
10. Unmount the file system
11. Change all timestamps, including trivial files, hidden files and deleted files, to correspond the scenario, in all three timestamp locations
12. Copy the first 16 MFT entries from $Mft to $MftMirr

3.4 Addition of Random Elements

For the tool to be useful, all images created to represent a scenario must be different, while maintaining the scenario structure. This is achieved by pulling trivial and hidden files from a pool and allowing random elements in the timeline. Trivial files are arranged by their kind, which include pictures, documents, audio, video and executables. The tool categorises files upon drag and drop upload, based on their file name and signature. A trivial strategy could, for example, be an instruction to create directory /holiday, set date to 10/02/2013 and place 10-20 picture files to the directory. If the user has uploaded 200 picture files to the repository, each image used would be a random selection chosen from this pool.

The secret file pool is not based on file type but grouping. Each secret strategy hides exactly one file from a chosen group using the chosen method. Groups are numeric values assigned to secret files. If a group has exactly one file, each image contains this file. If a group contains several files, one is chosen at random. Secret strategy implementations choose a destination file, directory or raw image location randomly. If, for example, the hiding method "file slack" is being used, the target file, the slack of which is used, is selected randomly from existing trivial files already placed on the image.

Timeline randomisation is based on the addition of full weeks. Each trivial strategy and secret strategy contains timeline information and this is used as point zero in time. If a scenario allows a variance of a maximum of 30 weeks, a random number is chosen for each image and added to every timestamp henceforth. Weeks are used to preserve day of week and time of day information. In an educational setting, an example case might include suspicious activity happening outside working hours or during a weekend. This would be preserved despite providing a different timeline for each image to discourage plagiarism.

4 Implementation

The tool was implemented in Ubuntu 12.04 with Python 2.7.5. Its core processor implements the user interface, the correct order of actions, the handling of trivial strategies, random selection of hidden files, database management and timeline randomisation, while all file system operations and data hiding methods are executed in modules loaded dynamically during execution based on scenarion needs and database information. User interface was created with Django 1.5.1.

4.1 File Systems

File system modules need to implement a documented interface. To achieve this, the file system interface must be able to fully read and parse file system data structures on a raw image file. A limited write functionality is needed to write back timestamp information and handle slack space writing. The following list is an example of file system interface methods:

- fs_init(): reads in file system structures. Can be empty but the method must be present.
- mount_image(): mounts an image.
- dismount_image(): dismounts an image.
- get_list_of_files(flag): returns a list of files that have a certain flag (for example regular file, system file or directory) set.
- find_file_by_path(filename): locates a certain file and returns its data structures
- change_time(path, timedictionary): changes one or more time attributes of a file
- write_location(position, data): writes to raw image space

Linux is dependent on the Tuxera-3G NTFS driver [13]. Tuxera versions prior to 2013.1.13 destroy $FILE_NAME attributes when deleting files, which is not a typical file deletion behaviour in Windows systems [7, p. 41]. The requirement is thus to use Tuxera version 2013.1.13 or newer.

4.2 Hiding Methods

A data hiding method module needs to implement a class with a single method hide_file(file, parameterblock). Data hiding methods return a dictionary containing a human readable string to be inserted into the database, to facilitate displaying image contents. An example of this would be *"File foo.txt hidden in file slack, position nnnnn length zzzz"*. The dictionary can also contain instructions to the core processor if the hiding method requires either timestamp information modifications or file deletions. An example of a hiding method that "hides" a file by deleting it, is provided:

```
def hide_file(self, hfile, param = {}):
    hf = None
    dirs1 = self.fs.get_list_of_files(FLAG_DIRECTORY | FLAG_REGULAR)
    dirs2 = self.fs.get_list_of_files(FLAG_DIRECTORY | FLAG_SYSTEM)
    dirs = dirs1+[dirs2[0]]
    try:
        dpr = choice(dirs)
        if dpr.filename != ''/.'':
            targetdir=dpr.filename
        else:
            targetdir=''''
        internalpath = targetdir + ''/'' + os.path.basename(hfile.name)
        targetfile = self.fs.fs_mountpoint + internalpath
        hf = internalpath
    except IndexError:
        raise ForensicError(''No directory for hiding'')
```

The above code snippet is a typical starting point for any hiding method. It needs to write the hidden file to the filesystem, and the first task is to find a directory where the file should be written. The list of existing directories is queried from the file system module and one is then chosen by random by the *choice()* function. If the file system is empty and no directories can be found, an exception is raised.

The rest of the method handles the actual file processing and return value generation:

```
try:
    if self.fs.mount_image() != 0:
        raise ForensicError(''Mount failed'')
    tf = open(targetfile, ''w'')
    tf.write(hfile.read())
    tf.close()
    if self.fs.dismount_image() != 0:
        raise ForensicError("Dismount failed")
except IOError:
    errlog(''cannot write file'')
    raise ForensicError(''Cannot write file'')
if internalpath.find(''/./'') == 0:
    internalpath = internalpath[2:]
return dict(instruction=hf, path=internalpath,
        todelete=[targetfile])
```

The file is initially written to the file system and exceptions caught. An exception could be raised, for example, if the file does not fit into the image. The file system is mounted using file system class methods but the actual writing of a regular file is done with Python file operations. The results dictionary contains the file name as a reference to be inserted to database, but also the instruction that the file should be deleted. The hiding method cannot do the deletion itself, as doing it at this stage could cause contamination. Due to the modular structure and strong supporting functionality from the core processor and file system module, actual data hiding methods require little programming.

ForGe implements various data hiding methods that can be considered stable [8]. The selected methods are *deleted file, extension change, alternate data streams, concatenation of files, file slack, steganography* and *unallocated space*. A hiding method of "not hidden" is provided to allow placement of scenario related files into plain sight, with full control over their timelines. *ForGe* is a proof of concept and different data hiding methods were chosen to highlight versatility. For example, file extension change and alternate data streams modify files or file metadata, steganography uses an external open source tool (steghide) and file slack modifies disk space directly instead of with file system tools. *ForGe* offers a framework to do this. It provides access to image files, file metadata and raw disk space. For example in steganography, the framework is used to randomly choose a target file, and to raise an exception if no such files exist, and finally reset timeline in such a way that the modified file cannot be spotted by timeline analysis (Fig. 2).

5   Example

A simple example is provided as a proof of concept. A case of 5 NTFS images is created, with image size of 10 megabytes and cluster size 8. Timestamp variance is set to 26 weeks. Two trivial strategies are created: one to set up */holiday* with 3-6 pictures, and */PDF* to contain exactly two documents.

Trivial strategies provide two directories with random irrelevant files (Fig. 3) as the foundation of images. Three secret strategies are created as illustrated in Fig. 4. The first hides a file by changing its extension, the second places it in unallocated space and the third creates an alternate data stream. Extension

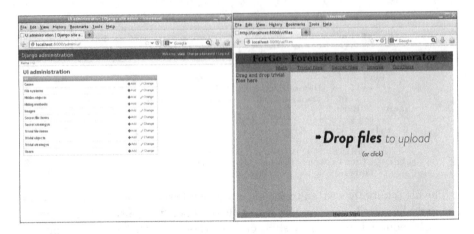

Fig. 2. Main user interfaces

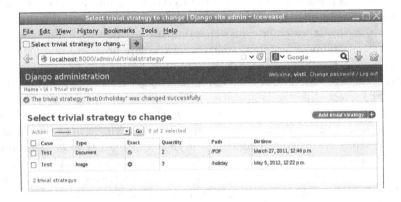

Fig. 3. Trivial strategies of the example case

change and alternate data streams also utilise optional instructions. The extension change hiding method has an option to exclude the root directory from hiding directory candidates. It also has an option to delete the file afterwards. Alternate data streams allows defining the stream name to override the default name "ads".

An example result sheet (Fig. 5) displays contents of the file system and an exact location and timestamp (if relevant) of each hidden file. A simple file extraction test to images 1 (result sheet not included) and 2 demonstrate the result.

Istat displays the NTFS attributes in human readable format (Fig. 6). Timestamps correspond to result sheets and the named $DATA attribute confirm the presence of an alternate data stream. Stream name "foo" is displayed as the attribute name, which corresponds to NTFS alternate data streams functionality.

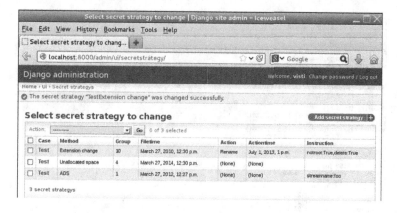

Fig. 4. Secret strategies of the example case

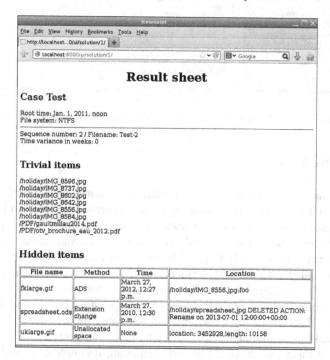

Fig. 5. Contents report of an example image

Creating this case requires only six database entries: One for case, two for trivial strategies and three for secret strategies. Image creation and result sheet display are functions of the *ForGe* application; SQL database access is not needed to analyse results. The only command line interaction would be to copy the created images to a location where they would be used. Access to images is not provided through the user interface.

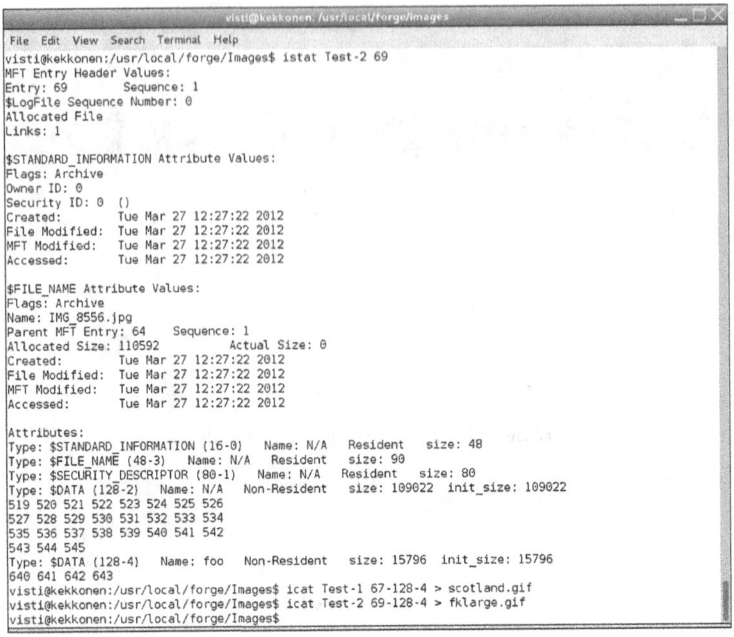

Fig. 6. Timestamps and contents of alternate data streams hiding

6   Conclusions

ForGe is a fast mass image generator with a graphical user interface. It is a fully functional prototype. It lacks some finesse in error handling, and no installation or removal procedures are provided for the program. *ForGe* provides an extensible framework that has built-in mechanisms to avoid contamination and provide full timeline control. It provides information sheets about the images that are created, thus enabling verification of results. Its strength is in rapid mass creation of "similar but not identical" images for forensic software testing or education purposes. Its main weakness is its operation on file and file system level. Higher abstraction level concepts, for example mail folders, web browser caches or backups of mobile devices are not readily supported.

Suggested future work would include removing its current focussing on the placement within an image of individual files, as this would extend its area of usefulness to the creation of, for example, databases and web browser histories.

References

1. Guo, Y., Slay, J., Beckett, J.: Validation and verification of computer forensic software tools-Searching Function. Digital Invest. **6**, S12–S22 (2009)
2. Duffy, K.P., Davis Jr., M.H., Sethi, V.: Demonstrating operating system principles via computer forensics exercises. J. Inf. Syst. Educ. **21**(2), 195–202 (2010)

3. Agarwal, R., Karahanna, E.: Time flies when you're having fun: cognitive absorption and beliefs about information technology usage. mis quarterly **24**(4), 665–694 (2000)

4. Carrier, B.: Digital forensics tool testing images, August 2010. http://dftt. sourceforge.net, Accessed 20/03/2014

5. Moch, C., Freiling, F.C.: The forensic image generator generator (forensig2). In: 2009 Fifth International Conference on IT Security Incident Management and IT Forensics, pp. 78–93. IEEE, September 2009

6. Moch, C.: Der festplatte forensik fall generator, Master's thesis, University of Mannheim (2009)

7. Visti, H.: Automatic creation of computer forensic test images, Master's thesis, University of Westminster (2013)

8. Huebner, E., Bem, D., Wee, C.K.: Data hiding in the NTFS file system. Digital Invest. **3**(4), 211–226 (2006)

9. Carrier, B.: File System Forensic Analysis. Addison-Wesley Professional, Boston, London (2005)

10. Hayes, D., Reddy, V., Qureshi, S.: The impact of microsoft's windows 7 on computer forensics examinations. In: Applications and Technology Conference, pp. 1–6, IEEE, May 2010

11. Bang, J., Yoo, B., Lee, S.: Analysis of changes in file time attributes with file manipulation. Digital Invest. **7**(3), 135–144 (2011)

12. Anon, Timestomp, November 2010

13. Tuxera, NTFS-3G manual (2014). http://www.tuxera.com/community/ntfs-3g-manual, Accessed 20/03/2014

Art Forgery Detection
via Craquelure Pattern Matching

Jason R.B. Taylor$^{(\boxtimes)}$, Aryaz Baradarani, and Roman Gr. Maev

Institute for Diagnostic Imaging Research, University of Windsor, Windsor, Canada
j.r.taylor@ieee.org,
{baradar,maev}@uwindsor.ca

Abstract. This work proposes using the craquelure pattern of a painting as a fingerprint to verify its authenticity against prior records. Craquelure are extracted and matched from photographs in a manner robust to illumination, scale, rotation and perspective distortion. A new crack extraction technique is introduced which uses multi-scale multi-orientation morphological processing and shape analysis in each orientation sub-band. Feature extraction – a Radon-transform based local descriptor at the crack junctions – and matching are described. Matching accuracy was 98.69 % on our database of 151 genuine unique craquelure images with simulated multiple copies of each pattern.

Keywords: Crack extraction · Craquelure · Feature extraction · Forgery detection · Image matching · Morphological filters

1 Introduction

Art crime ranks behind only drugs and weapons trades as the largest criminal markets in monetary value according to the U.S. Department of Justice [1]. Art forgeries, a subset of these crimes, can also degrade the cultural value of a piece of art by raising doubts about its authenticity. This work presents a system for recording and comparing the craquelure pattern of an artwork as a kind of fingerprint for the painting [2]. This allows for the verification of a painting's authenticity at a later date against a prior record, for example, after it has been leant out on exhibit.

Craquelure refers to a pattern of cracks which have formed on a painting due to age. The formation of craquelure can be affected by several factors: the varying rates of drying and contraction over time of the different layers of pigment, both with respect to each other and to the base; aging of the canvas or support; and macro-level mechanical stresses – for example, the stretching of a canvas at the corners of the frame [3]. Art historians have long exercised a manual visual classification of craquelure patterns by geographical region and time-period, owing to the dependence of the craquelure formation on the methods and materials used by the painter [3]. Regional classification of craquelure has also been adopted by the image processing community and implemented in an automated manner, eliminating the possibility of examiner bias [4,5].

© Springer International Publishing Switzerland 2015
U. Garain and F. Shafait (Eds.): IWCF 2012 and 2014, LNCS 8915, pp. 176–187, 2015.
DOI: 10.1007/978-3-319-20125-2_15

The first objective of this work is to develop a robust technique for craquelure extraction from grayscale photographs of paintings, without the need for specialized equipment or carefully controlled imaging conditions. The desired implementation would allow a museum employee to conveniently photograph the painting while on display, for which the craquelure extraction should be suitably robust to variations in scale, rotation, lighting or perspective distortion. A robust craquelure extraction would aid not only craquelure matching for authenticity verification, but also monitoring of crack spread. The second objective of this work is to match the obtained craquelure pattern against prior craquelure records to detect forgery, which to the authors best knowledge is a novel concept. Likewise, there are two contributions in this work: a craquelure extraction technique; and a scheme for craquelure feature detection and matching.

The layout of this paper is as follows: Sect. 2 introduces a new craquelure extraction scheme; Sect. 3 provides details on feature detection, local descriptors and matching; Sect. 4 discusses our experiment and presents matching accuracy in a receiver operating characteristic (ROC) graph; and Sect. 5 concludes this work.

2   Craquelure Extraction

2.1   Prior Work

Let $I(x, y)$ represent a grayscale image and $m(x, y)$ denote a grayscale structuring element, where (x, y) are spatial coordinates. Grayscale morphological dilation and erosion are defined respectively as

$$(I \oplus m)(x, y) = \sup_{u,v}\{I(x - u, y - v) + m(u, v)\} \tag{1}$$

$$(I \ominus m)(x, y) = \inf_{u,v}\{I(x - u, y - v) - m(-u, -v)\}. \tag{2}$$

Grayscale morphological opening and closing are defined respectively as

$$I \circ m = (I \ominus m) \oplus m \tag{3}$$

$$I \bullet m = (I \oplus m) \ominus m. \tag{4}$$

The white top-hat and black top-hat transforms are defined as

$$T_w(I, m) = I - I \circ m \tag{5}$$

$$T_b(I, m) = I \bullet m - I. \tag{6}$$

The white (or black) top-hat transform enhances details in the image that are smaller than the structuring element and lighter (or darker) than their surroundings.

Most prior craquelure extraction techniques, such as [4–7], apply the morphological top-hat transform. The fundamental assumption for its use as a preprocessing step in craquelure extraction is that cracks are thinner than most details in the painting. However, small-scale textures in the painting such as brush strokes and canvas texture can also be enhanced.

Both [4,5] utilize the top-hat transform with a flat square- or disk-shaped structuring element, followed by block-based automatic thresholding. In [6,7] another assumption is added: cracks, unlike some small-scale textures, exhibit connectivity. In [6], user-selected seed points are input to a region-growing algorithm to trace the cracks after pre-processing with the top-hat transform. Similarly, [7] applies a region-growing algorithm to trace the cracks, but utilizes a decision-tree for pixel segmentation rather than manually marked seed points.

2.2 Proposed Craquelure Extraction

The operator of the proposed system is instructed to take the craquelure photographs at approximately a predetermined distance from the painting, with the same camera. Variation in scale between multiple captures of the same craquelure pattern occurs due to human error in visually estimating that instructed distance. The shortcoming of the methods in the preceding discussion with respect to this application is the need to manually select a structuring element size – the top-hat transform enhances the cracks only if the structuring element is larger than the crack width and smaller than the background features. A fixed structuring element size may be suitable when all photos are taken at the same scale – crack widths do not vary significantly – but, for instance, if the image is increased or decreased in scale, the top-hat transform could miss the cracks entirely or enhance background features, respectively.

Scale invariant craquelure extraction may not be practical over an arbitrary range of scales. Assuming the proposed system requires photography from a distance of approximately 1 m, we estimate empirically that an operator would take the photographs from distances of 0.5–1.5 m – the expected range of relative scale is ±50 %. At this range of image scales it was found that a fixed structuring element size did not consistently enhance the cracks relative to the background. Instead, a quasi-scale-invariance may be achieved by selecting several fixed structuring elements and combining their results.

Improving the underlying assumptions in prior literature on craquelure characteristics – general connectivity and small size – the proposed work assumes: cracks have a local orientation – at some scale a crack can be locally approximated as a straight line; and cracks are significantly longer than they are wide – i.e. the size along their direction of orientation as well as perpendicular to it should be considered. From this assumption, the proposed method forgoes the square- or disk-shaped structuring elements and top-hat transform of the aforementioned prior works and instead uses morphological opening with line-shaped structuring elements, operating across a range of orientations.

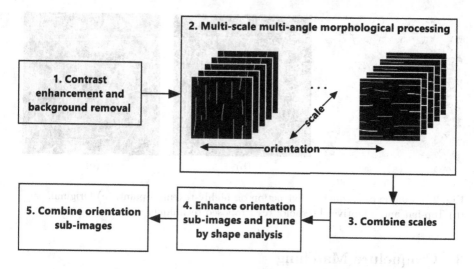

Fig. 1. Block diagram of craquelure extraction.

A block diagram of the proposed craquelure extraction technique is shown in Fig. 1 with a summary of each block following.

1. Contrast enhancement and background removal: adaptive histogram equalization [8] and top-hat transform with a large disk structuring element, approximately 10 times the expected crack width, to mitigate the effects of uneven lighting and background.
2. Multi-scale multi-angle morphological processing: morphological opening with a linear structuring element through a range of angles (orientation sub-bands) and line lengths (scales).
3. Combine scales: summation.
4. Enhance orientation sub-images and prune by shape analysis: subtract perpendicular sub-images to take advantage of the narrowness of the crack – as opposed to large objects where the structuring element can fit inside at both angles. Threshold each resulting sub-image by [9]. Approximate the length-to-width ratio of each connected component as the ratio of major axis length to minor axis length of an ellipse with the same second moments. Remove (by setting to zero) all objects with length-to-width ratios below some threshold.
5. Combine orientation sub-images: calculate standard deviation with respect to orientation. As above, the narrowness of the crack, its sensitivity to the alignment of the structuring element, is a fundamental assumption. Note the result is a grayscale image, where the gray-level is considered during matching as the strength or certainty of the crack.

The result of the proposed method is compared to the top-hat and adaptive threshold approach by our group from [4] in Fig. 2. This example is highly textured and challenging. The images are truncated for visual clarity.

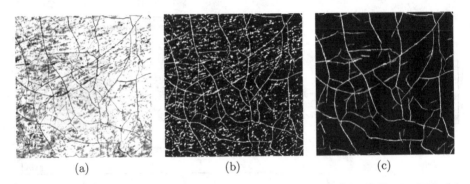

(a)   (b)   (c)

Fig. 2. Example of craquelure extraction on highly-textured paint. (a) Original; (b) Top-hat and adaptive threshold; (c) Proposed technique.

3   Craquelure Matching

In the intended application of a photograph taken in a museum without the need for specialized equipment or precisely controlled imaging conditions, the craquelure matching must be robust to:

1. Uneven or non-ideal lighting.
2. Scale, due to varying distance of the photographer from the painting.
3. Perspective, particularly as the photographer may change the angle due to light reflecting off the painting which can otherwise obscure the craquelure.
4. Rotation.
5. Incomplete overlap between query and database craquelure images – i.e. partialness.

Due to partialness and the variability of craquelure characteristics across an individual painting caused by varying materials and mechanical stresses, local feature points, rather than global features, are needed.

In contrast to the global features in [4] our objective is not to detect forgeries by sorting in to broad classes of craquelure patterns, estimating the origin and/or time-period of a painting, but to directly establish 1-to-1 correspondence of feature points between matching craquelure patterns. Forgery with artificial craquelure similar in overall characteristic to the desired region and time-period may someday be possible for criminals, fooling a region-based classifier. However, point-by-point reproduction of a craquelure pattern would be far more challenging to artificially introduce to a forgery; from both mechanical considerations as well as the requirement of a detailed craquelure record. Similarly, a 1-to-1 matching for authenticity verification necessitates such a prior record, which may not be available if the system was not previously in place. The two approaches may thus work in tandem.

3.1   Feature Point Detection

Using the craquelure pattern as a fingerprint of the painting, crack terminations and junctions are analogous to ridge endings and bifurcations. However, due to the continual spreading of the cracks over time as well as noise inherently added by morphological processing and thresholding, crack terminations cannot be reliably located as feature points. Crack junctions are the only feature points used in this work.

Crack junctions are detected by calculating the crossing number [10] after binarization and thinning of the enhanced crack pattern. The crossing number C of a pixel P is defined from its 8-connected neighborhood as

$$C(P) = \frac{1}{2} \sum_{k=1}^{8} |P_k - P_{k+1}|, \text{for} \begin{bmatrix} P_8 & P_1 & P_2 \\ P_7 & P & P_3 \\ P_6 & P_5 & P_4 \end{bmatrix} \text{ and } P_9 = P_1. \tag{7}$$

However, the thinning process introduces numerous false spurs, which are pruned by length to prevent a large number of false detections. Spurious junctions are also detected by the average Euclidean distance to the nearest n neighbors of each junction: tightly clustered junction points, relative to the rest of the image, are likely caused by noise. The feature detection is summarized in Fig. 3. An example follows in Fig. 4.

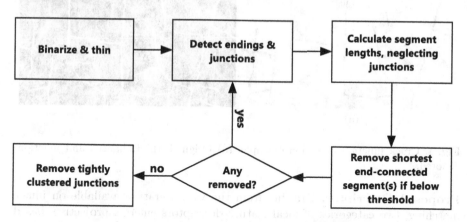

Fig. 3. Block diagram of crack junction detection.

3.2   Feature Descriptors

Scale Invariance. The challenge of designing a scale invariant descriptor for the intended application is the lack of external reference or well-documented assumptions by which to approximate image scale – craquelure patterns have a relatively wide range of densities. However, if the craquelure extraction and junction detection are sufficiently robust with respect to scale, a relative scale between two images of the same painting can be estimated by comparing their junction point densities; Let the window size for calculating the local feature descriptor, w, be defined as a base amount, w_0, multiplied by the ratio of the junction density to an expected typical value – the feature vector can then be interpolated back to the length dictated by w_0 to maintain a fixed descriptor length to facilitate matching.

Rotation Invariance. A major consideration in designing a local descriptor for craquelure matching is the lack of a direction attributable to each junction point, being by definition the intersection of cracks with different orientations. Without a global reference or local characteristic direction, we settle for a descriptor for which a rotation results in a shift of the feature vector. The feature-space distance is defined as the minimum ℓ_2 distance obtained by shifting one feature vector relative to the other.

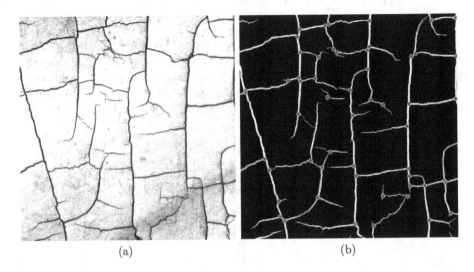

(a)   (b)

Fig. 4. Crack junction detection example. (a) Original; (b) Enhanced and junction-denoted.

Proposed Descriptor. Drawing from the vast literature available on image matching, two categories of local feature descriptors emerge: projective, based on some transformation of the pixel values within a window around each feature point [11–13]; and neighbor-based, where the feature descriptor depends solely on the relative location of nearby features, for example [14]. Neither is highly descriptive for craquelure patterns: crack junctions are highly self-similar, typically being either an 'X' or 'T' formation where the perpendicularity of the junction is characteristic to the region and time-period of the painting rather than a specific location on the painting; and the crack density is approximately piece-wise constant within a painting, with variations due to the chemical compositions of different colored paints.

This work uses a projective feature, similar to that used in [13] for veins in retinal images, due to the simplicity of its calculation – modifying this descriptor to be scale and rotation invariant as described above is straightforward. The Radon transform, a popular shape descriptor, of an image $I(x, y)$ is defined as

$$\mathcal{R}(I)(r, \theta) = \iint I(x, y)\delta(x\cos\theta + y\sin\theta - r)dxdy, \qquad (8)$$

where r is the radius from the center of the image, θ is the projection angle and δ is the Dirac delta function. Rotation of the image results in a shift of its Radon transform along the θ-direction, which meets the requirement of rotation invariance described above. Translation of the image shifts its Radon transform in the r-direction, (non-uniformly) as a function of θ. To make the descriptor insensitive to small location errors in feature detection, we use the translation-invariance of the amplitude Fourier spectrum, as described in [13].

The local feature descriptor in the proposed work is calculated as:

1. Let window size $w = w_0 d/d_0$, where w_0 is a typical window size, d is the crack junction density in the current image and d_0 is a typical crack junction density.
2. Calculate the discrete Radon transform of the local image window, $\mathcal{R}(I_w)$.
3. For small shift invariance: $|\mathcal{F}_r(\mathcal{R}(I_w))|$, where $\mathcal{F}_r$ denotes the discrete Fourier transform along the r-direction. The negative frequency components are discarded due to the symmetry of the amplitude Fourier spectrum.
4. Concatenate, normalize (for robustness to illumination and noise) and interpolate (linearly) to a fixed descriptor length n_f.

3.3   Feature Correspondence

Robustly matching two craquelure patterns necessitates a 1-to-1 correspondence of local features such that the maximum number of features is matched with the minimum feature-space distance between them. Spatial relations between neighboring features are accounted for via application-specific constraints on the isomorphism between paired features – in this case, a co-planar projective transform. The feature correspondence is summarized as follows.

1. Calculate the feature-space distances d_{ij} of all pairs of features (f_i, f_j) in the two images:

$$D = \left\{ d_{ij} = \min_\theta \sqrt{\sum_{k=1}^{n_f}(f_i(k) - f_j(k - \theta))^2}, \forall i \in I, \forall j \in J \right\} \qquad (9)$$

2. Candidate correspondences are those within some threshold ε of their bidirectional minimum, to account for noise added by morphological processing and thresholding:

$$D_\varepsilon = \left\{ d_{ij} | d_{ij} \le (1 + \varepsilon) \min\{\min_i d_{ij}, \min_j d_{ij}\} \right\} \qquad (10)$$

3. Refine final correspondences, $D_{\text{match}} \subseteq D_\varepsilon$, via Random Sample Consensus (RANSAC) – an iterative, outlier-robust parameter estimation – fitting a homography, $p \colon F_i \to F_j$, to the sampled points at each iteration [15].

An example of the resulting correspondences is shown in Fig. 5.

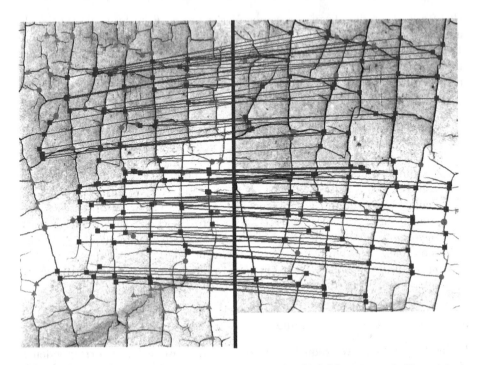

Fig. 5. Example of local feature correspondences. Matched (blue squares); Unmatched (red circles); Not in mutual foreground (magenta triangles) (Color figure online).

3.4 Similarity Measure

A global similarity measure between two craquelure images is consolidated from the correspondences found via RANSAC. Denoting the number of correspondences as $N_c = |D_{\text{match}}|$, the similarity of the two images is given as a vector:

$$
s = \begin{bmatrix} N_c \\ \displaystyle\sum_{D_{\text{match}}} d_{ij}/N_c \\ \sqrt{\sum p^2} \end{bmatrix}
\tag{11}
$$

where the last term represents the energy in the deformation field mapping corresponding feature point locations from set F_i to F_j. The domain of p is the area of overlap between the two images. For an ideal match, this energy term is zero, as the mapping is rigid.

Linear discriminant analysis [16] is applied to the similarity-score vectors from a training set of craquelure patterns to obtain a scalar similarity measure from (11).

4 Experiment and Results

4.1 Craquelure Database

From an initial database of 151 unique grayscale craquelure images, a larger database was generated to simulate multiple captures of each craquelure pattern under the conditions of the target application – as if photographed on different occasions without specialized equipment or precisely controlled imaging conditions. All original photographs were approximately 40×60 mm in area on the painting. Only grayscale images were available and to the authors' best knowledge, no publicly available craquelure database exists, nor has such a craquelure pattern matching system been published.

The probability density functions for in-plane rotation, angle of perspective and scale under these conditions were all approximated as Gaussian distributions of means 1, 0° and 0°, respectively, and standard deviations 0.15, 3°, and 5°, respectively. These values were chosen empirically, based on the assumption that operator error in visually estimating the instructed distance of photography would be the dominant factor over correctly aligning the vertical and perpendicular viewpoint. The larger variance in perspective distortion compared to in-plane rotation is to allow for the possibility of light reflecting off the painting which can obscure the craquelure and require the operator to change the angle of photography. All distributions were limited to 3 standard deviations from the mean to avoid anomalous cases in the generated database. The direction of the perspective view – i.e. from either side, from the top or bottom, or any combination thereof – was uniformly random over 0 to 360°.

The percentage of overlap between multiple captures of the same painting was approximated as a uniform distribution from 50 % to 100 %. This was selected empirically as a reasonable expectation for an operator instructed to photograph approximately the same portion of the painting on separate occasions.

Each distribution was independently sampled 1510 times to generate 10 simulated captures per original image, for 1661 total images.

4.2 Test Protocol

The first 10 original images and their copies, 110 images total, were used as a training set and excluded from the test set. Matching was performed between each original image and its 10 copies (for 1410 true matches), and between each original image and the first simulated copy of the next 10 images in the database (wrapping around at the end, for 1410 false matches).

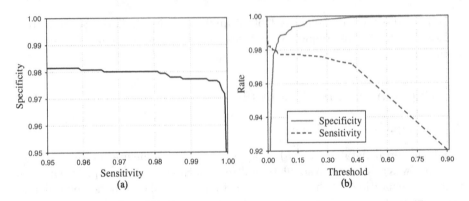

Fig. 6. Craquelure matching accuracy. (a) ROC graph; (b) Specificity and sensitivity vs decision threshold.

4.3 Accuracy

Each original matched against its 10 simulated copies determines the sensitivity, or true positive rate. Each original matched against a simulated copy of the proceeding 10 originals determines the specificity, or true negative rate. Sensitivity and specificity are plotted in Fig. 6 against each other (ROC) as well as against the decision threshold. The maximal accuracy is 98.69 % (97.52 % sensitivity, 99.86 % specificity).

5 Conclusion

This work is an early investigation of the distinctiveness and robustness of craquelure identification for authenticity verification in art. Novel multi-scale multi-angle morphological processing was presented for craquelure extraction, and a Radon transform based descriptor was calculated at the craquelure junction points.

As the results, 98.69 % accuracy, are promising, the authors hope for increased partnership with the art community to build a larger database of craquelure patterns to further develop this idea; The simulated database can be exchanged for real-world operating conditions and the image processing community can gain from the expertise of art historians. Additionally, we propose to extend these concepts as well as those discussed in the introduction – craquelure matching for forgery detection, time-period and geographical region verification, and monitoring of crack growth – to ceramics.

Acknowledgements. The authors thank the Institute for Diagnostic Imaging Research of the University of Windsor for financial support of this research. Our special thanks go to Dr. Spike Bucklow and the Hamilton Kerr Institute of the University of Cambridge for their support in providing the craquelure images.

References

1. Charney, N., Denton, P., Kleberg, J.: Protecting Cultural Heritage from Art Theft (2012). http://www.fbi.gov/stats-services/publications/law-enforcement-bulletin/march-2012/. Accessed March 2014
2. Taylor, J.R.B., Severin, F., Baradarani, A., Maev, R.: 3D ultrasonic system for finger-print imaging. In: Military Health Systems Research Symposium, Fort Lauderdale, FL, USA (2013)
3. Bucklow, S.: A stylometric analysis of craquelure. Comput. Humanit. **31**, 503–521 (1998)
4. El-Youssef, M., Bucklow, S., Maev, R.: The development of a diagnostic method for geographical and condition-based analysis of artworks using craquelure pattern recognition techniques. Insight Nondestr. Test. Condition Monit. **56**(3), 124–130 (2014)
5. Abas, F.S., Martinez, K.: Classification of painting cracks for content-based analysis. In: Electronic Imaging 2003, pp. 149–160. International Society for Optics and Photonics (2003)
6. Giakoumis, I., Nikolaidis, N., Pitas, I.: Digital image processing techniques for the detection and removal of cracks in digitized paintings. IEEE Trans. Image Process. **15**(1), 178–188 (2006). IEEE Press, New York
7. Gancarczyk, J.: Feature vector definition for a decision tree based craquelure identification in old paintings. In: Fusiello, A., Murino, V., Cucchiara, R. (eds.) ECCV 2012 Ws/Demos, Part I. LNCS, vol. 7583, pp. 542–550. Springer, Heidelberg (2012)
8. Zuiderveld, K.: Contrast Limited Adaptive Histograph Equalization. Graphic Gems IV, pp. 474–485. Academic Press Professional, San Diego (1994)
9. Otsu, N.V.: A threshold selection method from gray-level histograms. IEEE Trans. Syst. Man Cybern. **9**(1), 62–66 (1979). IEEE Press, New York
10. Arcelli, C., Di Baja, G.S.: A width-independent fast thinning algorithm. IEEE Trans. Pattern Anal. Mach. Intell. **7**(4), 463–474 (1985). IEEE Press, New York
11. Lowe, D.G.: Distinctive image features from scale-invariant keypoints. Int. J. Comput. Vis. **60**(2), 91–110 (2004). Springer, Heidelberg
12. Bay, H., Tuytelaars, T., Van Gool, L.: SURF: speeded up robust features. In: Leonardis, A., Bischof, H., Pinz, A. (eds.) ECCV 2006, Part I. LNCS, vol. 3951, pp. 404–417. Springer, Heidelberg (2006)
13. Bathina, Y. B., Medathati, M. V., Sivaswamy, J.: Robust matching of multi-modal retinal images using radon transform based local descriptor. In: Proceedings of ACM International Health Informatics Symposium, vol. 1, pp 765–770. ACM, New York (2010)
14. Cappelli, R., Ferrara, M., Maltoni, D.: Minutia cylinder-code: a new representation and matching technique for fingerprint recognition. IEEE Trans. Pattern Anal. Mach. Intell. **32**(12), 2128–2141 (2010). IEEE Press, New York
15. Kovesi, P. D.: MATLAB and Octave Functions for Computer Vision and Image Processing. School of Computer Science and Software Engineering, University of Western Australia. http://www.csse.uwa.edu.au/~pk/research/matlabfns. Accessed March 2014
16. Izenman, A.J.: Linear Discriminant Analysis, pp. 237–280. Springer, New York (2008)

Forensics Acquisition and Analysis of Instant Messaging and VoIP Applications

Christos Sgaras[1], M-Tahar Kechadi[2], and Nhien-An Le-Khac[2(✉)]

[1] Europol, Eisenhowerlaan 73, 2517 KK, The Hague, Netherlands
christos.sgaras@europol.europa.eu
[2] School of Computer Science & Informatics,
University College Dublin Belfield, Dublin 4, Ireland
{tahar.kechadi,an.lekhac}@ucd.ie

Abstract. The advent of the Internet has significantly transformed the daily activities of millions of people, with one of them being the way people communicate where Instant Messaging (IM) and Voice over IP (VoIP) communications have become prevalent. Although IM applications are ubiquitous communication tools nowadays, it was observed that the relevant research on the topic of evidence collection from IM services was limited. The reason is an IM can serve as a very useful yet very dangerous platform for the victim and the suspect to communicate. Indeed, the increased use of Instant Messengers on smart phones has turned to be the goldmine for mobile and computer forensic experts. Traces and Evidence left by applications can be held on smart phones and retrieving those potential evidences with right forensic technique is strongly required. Recently, most research on IM forensics focus on applications such as WhatsApp, Viber and Skype. However, in the literature, there are very few forensic analysis and comparison related to IM applications such as WhatsApp, Viber and Skype and Tango on both iOS and Android platforms, even though the total users of this application already exceeded 1 billion. Therefore, in this paper we present forensic acquisition and analysis of these four IMs and VoIPs for both iOS and Android platforms. We try to answer on how evidence can be collected when IM communications are used. We also define taxonomy of target artefacts in order to guide and structure the subsequent forensic analysis. Finally, a review of the information that can become available via the IM vendor was conducted. The achieved results of this research provided elaborative answers on the types of artifacts that can be identified by these IM and VoIP applications. We compare moreover the forensics analysis of these popular applications: WhatApp, Skype, Viber and Tango.

Keywords: Voip · Forensic acquisition analysis and comparison · Whatsapp · Skype · Viber · Tango

1 Introduction

One of the daily activities that has seen significant changes due to service introduced via the Internet is the social networking and communication amongst people [1, 2, 4]. Various Internet based communication services have been introduced that offer diverse

© Springer International Publishing Switzerland 2015
U. Garain and F. Shafait (Eds.): IWCF 2012 and 2014, LNCS 8915, pp. 188–199, 2015.
DOI: 10.1007/978-3-319-20125-2_16

methods of communication such as instant messaging, audio, video, file exchange and image sharing. The term *"Instant Messaging application"* or *"IM applications"* will be used throughout this text in order to refer to this category of Internet based communication services.

However, it was not only the legitimate activities that shifted to Internet based services. Eventually, criminal activities started being facilitated or taking place over the Internet [5] and criminals started using IM applications to communicate, either with potential victims [6] or amongst themselves to avoid interception [7]. It becomes obvious that, due to their popularity, IM applications have the potential of being a rich source of evidential value in criminal investigations. Moreover, for most of these applications, the type of information that can be collected in the context of an investigation can span beyond text messages. Europol has identified the threat of misused IM communications by criminals to facilitate their illegal activities due to the fact that it is harder to monitor or regulate these services [8].

Despite the wide prevalence of IM applications, there has been limited published research towards the assessment of their evidential value in criminal investigations. Moreover, the existing published research has not addressed all the popular OS platforms and IM applications, either due to the fact that they did not all exist at the time the research was conducted or the specific IM application was not that prevalent at that point to attract the attention of deep investigations.

As a result, this acted as the main motivation in proceeding with this specific problem since any solution to it would address the gap in the existing published research and contribute to its further progress. In this paper, we present forensic acquisition and analysis of four VoIPs: WhatsApp, Skype, Viber and Tango for both iOS and Android platforms. They are the most popular IM apps as their total users already exceeded 1 billion [23, 24, 26]. Indeed, to the best of our knowledge, there is no published research regarding forensic artefacts of Tango as well as a comparison of forensics analysis of these four IMs. Indeed, most of the published research has been focusing on Android devices whereas iOS based devices have not been extensively examined. In this paper we aim to answer how evidence can be collected when these IMs' communications are used. In order to provide answers to this problem, the idea is to select a number of IMs services and operating systems based on current popularity and conduct test communications for further analysis. Furthermore, a taxonomy of target artefacts was defined in order to guide and structure subsequent forensic analysis. Additionally to the forensic analysis, alternative sources of evidence were examined such as the possibility to clone IM session and perform communication interception. Finally, a review of the information that can become available via the vendor was conducted. Based on this approach, experimental tests were also conducted in order to identify potential forensic artefacts for these IM applications.

The rest of this paper is structured as follows: Sect. 2 looks at the literature survey and relevant work that has been conducted in the field. Section 3 describes the acquisition techniques in order to address the problem as identified in this section. Section 4 presents the evaluation and discussion of the outcomes of applying the adopted approach to solve the problem. Finally, Sect. 5 summarises some concluding remarks and discusses some future work.

2 Background

Although IM and VoIP applications were not very widespread in 2006, Simon & Slay [9] had already identified that the use of VoIP communications poses new challenges to law enforcement authorities. Specifically, they pointed out that new methods for collecting evidence were needed due to the fact the VoIP communications are based on a decentralised data network and can be easily encrypted. In the same paper, the authors described the challenges of performing call interception due to VoIP architecture of non-carrier solutions with a special reference to Skype, which was one of the few VoIP applications at that time. They present a potential real life scenario where criminals could avoid the traditional PSTN network and communicate via Skype in order to avoid interceptions and achieve the necessary obscurity required to remain undetected [10]. Moreover, they referred to the immaturity of legislation regarding the regulation of non-carrier VoIP and the complexity of introducing relevant legislation at an international level. Finally, they proposed memory forensics as a potential direction in retrieving volatile evidence related to running VoIP software, although they do not present a concrete methodology since their research was still incomplete at that point.

Kiley et al. [11] conducted some research on IM forensic artefacts and they also pointed out that IM is being exploited by criminals due to its popularity and privacy features. However, their research focused on, what they named, volatile instant messaging which described the IM services operating via a web interface, without requiring a fat client. They analysed four popular web-based IM services on Windows desktop environments and concluded that it is possible to retrieve forensic artefacts via the browser cache files and the Windows page files. The identified forensic artefacts included communication timelines, usernames, contact names and snippets of conversation. However, the entire conversation was never possible to be retrieved. The authors concluded their paper by presenting an investigative framework for addressing volatile messaging, which consists of three phases: recognition, formulation and search.

Simon & Slay [12] continued their work on investigative techniques for VoIP technologies by conducting experiments in order to identify traces left by Skype in the physical memory. They drew their inspiration from similar research on the operating system recovery level information from the physical memory and expanded the approach to application level information. To better structure the objectives of their proposed investigative approach, the authors defined a number of data type categories that could be identified in the context of an investigation: Communication Content, Contacts, Communication History, Passwords and Encryption Keys. In order to capture the memory of the system under investigation, they leveraged virtualisation and the inherent functionalities of memory extraction. They concluded that it is possible to retrieve useful information about the use of Skype via the physical memory and specifically: information about the existence of the Skype process, the password and the contact list of the Skype account that was used. However, it was not possible to retrieve any encryption keys although it is known that Skype uses encryption.

Vidas et al. [13] conducted work towards the definition of a general methodology for collecting data on Android devices. Although not directly relevant to the IM investigation issue, their work provides useful information that assisted in developing our approach. More precisely, the authors have provided a comprehensive overview of an Android device and proposed specific data collection objectives and processes that were taken into account in our experiments, which are described in Sect. 4.

Alghafli et al. [14] gave guidelines on the digital forensic capabilities in smartphones where they considered Skype as a source of evidence. They also referred to VoIP applications being used to communicate without leaving logs in the traditional phone functions of the smartphones.

Carpene [15] and Tso et al. [16] approached the evidence extraction for iOS based devices from a different perspective, which does not require the actual seizure of the device. Their approach was to leverage the backup files created via the iTunes application, the PC companion software for managing iOS devices. In [15] the author took a more generic approach in an attempt to create taxonomy for all potential evidence that can be extracted from the iTunes backup file. Skype is one of the applications that were included in this taxonomy and the potential evidence identified is limited call history and limited contact data. The same approach was followed in [16] to investigate the iTunes backup files. Nevertheless, their research focused in identified forensic artefacts of five popular IM devices: Facebook, Skype, Viber, Windows Live Messenger, and WhatsApp Messenger. They concluded that it is possible to retrieve the content of IM communications via the backup files. Since three of these IM applications are included in analysis, their outcome will be taken into consideration.

Schrittwieser et al. [17] conducted a security assessment of nine popular IM and VoIP applications, including Viber, WhatsApp and Tango. Although their approach is stemming from a vulnerability assessment perspective, the outcome could also be valuable in a law enforcement investigation context. For instance, their results about weak authentication mechanisms could be used in order to perform session cloning and intercept the communication, wherever the applicable legislation allows for such activities by law enforcement authorities.

Chu et al. [18] examined the possibility of retrieving Viber communication content via the Random Access Memory (RAM) in Android devices. They concluded that it is possible to retrieve partial evidence via the RAM and, furthermore, that the evidence is present even after resetting the device.

Mahajan et al. [19] conducted forensic analysis for both Viber and WhatsApp on Android devices, using forensic acquisition equipment to perform the file system extraction of the smartphones. Their research concluded that for both IM applications it is possible to retrieve useful information about the user's activities such as communication content, communication history and the contact list.

We also want to validate what has been concluded in [19] and go beyond by expanding it to issues that they have not been addressed such as the recovery of deleted messages or factory reset phones. Moreover, we will expand further to more platforms and more IM applications. As presented above, IM and VoIP applications are in the rise within the last few years and most likely will remain popular in the future. The shift from traditional communications (i.e. over PSTN or GSM networks) to IM and VoIP services calls requires new ways of collecting evidence.

The existing literature has identified the issue of identifying and monitoring VoIP traffic [9, 10, 20] and some research has been conducted towards the retrieval of evidence from IM and VoIP services [11, 12, 15, 16, 19]. Nevertheless, there are gaps in the existing research and developments on this field, which have yet to be addressed. For instance, the investigating forensic artefact of Tango, which is popular amongst Android users or the desktop version of Viber which was only released in May 2013 is highly required. Moreover, very little is known about alternative investigation techniques which is often used by law enforcement for Skype investigations. Indeed, there is no research that compares forensics analysis of four applications: WhatsApp, Skype, Viber and Tango. Finally, most of the published research has been focusing on Android devices whereas iOS based devices have not been extensively examined.

These open issues formulate the problem statement of this work, which can be summarised in the following questions:

- What types of forensic artefacts can be found in the most popular IM services?
- How and where can evidence be collected from the most popular IM services?
- What alternative sources exist in order to capture evidence from IM services?

In order to address these questions we follow the approach that is described in the following Section.

3   Acquisition Techniques

The first step is to set-up an investigation environment for various mobile devices in with WhatsApp, Skype, Viber and Tango are installed. Following the environment setup and the definition of the list of target artefacts, the next steps are dedicated to the whole investigation itself; from the data collection to the extraction of evidence (artefacts in this case). We perform the forensic analysis on the data. This approach implies that a device has been seized and therefore we can conduct a forensic analysis on it in order to extract evidence in a post mortem fashion.

3.1   Forensics Analysis

The objective of this analysis is to identify the artefacts stored by each IM application in the file system of every seized device. The following questions are usually expected to be answered during this analysis.

- What data is generated and stored on the device for each of the used IM functionality?
- Where is this data stored on the file system?
- In what format is the data stored?
- How can the data be retrieved, accessed and analysed?

For the data extraction and analysis from the devices, we use specialised mobile forensic tools:

- Cellebrite UFED Touch Ultimate - data extraction/acquisition – with the following extraction modes:
  - Logical extraction: Quick extraction of target data (e.g. sms, emails, IM chats) performed at the OS level.
  - File system extraction: In depth extraction of the entire file system of the device.
- Cellebrite UFED Physical Analyzer - data analysis

Following the data extraction, we use SQLiteStudio as a main tool for opening and parsing the SQLite databases that are mainly used for storing data in IM applications. Further we use other software applications for opening image, audio and video files that have been identified.

3.2   Taxonomy of Target Artefacts

In this subsection, we describe taxonomy of target atefacts that we use in our forensics analysis (Table 1).

Table 1. Target artefacts

Target Artefacts	Definition
Installation data	Data related to the installation of an IM client on a specific device. It can be very useful in the initial phase of an investigation, as it can lead to further queries related to IM data.
Traffic data	According to the European Data Protection Supervisor [27], *traffic data are data processed for the purpose of the conveyance of a communication on an electronic communications network. According to the means of communication used, the data needed to convey the communication will vary, but may typically include contact details, time and location data.* Therefore it is crucial for forensic analysis.
Content data	The actual content of a communication, which can be text, audio, video, or any other format of the data. In the context of this study, we do not categorise attachments or exchanged files as content data but we establish category for them.
User profile data	Information related to the profile of the IM user such as name, surname, birthdate, gender, picture, address, phone number and email.
User authentication data	Data that is used to authenticate the user to a service or an application such as a password, session key, etc.
Contact database	The list of contacts associated to the IM user.
Attachments/Files exchanged	Data files that were exchanged via a file transfer functionality.
Location data	According to the UK Information Commission Officer [28], *location data means any data processed in an electronic communications network or by an electronic communications service that indicates the geographical position of the terminal equipment of a user of a public.*

3.3 Discussion

The approach adopted in order to conduct this study is influenced by Simon & Slay [12] with regards to the definition of data categories of expected evidence. Moreover, the adopted approach for the data acquisition from the mobile devices is based on the same technique used in [19]. Nevertheless, the adopted approach differs from these previous studies in the following:

- It covers both iOS and Android platforms. Previous work mainly focused either on Android devices [19] or the backup files of iOS devices [15] [16], but not both at the same time.
- It covers the four most popular IM applications; in total more than 1 billion users, on the two most popular mobile platforms, covering 63 % of the market share as described earlier. Overall, the scope of the examined IM and mobile OS platforms should cover the vast majority of IM based communications via mobile devices.
- With the exception to the study presented in [19], none of the previous work was based on the file system forensic analysis of data images acquired by mobile devices.
- Although mostly focusing on the mobile file system forensic analysis, it addresses the IM communications from file system forensic analysis. Previous work was focused only on the technical forensic analysis of the file system [19], backup files [15, 16] or the physical memory [12] [18].

4 Description of Results and Analysis

4.1 Test Environment

In order to examine the four IM applications and answer the questions posed in the problem statement, a testing environment is setup, based on two different mobile devices with all the four IM applications installed (Fig. 1). The communications between the two devices was conducted for a week using all features of IM applications.

We used the iOS version 6.1.3 and the Android version 2.3.5 (Gingerbread) during the testing. Although the Android operating system is characterised by considerable fragmentation in terms of versions, it can be assumed that the results of the tests can be extended to all current versions of Android as it was also concluded in [19]. It must be noted that both devices were neither jail-broken nor rooted. In the case of a jail-broken or rooted device, the test would result in at least the same amount of evidence, if not more due to the more uncontrolled environment in a jail-broken or rooted device. Moreover, the devices used were not locked with a passcode, although the equipment we used was able to retrieve almost the same data when the devices were locked. Nevertheless, the passcode recovery or cracking of the devices is out of the scope of this study.

4.2   IOS Forensic Analysis

Logical Extraction Analysis. The Logical Extraction of information from the iPhone did not produce any IM related results. The analysed data from UFED Physical Analyser do not include any explicit information related to the four IM applications under investigation.

Filesystem Extraction Analysis. On the other hand, when a File System Extraction was performed with UFED, the UFED Physical Analyzer was able to identify relevant information for Skype, Viber, Tango and WhatsApp (Table 2).

Manual Filesystem Analysis. In order to further investigate for potential file system artefacts generated by facts, it was required to proceed with a manual analysis of the file system. The most valuable information in the Skype user folder is found at the following locations: main.db.EMBEDDED that contains the profile pictures of all the Skype contacts and main.db that contains information about the Skype account, list of contacts that participated in a call, list of Skype contacts, list of conversations, messages and SMS, list of transferred files from and to the user, list of voicemails sent to the user and list of video calls.

The most important file of Viber is Contacts.data that is at the core of the application and comprises the main data repository where valuable information can be found such as a list of all contacts; list of all the attachments exchanged, including pictures, video, stickers and custom locations; list of unique conversation; list of phone numbers; list of recent calls and their duration; data related to the sticker icons and packages; the latitude and longitude of each message that was sent with the location service enabled; list of messages exchanged.

The first remark that was made when researching the Tango application in the iOS device was the fact that the application is registered with the name 'sgiggle' instead of tango in the file system. Secondly, it has to be noted that Tango's application folder 'sgiggle' was the only one of the IM applications in scope that was hidden in the file system. While analysing the files included in Tango's application folder, it was initially noticed that mainly comprises of SQLite .db files like all the other examined applications. However, when attempting to parse the database files, it was noticed that the content of the databases are not in clear text. For instance, the database file tc.db appears to be the one storing the communication content in Tango. When examining the data of the table 'messages', the content of the fields 'conv_id' and 'payload' appear to be unintelligible which leads to the conclusion that they are stored in an encrypted form. The same kind of encryption was encountered with all other database files in the Tango application folder which made the further analysis of the data not

Table 2. iOS filesystem extraction analysis

Target artefacts	Skype	Viber	Tango	WhatsApp
Installation data	Yes	Yes	Yes	Yes
Traffic data	Call/Chat history	Call/Chat history	No	Chat history
Content data	Chat/Image	Chat/Image	Image	Chat/Image
User profile data	Yes	No	Yes	No
Contact database	Yes	No		No

feasible in the context of this research, as it would require extensive cryptanalysis attacks.

The manual file system analysis identified that the WhatsApp application files reside in an iOS folder in the /var/mobile/Applications/directory. The application files are contained in two subfolders 'Documents' and 'Library', with the first one storing all the database and iOS plist settings files while the latter contained media files such as images and videos. The subfolder Library/Media contained the following subfolders: <contact_number>@s.whatsapp.net that contains all the media files exchanged in conversations with the specific contact; profile that contains thumbnail images of the profile pictures of all contacts. Nevertheless, the database files storing the activity and contact information for WhatsApp reside in the Documents folder. Specifically, the communication activity is stored in the database called ChatStorage.sqlite and the WhatsApp contact information is stored in the Contacts.sqlite database file.

4.3   Android Forensic Analysis

Logical Extraction Analysis. Contrary to the results retrieved for iOS via the UFED Logical Extraction analysis, the equivalent results for Android are much more extensive with a considerable amount of IM related information been identified. However, the logical extraction analysis of the Android device did not produce any information regarding Viber. Besides, the only related information to Tango was a record in the 'User Accounts' section of an account titled "Sync Tango friends". Similarly to Skype, information related to WhatsApp includes all the chat history and its content. Moreover, the WhatsApp chat content also includes the attached files (Table 3).

Filesystem Extraction Analysis of the Android device did not produce significantly different results compared to the Logical Extraction analysis described in Sect. 4.2. For Skype, File System Extraction analysis provides more information contained in the chat content. Specifically, while the attachments were missing in the Logical Extraction analysis, most of them were embedded in the conversations retrieved by the File System Extraction analysis. Nevertheless, this information can also be retrieved vie the Logical Extraction analysis under the Videos section.

Similarly, the only possibility of retrieving Viber's data was by searching for "viber" in the Images and Videos section which returned the image and video files. Nevertheless, it only provided an initial identification of related data without providing a lot of context.

For Tango, additionally to the information retrieved by the Logical Extraction Analysis, the File System Extraction Analysis revealed an entry of the Tango

Table 3. Android logical extraction analysis

Target artefacts	Skype	Viber	Tango	WhatsApp
Traffic data	Call/Chat history	N/A	N/A	Chat history
Content data	Chat/Image/Video	N/A	N/A	Chat/Image
User profile data	Yes	N/A	N/A	No
Contact database	Yes	N/A	N/A	No

application in the 'Installed Applications' section of the UFED Physical Analyzer. Finally, for WhatsApp, this analysis does not produce significantly different results compared to the Logical Extraction analysis described above. The same data was identified with regards to WhatsApp as the ones described with the Logical Extraction analysis.

Manual Filesystem Analysis. With the exception of the location in the file system, the Android folder structure of Skype application data is similar to the one described for iOS. As a result, the main bulk of the information is stored in the main.db SQLite database which is located in the Skype user folder. The Skype user folder in an Android device is located at the following path /data/data/com.skype.raider/files/ <username>. Apart from the information contained in the main.db database and already analysed in the iOS section, the following folders can be of interest in the Android filesystem: media that contains media files that have been exchanged via Skype and / mnt/sdcard/Android/data/com.skype.raider/cache that is located in the SD card of the device and contains cached media files that were sent by the Skype user.

Since the analysis performed by the UFED Physical Analyzer did not yield any results related to Viber, the manual file system analysis is the only possible way of retrieving evidence coming from IM communications over Viber. Contrary to Skype where the databases between iOS and Android were almost identical, the situation with Viber was identified to be considerably different between the two operating systems. In the case of Android, the information is mainly stored in the following locations:

- Folder /mnt/sdcard/viber that locates in the SD card of the device and contains the following subfolders which might be of interest in an investigation: User photos-profile photos of all the Viber contacts, Viber Images- Image files exchanged via Viber, Viber Video-Video files exchanged via Viber
- Folder /data/data/com.viber.voip: Located in the device's internal memory and containing the following database files

When analysing the two database files, we notice that the viber_message is used for storing information related to text communications whereas the viber_data for the rest such as the call log and the phonebook.

The manual file system analysis in the Android file system resulted in identical conclusions as the one described in the iOS section. All the Tango database files contained encrypted content and TangoCache.db was the one in cleartext pointing to exchanged media files. The difference compared to the iOS analysis was the fact that the folder TCStorageManagerMediaCache and the contained media files were available locally.

Mahajan et al. had identified the artefacts produced in WhatsApp in their research [19]. However, they do not include the exact structure of the WhatsApp data stored in the Android file system and neither did they provide the detailed table structure of the database files used by WhatsApp in Android. The folder 'databases' was identified as storing the most valuable information in order to reconstruct the communication history in WhatsApp, which were the two main database files: msgstore.db and wa.db that contain all the exchanged attachments, such as images, video and contact cards. Similarly to the iOS findings, the communication activity is stored in the database called msgstore.db and the WhatsApp contact information is stored in the wa.db database file. However, compared to the WhatsApp database table structure in iOS, the Android ones contained far less tables.

5   Conclusion and Future Work

This research was mainly motivated by the fact that despite the fact that IM applications are a ubiquitous communication tool nowadays, there was in-depth research on the topic of evidence collection from IM services. In this paper, we take into account the fact that criminal activities are taking place over IM communications in an increased frequency, the problem statement was created around providing answers on how evidence can be collected when IM is used. To that end, this research has provided elaborate answers on the types of artefacts that can be identified by the four most prevalent IM applications. Specifically, the following should now be well known for each of the investigated IM applications such as (i) the types of artefacts that can be collected in both iOS and Android devices, (ii) the location of the artefacts in each of the aforementioned file systems, (iii) the format of the artefacts and how to analyse them, (iv) a comprehensive description of the internals of every important application database with an explanation of what is stored in each database table for every IM application in both operating systems.

There are still a few remaining parts of the problem statement to be solved which could formulate future research work such as (i) the possibilities and limitations of using session cloning as an alternative investigation method in order to perform IM communication interception and (ii) the possibilities and limitations of retrieving information via the IM vendors.

References

1. European Commission, Digital Agenda for Europe - Telecoms and the Internet. http://ec.europa.eu/digital-agenda/en/telecoms-and-internet
2. ITU (International Telecommunication Union), Global ICT developments, 2001–2013. http://www.itu.int/en/ITU-D/Statistics/Documents/statistics/2012/stat_page_all_charts.xls
3. Portio Research, Portio Research Mobile Factbook 2013 (2013)
4. Eurostat, Internet use in households and by individuals in 2012 (2012)
5. UNODC, Comprehensive Study on Cybercrime (2013)
6. McAfee, Hackers Using IM for Cyber Crime (2013). http://home.mcafee.com/advicecenter/?id=ad_cybercrime_huifcc
7. The Register, Italian crooks use Skype to frustrate wiretaps (2009)
8. Europol, Threat Assessment - Italian organised crime (2013)
9. Simon, M., Slay, J.: Voice over IP: Forensic computing implications (2006)
10. Simon, M., Slay, J.: Investigating modern communication technologies: the effect of internet-based communication technologies on the investigation process. J. Digital Forensics Secur. Law 6(4), 35–62 (2011)
11. Kiley, M., Dankner, S., Rogers, M.: Forensic analysis of volatile instant messaging. In: Ray, I., Shenoi, S. (eds.) Advances in Digital Forensics IV, vol. 285, pp. 129–138. Springer, USA (2008)

12. Simon, M., Slay, J.: Recovery of skype application activity data from physical memory. In: 2010 International Conference on Availability, Reliability and Security, pp. 283–288, February 2010

13. Vidas, T., Zhang, C., Christin, N.: Toward a general collection methodology for Android devices. Digit. Invest. **8**, S14–S24 (2011)

14. Alghafli, K., Jones, A., Martin, T.: Guidelines for the digital forensic processing of smartphones. In: 9th Australian Digital Forensics Conference, vol. 1, pp. 1–8 (2011)

15. Carpene, C.: Looking to iPhone backup files for evidence extraction. In: Proceedings of the 9th Australian Digital Forensics Conference, pp. 16–32 (2011)

16. Tso, Y.-C., Wang, S.-J., Huang, C.-T., Wang, W.-J.: iPhone social networking for evidence investigations using iTunes forensics. In: Proceedings of the 6th International Conference on Ubiquitous Information Management and Communication - ICUIMC 2012, p. 1 (2012)

17. Sebastian Schrittwieser, E.R.W., Fruehwirt, P., Kieseberg, P., Leithner, M., Mulazzani, M., Huber, M.: Guess who's texting you? evaluating the security of smartphone messaging applications. In: Proceeding of: Network and Distributed System Security Symposium (NDSS 2012) (2012)

18. Chu, H., Yang, S., Wang, S., Park, J.: The partial digital evidence disclosure in respect to the instant messaging embedded in viber application regarding an android smart phone. In: Proceedings of the 4th FTRA International Conference on Information Technology Convergence and Services (ITCS 2012), pp. 171–178 (2012)

19. Mahajan, A., Dahiya, M., Sanghvi, H.: Forensic analysis of instant messenger applications on android devices. Int. J. Comput. Appl. **68**(8), 38–44 (2013)

20. Leung, C., Chan, Y.: Network forensic on encrypted peer-to-peer voip traffics and the detection, blocking, and prioritization of skype traffics. In: Enabling Technologies: Infrastructure for Collaborative Enterprises, pp. 1–6 (2007)

21. Aouad, L.-M., Tahar Kechadi, M., Trentesaux, J., Le-Khac, N-A.: An Open Framework for Smartphone Evidence Acquisition. In: IFIP International Conference on Digital Forensics, pp. 159–166 (2012)

22. Xyologic Mobile Analysis GmbH, IM application usage statistics. http://xyo.net/

23. Wall Street Journal, WhatsApp Surpasses 250 Million Active Users. http://blogs.wsj.com/digits/2013/06/20/whatsapp-surpasses-250-million-active-users/

24. The Verge, Viber expands to PC and Mac as competitors preach 'mobile only'. www.theverge.com/2013/5/7/4305350/viber-pc-and-mac-apps-200-million-users

25. Microsoft, Earnings Release FY13 Q1. http://www.microsoft.com

26. Digital Trends, Messaging app Tango steps into social network status with new photo filters and 100 M users

27. EDPS Glossary - Traffic Data

28. Location Data - ICO. http://www.ico.org.uk/for_organisations/ privacy_and_electronic_communications/ the_guide/location_data

29. Skype Forensic Artifacts. http://forensicartifacts.com/2010/08/skype/

30. Chu, H.-C., Deng, D.-J., Chao, H.-C.: The digital forensics of portable electronic communication devices based on a Skype IM session of a pocket PC for NGC. Wireless Commun. Mob. Comput. **11**, 211–225 (2011)

Biografo: An Integrated Tool for Forensic Writer Identification

Javier Galbally[✉], Santiago Gonzalez-Dominguez, Julian Fierrez,
and Javier Ortega-Garcia

Biometric Recognition Group-ATVS, EPS, Universidad Autonoma de Madrid,
C/Francisco Tomas y Valiente 11, 28049 Madrid, Spain
javier.galbally@uam.es

Abstract. The design and performance of a practical integrated tool for
writer identification in forensic scenarios is presented. The tool has been
designed to help forensic examiners along the complete identification
process: from the data acquisition to the recognition itself, as well as with
the management of large writer-related databases. The application has
been implemented using JavaScript running over a relational database
which provides the whole system with some very desirable and unique
characteristics such as the possibility to perform all type of queries (e.g.,
find individuals with some very discriminative character, find a specific
document, display all the samples corresponding to one writer, etc.), or
a complete control over the set of parameters we want to use in a specific
recognition task (e.g., users in the database to be used as control set, set
of characters to be used in the identification, size of the ranked list we
want as final result, etc.). The identification performance of the tool is
evaluated on a real-case forensic database showing some very promising
results.

Keywords: Forensics · Writer identification · Data acquisition · Database management

1 Introduction

Analysis of handwritten documents with the aim of determining the writer identity is an important application area in forensic casework, with numerous cases
in courts over the years that have dealt with evidence provided by these documents [1]. Handwriting is considered individual, as shown by the wide social and
legal acceptance of signatures as a mean of identity validation, which is also supported by experimental studies [2]. The goal of writer recognition is to determine
whether two handwritten documents, referred to as the *control* document (i.e.,
generated by a known writer) and the *questioned* document (i.e., generated by
an unknown writer), were written by the same person or not. For this purpose,
computer vision and pattern recognition techniques have been applied to this
problem to support forensic experts [3, 4].

© Springer International Publishing Switzerland 2015
U. Garain and F. Shafait (Eds.): IWCF 2012 and 2014, LNCS 8915, pp. 200–211, 2015.
DOI: 10.1007/978-3-319-20125-2_17

The forensic scenario presents some difficulties due to its particular characteristics in terms of [5]: frequently reduced number of handwriting samples, variability of writing style, pencil or type of paper, the presence of noise patterns, etc. or the unavailability of online information. As a result, this application domain still heavily relies on human-expert interaction. The use of semi-automatic recognition systems is very useful to, given a questioned handwriting sample, narrow down a list of possible candidates which are comprised in a database of known identities, therefore making easier the subsequent confrontation for the forensic expert [4,5].

However, before reaching the recognition phase itself, forensic examiners have to manually go through a number of steps which include: labeling the data, segmenting the characters of the new handwriting samples or manually handling all the data of large databases. Although some efforts have been made in the automation of several of these steps [6,7], usually, for each of the stages, different independent tools are used or, in the worst cases, no practical applications are available. This fact hinders and slows down the already difficult task of the forensic specialists and increases the chances of human errors.

In this context, we have developed Biografo, a tool that integrates over a relational database the different steps involved in the forensic identification of unknown writers, automating all the tasks related to the management of data and presenting a number of functionalities thought to make more efficient the work of forensic examiners. The application intends to give practical solutions to problems encountered by examiners in real-world case scenarios and has been designed based on a previous very schematic and simple software [8], according to the advice and suggestions received from the experts of the Spanish forensic laboratory of the National Police Force (*Dirección General de la Guardia Civil, DGGC*).

The present contribution also includes some preliminary results on the performance of the recognition module included in Biografo, based on the extraction of gradient-related features of individual characters. The evaluation has been carried out on a subset of a real forensic database comprising original confiscated/authenticated documents, which has been captured by trained operators using the acquisition tool integrated in Biografo.

The rest of the paper is structured as follows. The general tool is introduced in Sect. 2. Each of the two specific modules comprised within Biografo are described in Sects. 3 and 4 respectively. The preliminary performance results are presented in Sect. 5. Finally conclusions are drawn in Sect. 6.

2   Biografo

Biografo is a forensic tool formed by a client application programmed in JavaScript running over a relational database implemented in the platform MySQL Server 5.5. As shown in Fig. 1, Biografo presents two different operating modes: (*i*) *local*, in which both the client application and the database run on the same machine, and (*ii*) *remote*, in which several copies of the client

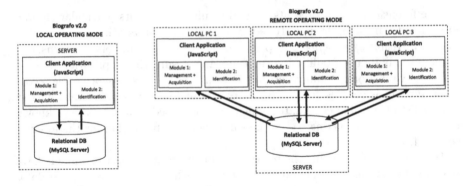

Fig. 1. General diagram of Biografo local (left) and remote (right) operating modes.

application installed in different local machines communicate with one single copy of the database installed in a remote server. In the second case different forensic experts (that may be located at any point in the globe) can use the tool at the same time (e.g., launching queries or introducing new data) without compromising the consistency of the data.

Biografo has two main functionalities which are intended to help the forensic experts over the whole examination process, from the acquisition of the data to the identification of the individuals: (*i*) acquisition of handwritten characters of individuals from control or questioned documents, and management within a relational database of the acquired data; (*ii*) run automatic identifications of individuals based on the samples acquired and handled within the database. Each of these functionalities is implemented in two separate modules that form the core of the client application as shown in Fig. 1.

Before describing in the next sections the specific functionalities of both modules, and in order to better understand the design of Biografo, it is important to clarify at this point that the identification module of Biografo works at the character level, that is: identification is performed comparing the samples of each character of the questioned individual to those of the known individuals, and performing a majority voting. The questioned individual will be identified with the known individual which has given a highest similarity score for the most number of characters.

Therefore, it is important to understand the difference that will be made throughout the document between: *character*, referring to each of the elements in the occidental written alphabet (i.e., we will consider 62 characters corresponding to the uppercase letters "A–Z", lowercase letters "a–z", and the ten digits "0–9"); *sample*, referring to each of the particular executions of a character carried out by a writer.

In general, for each individual several samples of one same character will be acquired. Each of these samples will have been captured from a digitalized document which, in turn, will be associated with a given individual. This link individual-document-sample is the basis of the tool operation.

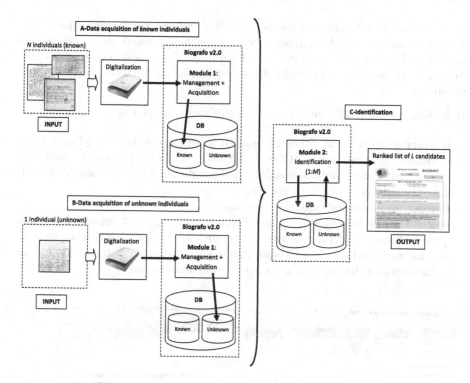

Fig. 2. General diagram of a typical use-case for Biografo.

In this scenario, a typical use-case for Biografo would be as follows (see Fig. 2):

- A. Data acquisition from documents of *known origin*. We will assume that a certain forensics laboratory has a number of handwritten documents coming from N known individuals. These documents are digitalized and, using the acquisition and management module in Biografo, several samples for each character are acquired and stored in the relational database.
- B. Data acquisition from *questioned* documents. Now lets assume that a handwritten document found in a crime scene is sent to the forensics laboratory for identification. Again, the experts will digitalize the document and store the acquired samples into the database.
- C. Identification. The forensic examiners will run the identification module in Biografo comparing the data corresponding to the questioned document to that of M known subjects, being M a subset of N, i.e., $M \leq N$. The identification module will give as output a ranked list of the L most probable candidates, where $L \leq M$.

3   Module 1: Management and Acquisition

This module of the client application is responsible for the acquisition of the data (samples) from documents written by known or unknown individuals, and managing all these data maintaining at all times the consistency individual-document-sample. For this purpose the tool has implemented three main menus labeled as Individuals, Documents, and Samples (*Individuos, Documentos* and *Muestras* respectively in Spanish). Each of these menus presents the next functionalities:

Individuals. Different screenshots from this menu are shown in Fig. 3.

- Register new known or unknown individuals in the database (see Fig. 3, left). A unique alphanumeric identifier is assigned to each subject and we may also include other meta data associated to the individual such as name, id-card, date of birth, general comments etc.
- Remove an individual from the database.
- Search for a certain individual (see Fig. 3, right). The tool permits to launch queries attending to different parameters such as the date in which the subject was incorporated to the database, name, surname, date of birth, those who write a certain character in a very particular manner, etc.

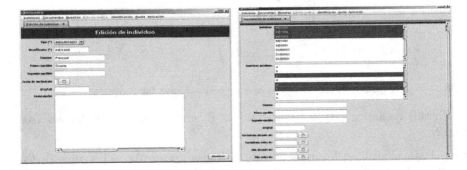

Fig. 3. Screenshots from the individuals menu in Biografo corresponding to the options: registration (left) and search (right) of an individual.

Fig. 4. Screenshots from the document menu in Biografo corresponding to the options: search (left) and visualization (right) of a document.

- Retrieve and print information of a given individual. Once an individual has been found with the search option, the tool can generate a document with all the data comprised in the database related to that subject: number of acquired samples of each character, number of handwritten documents, meta data, etc.

Documents. Different screenshots from this menu are shown in Fig. 4.

- The main purpose of this menu is to import a previously digitalized document into the database and assign it to a given individual. Documents accepted by Biografo are greyscale images in bmp format.
- This menu also has the option to search for documents within the database for their visualization (see Fig. 4 right). The search can be performed in terms of: the date in which the document was imported to the database, the individual to whom they are assigned, or directly with the name of the document (see Fig. 4 left).

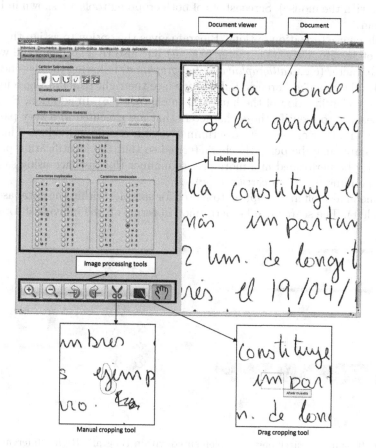

Fig. 5. Screenshots from the samples menu in Biografo corresponding to the acquisition options.

Samples. Different screenshots from this menu are shown in Fig. 5.

- The main functionality of this menu is to manually acquire the samples of the different 62 handwritten characters (i.e., uppercase and lowercase letters and the ten digits) of a certain individual. These samples may be captured from any of the documents associated to that subject. Prior to the acquisition of a given sample, the operator selects on the labeling panel (see Fig. 5) the character to which it has to be assigned. On this panel the expert can see the number of samples already captured from each of the characters. On top of the labeling panel the last 5 acquired samples of the selected character are shown.
- Graphical processing tools. To assist the forensic expert in the acquisition process, Biografo has implemented different graphical tools such as: a hand tool to move the document, zoom in and out, a document viewer with your current location, rotation tools, drag cropping tool (i.e., acquires what is inside a rectangle), manual cropping tool (i.e., acquires what is inside a contour drawn with the mouse). Screenshots of both cropping tools are shown in Fig. 5 (bottom).
- Sample characterization options. Biografo gives the option to assign the samples not just to a given character (e.g., *a*) but also to a specific type within that character (e.g., *calligraphic a* or *typographic a*) following the classification used by the Spanish Forensic Laboratory (see the right panel in Fig. 6 for the complete classification of the handwritten character *a*). In addition, Biografo also permits to identify those characters that are executed in a very particular way and that can be very discriminative of a certain individual. This way each sample may be perfectly characterized so that the identification process can later be performed in a more precise manner (for instance using samples corresponding only to a certain type).
- This menu also offers the option to search for samples within the database (see Fig. 6 left). The search can be performed in terms of: the individual to whom

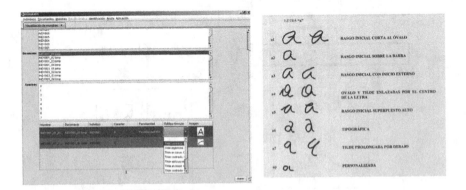

Fig. 6. Left, sample search engine implemented within Biografo. Right, different types of the character 'a' that may be selected by the operator to classify the different samples.

they are assigned, the documents from which they were acquired, and the character they represent. Once the samples are retrieved from the database, the tool gives the possibility to visualize them, print them, or update them (e.g., changing the character they represent in case of an acquisition error.)

4   Module 2: Identification

This module of the client application is responsible for the identification of unknown individuals within the database. Biografo permits to fix a number of parameters before running the identification in order to restrict the search options or to discard *a priori* unfeasible candidates: (i) unknown individual that we want to identify; (ii) subset of M known individuals (from the total N available in the database) among which we want to run the identification (e.g., all of them, only those registered in the database prior/after a certain date); (iii) characters that we want to use in the identification (e.g., all of them, only the lowercase letters, only the uppercase letters); (iv) number of ranked candidates L that we want to obtain in the output list.

Once the parameters above mentioned have been selected, the identification of writers is performed at the character level. Lets assume that we are using for identification the character subset composed of the 26 lowercase letters. All the samples of each of the 26 characters of the unknown individual are compared according to a certain matching function (described below) with all the samples of each of the 26 characters of the M known individuals selected for the search. The closest identity for each character is computed based on the majority rule: the winning identity for a certain character will be the writer having the maximum number of winning samples (i.e., highest similarity score given by the matching function). In case of writers having the same number of winning samples, they are ranked according to the average of the winning scores. Finally, identification is based again on the majority rule, applied in this case to the characters: the winning output identity will be the writer having the maximum

Fig. 7. Left, identification module implemented within Biografo. Right, output document with a summary of the results obtained in an identification test.

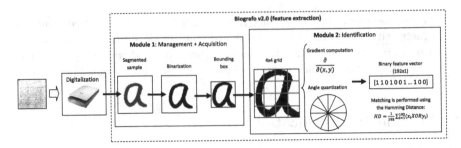

Fig. 8. Diagram of the feature extraction process followed by Biografo.

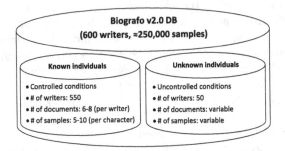

Fig. 9. Diagram showing the distribution of the Biografo DB.

number of winning characters. In case of writers having the same number of winning characters, the same above criterion is applied.

A screenshot of the identification tool with the different parameter options to be selected is shown in Fig. 7 left, while on the right appears a document given as output by Biografo with a summary of the results of an identification test.

The current matching function implemented in Biografo is based on gradient-related features [2]. After the manual segmentation and labeling of the samples from a given document, they are binarized using the Otsu algorithm [9], followed by a margin drop and a height normalization to 120 pixels, preserving the aspect ratio. Elimination of noise of the binary image is then carried out through a morphological opening plus a closing operation [10]. After these preprocessing steps the feature vectors are computed as follows (see Fig. 8):

- The processed samples are divided into a grid of 4×4 cells.
- The gradient is computed in each cell using 3×3 vertical and horizontal Sobel filters [10]. The direction of the gradient vector is quantized to 12 values (i.e., multiples of $\pi/6$).
- A histogram is computed for each cell, showing the number of times a certain direction appears in that given cell.
- All the 16 histograms are binarized according to the Otsu algorithm [9] so that for each cell we have a binary vector of length 12 showing if each of the possible directions are present (1) or not (0) in that cell.

– The final feature vector representing the sample is the binary vector of length $12 \times 4 \times 4 = 192$ that results from concatenating the individual binary vectors from each of the 16 cells.

The similarity score between two binary feature vectors is finally computed according to the Hamming distance.

5   Performance Evaluation

In order to evaluate the recognition performance of the identification module, a real forensic database from original confiscated/authenticated documents provided by the Spanish forensic laboratory of the Dirección General de la Guardia Civil (DGGC) was captured using the acquisition and management module of Biografo. Samples of the handwritten alphanumeric characters were segmented and labeled by trained operators of the DGGC. The database contains a set of 550 known individuals and a set of 50 unknown writers (see Fig. 9):

– Set of *known* individuals. The documents in this set were written under controlled conditions (type of paper, pen, writing position, etc.) in the police premises after the criminal had been arrested. This way the available data is very large and very consistent for all the writers in this set, with 6–8 documents per subject, and with 5–10 acquired samples per character (except those that are rare in Spanish such as the 'w').
– Set of *unknown* individuals. The documents in this set were retrieved from crime scenes. This way the amount of data in this set is considerably smaller than in the case of the known individuals. Moreover, the variability of the available data among the writers is very big, in terms of amount of samples (some of them do not have samples of all the characters) and in terms of writing conditions (pen or pencil, type of paper, writing direction, etc.)

In Fig. 10 the samples of a known (top) and unknown (bottom) writer in the database are shown.

For the evaluation experiments, 30 out of the 50 unknown writers were manually identified with one of the known subjects in the database by forensic examiners from the DGGC. This correspondence between known and unknown individuals constitutes the ground truth for the performance evaluation of Biografo.

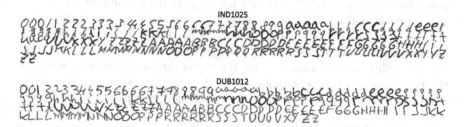

Fig. 10. Samples of a known (IND1025) and unknown (DUB1012) writer in Biografo DB.

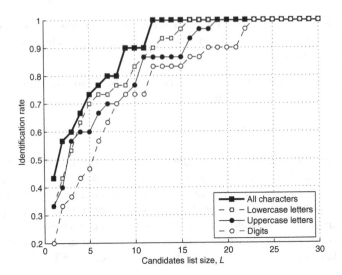

Fig. 11. Performance of the identification module in Biografo using: (*i*) all the 62 characters, (*ii*) only the lowercase letters, (*iii*) only the uppercase letters, and (*iv*) only the digits.

Given a writer of the unknown set, identification experiments are carried out by outputting the L closest identities of the known set. An identification is considered successful if the correct identity is among the L outputted ones. For this preliminary experiments only a subset of $N = 30$ writers from the known set was used (corresponding to those manually identified with the unknown individuals). Identification was performed using: (*i*) all the available characters, (*ii*) only the lowercase letters, (*iii*) only the uppercase letters, (*iv*) only the digits. Results are shown in the form of Cumulative Match Curves (CMC) in Fig. 11, from which two main observations may be extracted:

– Given the challenging nature of the database on which the evaluation was performed, specially for the subset of unknown individuals (with very few available data in some cases), the results show the high potential of the identification module to help forensic examiners narrowing down the search list of potential candidates (100 % accuracy for a top 12 list in the best case).
– The multiple options offered by Biografo to define the identification tests have shown that, as could be expected, the lowercase letters are the most discriminant characters, followed by the uppercase letters (which usually have less variability among writers), and the digits. Moreover, it is proven that the best option is to use samples of all the possible characters (lowercase, uppercase and digits), as this increases the chances of a positive recognition.

The design of Biografo also permits to add in the future new recognition approaches to be fused with the current gradient-related matcher in order to further improve the identification rates.

6 Conclusions

We have presented the new integrated tool for forensic writer identification Biografo. This software application runs over a relational database and is designed to assist the forensic experts in the whole examination process from the data acquisition to the identification of writers. Preliminary performance results of the tool have also been presented on a real-case database of original forensic documents.

Acknowledgements. This work has been partially supported by the Spanish *Dirección General de la Guardia Civil*, and projects Contexts (S2009/TIC-1485) from CAM, Bio-Challenge (TEC2009-11186) and Bio-Shield (TEC2012-34881) from Spanish MINECO, BBfor2 (ITN-2008-238803) from the European Commision, and *Cátedra UAM-Telefónica*.

References

1. Srihari, S., Huang, C., Srinivasan, H., Shah, V.: Biometric and Forensic Aspects of Digital Document Processing. In: Digital Document Processing, pp. 379–406. Springer, Heidelberg (2007)
2. Srihari, S., Cha, S., Arora, H., Lee, S.: Individuality of handwriting. J. Forensic Sci. **47**, 856–872 (2002)
3. Plamondon, R., Srihari, S.: On-line and off-line handwriting recognition: a comprehensive survey. IEEE Trans. Pattern Anal. Mach. Intell. **22**, 63–84 (2000)
4. Srihari, S., Leedham, G.: A survey of computer methods in forensic document examination. In: Proceedings of the International Graphonomics Society Conference (IGS), pp. 278–281 (2003)
5. Schomaker, L.: Writer identification and verification. In: Ratha, N.K., Govindaraju, V. (eds.) Advances in Biometrics: Sensors, Algorithms and Systems, pp. 247–264. Springer, London (2007)
6. Srihari, S.N., Ganesh, A., Tomai, C., Shin, Y.-C., Huang, C.: Information retrieval system for handwritten documents. In: Marinai, S., Dengel, A.R. (eds.) DAS 2004. LNCS, vol. 3163, pp. 298–309. Springer, Heidelberg (2004)
7. Franke, K., Schomaker, L., Veenhuis, C., Taubenheim, C., Guyon, I., Vuurpijl, L., Erp, M., Zwarts, G.: WANDA: a generic framework applied in forensic handwriting analysis and writer identification. In: Proceedings of the International Conference on Hybrid Intelligent Systems (HIS) (2003)
8. Tapiador, M.: Análisis de las Características de Identificación Biométrica de la Escritura Manuscrita y Mecanográfica. Ph.D. thesis, Escuela Politécnica Superior, Universidad Autónoma de Madrid (2006)
9. Otsu, N.: A threshold selection method for gray-level histograms. IEEE Trans. Syst. Man Cybern. **9**, 62–66 (1979)
10. Gonzalez, R., Woods, R.: Digital Image Processing. Addison-Wesley, Reading (2002)

Author Index

Printed in the United States
By Bookmasters